TREATING PEOPLE WITH PSYCHOSIS IN INSTITUTIONS

TREATING PEOPLE WITH PSYCHOSIS IN INSTITUTIONS

A Psychoanalytic Perspective

Belinda S. Mackie

Routledge
Taylor & Francis Group
LONDON AND NEW YORK

First published 2016 by
Karnac Books Ltd.

Published 2018 by Routledge
2 Park Square, Milton Park, Abingdon, Oxon OX14 4RN
711 Third Avenue, New York, NY 10017, USA

Routledge is an imprint of the Taylor & Francis Group, an informa business

British Library Cataloguing in Publication Data

A C.I.P. for this book is available from the British Library

ISBN-13: 9781782202240 (pbk)

Typeset by Medlar Publishing Solutions Pvt Ltd, India

To my family
this is an offering for the future

CONTENTS

ACKNOWLEDGMENTS

This book would never have been written if it were not for those psychoanalysts who published their work about psychiatric institutions making their experiences public. My gratitude goes to Monash University, Melbourne, Australia for providing me with the opportunity of writing my doctoral thesis on which this book is based. Also, thanks to the facilitators of the Psychoanalytic Research Seminar at Monash University, in particular Emeritus Professor Graeme Smith and to my doctoral colleagues. It was one of these colleagues, Dr Christine Hill, who urged me to undertake this journey in the first place. I would specifically like to express appreciation to Dr Leonardo Rodríguez, my thesis supervisor, for his direction and guidance. The editorial skills of Daryl Boyd were invaluable with his great attention to detail and I am most obliged to him for assisting me with the correct use of apostrophes and commas to which I am blind. I especially want to show recognition to Sharon Walker for the dedication she put into the artwork presented in this book—it is inspired. I am also very grateful to those friends who have helped so much in dragging me over the finish line, especially Dr Carmela Levy-Stokes. Thanks go to my family, friends and colleagues for their ongoing support and interest in the production of the PhD and then, finally, the book.

ABOUT THE AUTHOR

Belinda S. Mackie is a registered psychoanalyst with the Australian Centre for Psychoanalysis and is a member of the Forums of the Lacanian Field. She has worked as a psychoanalyst in private practice in Melbourne for over two decades. She supervises and teaches in the field, in addition to presenting regularly at conferences and publishing her work in Australia and internationally. Belinda completed her PhD, on which this book is based, in 2012 from Monash University. She has a background in mental health nursing and was a student in one of the old psychiatric hospitals of the past where she developed an interest in the positive and negative aspects of institutional care.

PREFACE

There are many paths that offer an understanding of the experience of people with psychosis, and numerous ways to consider the nature of institutional treatment approaches. Psychoanalysis is one path that provides a conceptual foundation for both the treatment of psychotic conditions and how to understand institutions that care for patients. Especially in relation to the structure of psychosis, psychoanalysis offers ways of affecting the clinical work in a treatment environment by helping to develop practice strategies that are strongly linked to a theoretical framework. This book focuses on the priority that psychoanalysis places on the individual, how the treatment is conceived theoretically and the ways it can be incorporated in the overall organisation of an institution. Psychoanalysis has its greatest efficacy in long-term treatments and has shown its suitability for patients diagnosed with psychosis when the method is adapted to the uniqueness of each person and is conducted by an experienced clinician. In many cases individual psychoanalysis is feasible but the treatment of psychosis cannot usually be conceived without considering some form of institutional care, although this does depend on the level of the individual's psychopathology. This is because the majority of people with a psychotic illness, especially those with schizophrenia, will be exposed to inpatient, community or outpatient treatment, in one form or other, during the course of their lives.

Therapy based on psychoanalysis permeates contemporary psychological approaches. It is over a century since Freud and his colleagues from the Burghölzli Clinic in Switzerland attempted the use of psychoanalysis in institutional treatment, laying the foundation for current practice in the mental health field. Major changes have occurred in treatment approaches since then and particularly since de-institutionalisation. The chapters of this book bring together the histories of a number of psychoanalytically informed hospitals, and provide a synthesis of the different theoretical underpinnings in the institutional practice of each. Here the institution is the subject of the case study. Institutions that are theoretically orientated to psychoanalysis were chosen and examined, taking into account their various approaches to the treatment of patients with psychosis. A number of institutional models that are informed by psychoanalysis offer a guide to the treatment and present a version of institutional practice that is different from the prevailing models in psychiatry. This has implications for health services in the current climate of mental health reform.

Of particular interest is how psychoanalysts and psychoanalytically trained staff working in institutions, apply their theoretical understanding, and in what ways the psychoanalytic technique has been modified or adapted to the treatment of individual patients and to the workings of an institution. In the recent past, institutional treatment took the form of large hospital complexes but post-deinstitutionalisation patients are treated in a range of outpatient and community based mental health services that remain institutional in nature, even though the original buildings have been demolished or reallocated. An understanding of institutions can be derived from the evolution of the asylums of the past through the more recent process of deinstitutionalisation to the current state of mental health services. In the process of deinstitutionalisation the stability, structure and respite that institutions provided were not considered in the overall drive to close them. Thus, the true concept of asylum was lost and the beneficial aspects of institutional care, such as security and protection, all but disappeared.

Therapy other than the classical method or standard technique of psychoanalysis is often given the global term psychotherapy even if it is significantly informed by psychoanalysis and conducted by a psychoanalyst. The term psychotherapy is often used in two distinct ways: one is psychotherapy as a broad category that encompasses a large array of talking therapies including psychoanalysis, and the other is a narrower meaning of psychotherapy that characterises a therapy other than psychoanalysis. Several of the analysts following Freud transformed his recommendations about psychoanalysis into rigid guidelines about what it was and the type of patient who would benefit from it. This process of reinterpretation has gradually created restrictions that were contradicted in Freud's own practice. Frieda Fromm-Reichmann applied a modified version of psychoanalysis to the institutional treatment of psychotic patients at Chestnut Lodge. She used the terms psychoanalysis, psychoanalytic therapy, and intensive psychotherapy alternately and synonymously to indicate that her approach in the treatment of psychosis was different from the psychoanalytic therapy of neurosis and that it required a modification of Freud's psychoanalytic techniques (Fromm-Reichmann, 1947, p. 333, footnote).

A working hypothesis is that for an institution to work effectively and ethically it needs a theoretical model to guide the work of a well-trained and supervised staff, together with an articulated approach to patient treatment and informed leadership. In addition, there must be an ethos that can be identified, understood and accepted by all those who populate the institution. The place of psychoanalysis in psychiatry, approaches to the structure and treatment of psychosis, relevant aspects of the history of psychoanalysis and the nature of institutions are all considered in the initial chapters of this book, so as to better facilitate an assessment of the selected institutions discussed in the chapters that follow. Given the considerable number of institutions and the different theoretical models used as frameworks to guide patient treatment and administrative practices, a selection of particular institutions was made for a more detailed analysis. This was based on the depth and diversity of material available about the chosen institution, the clinicians who worked there, and their ability to theoretically explain their praxis. People who are in psychoanalytic or psychiatric treatment are referred to here as patients, subjects, persons or individuals; other service providers may refer to them as clients, consumers, or service recipients.

Very few institutions or organisations are available for scrutiny: this work reports on the sociological, anthropological, and psychoanalytic investigations of some of those institutions that did expose their inner working life to public examination. In this investigative process questions arose concerning the function of individual institutions and how they differ from each other, especially in areas such as the prevailing philosophy that guides clinical practice and patient treatment models, treatment outcomes, historical perceptions, hospital administration, and the training of staff. Institutions that applied psychoanalysis to the whole institution, as much as this is possible, were foremost in the decision of which institutions to select for study. These institutions are and were located in North America, Continental Europe, and Great Britain, and they covered the treatment of adults, adolescents, and children. A list of these institutions can be found in the Appendix.

The following criteria were developed as a guide only to identifying common themes about the nature of institutions, how they functioned, their relationship to psychoanalysis, and to the treatment of psychotic patients:

(1) The institution's history and conceptual models that orient it towards psychoanalysis and psychiatry.
(2) The logic of the treatment of psychosis in its institutional application, including the influence of the psychiatric medical model.
(3) How the traditional psychoanalytic method is modified in its application to the treatment of patients. What makes the treatment strategies and programs unique? What is the place of the patient in the treatment?
(4) The institution's level of awareness and approach to examining itself psychoanalytically in the context of leadership and authority, administration, and fiscal decision-making.
(5) The institution's approach to staff and their education, analytic training, research, supervision, clinical meetings, case conferences, teamwork, etc.
(6) How research is conducted, how efficacy is measured and how treatment outcomes are used.

A Lacanian orientation is consistent with the author's training as a psychoanalyst and is central to the orientation of this book; the structure and treatment of psychosis is well elaborated by Lacan. In addition, there are a number of institutions whose practice and organisational administration are guided by Lacanian psychoanalysis. This creates interesting parallels with a number of other institutions in the area that apply alternate psychoanalytic models, such as object relations and post-Kleinian theory, interpersonal psychotherapy, and ego psychology, that have made significant contributions to the field in their understanding of institutions and the treatment of psychosis.

I have observed that terms such as severe pathology, seriously mentally disturbed, mentally ill, psychiatric disability, personality disorder, borderline psychotic, and others are frequently used and loosely applied in the literature. These terms are suggestive of psychosis without providing an adequate description of the phenomena under discussion or of the particular symptoms observed. From a Lacanian point of view, a diagnosis of psychosis occupies a broader category than that of the many versions of the *Diagnostic and Statistical Manual of Mental Disorders* (DSM) and specifically attempts to differentiate between the structures of psychosis, neurosis, and perversion in order to orient a treatment approach. Accordingly, a Lacanian understanding of psychosis generally places borderline personality disorder within a psychotic structure, but this is always dependent on a diagnosis drawn from the patient's unique psychopathology. Elementary phenomena, untriggered psychosis, and ordinary psychosis are Lacanian constructs that might help to understand borderline phenomena from a different perspective.

Opening up such a wide net for enquiry has enabled many questions, themes, and gaps in the literature to emerge. However, the vast amount of data that was identified made it difficult to filter the relevant information and remain focused on the overall aim; as a consequence some information had to be omitted. This work is therefore based on a selection of information. There is, of course, an unavoidable bias given the author's Lacanian orientation to psychoanalysis, which influences the generalisability of the findings; nevertheless, this would be the case for any psychoanalyst undertaking a study of the field. There has been a significant effort made to be inclusive of other schools of thought and this has been indispensable to understanding the diversity of approaches to institutional treatment. Similarly, there is a limitation in the method of research in another bias regarding the selection of data and the tendency to interpret case material in terms of a reigning theoretical orthodoxy. Approaches to the treatment of the patient are well conceptualised in Lacanian terms where clinical psychoanalytic research is based on psychoanalytic case studies and the complexity of the social reality being studied is maintained in the data.

The lack of a relationship between the psychoanalytic theories employed in a treatment approach and the way they inform the patients' treatment in an institution were encountered. Reports in the literature about institutional practices were often vague or absent; links to the theory behind institutional practice had to be extensively cross-referenced or assumed from other sources. In this way, certain approaches to language have been interpreted differently. The classical analytic method, for example, is understood and applied in different ways by different clinicians, as it should. However, the best way to proceed would be a method that can be understood, articulated and explained to others. Perhaps this has to do with the way psychoanalysts assume that their own favoured approach is the only worthwhile approach. To complicate the matter, literature that is translated from one language to another frequently has an interpreted meaning that can be different from the intended idea. This can be seen in the way Freud's words have been interpreted over one hundred years and the arguments that have ensued over his intended meaning in the original German. This is also the case with Lacan and translations from the original French where there is variation in the quality of translations into English; add to this is the fact that Lacan is notoriously difficult to fathom anyway.

The research themes identified in the concluding chapter have the potential to influence future considerations for the treatment of psychotic patients and institutional practices. These conclusions are not discipline specific; they have the possibility of informing an integrated multidisciplinary approach to knowledge about the patient's treatment, institutional practices and an understanding of the clinician's ethical responsibilities within the system. Further exploration is warranted in areas of reflective practice and supervision for individual mental health practitioners in the application of psychoanalytic theory adapted to the creation of thoughtful and dynamic learning environments, as part of an institution that is inclusive of, and responsive to, the patient. Most of the hospitals identified in this book conducted a significant amount of research that proved to be beyond the scope of this project to examine in depth. Thus, future research might be able to more fully investigate the research outcomes of the hospitals and clinics oriented towards psychoanalysis and compare them.

Outline of chapters

The introductory chapter outlines a framework for the central premise of the book, that is that psychoanalysis provides an understanding of the structure and treatment of psychosis and this is manifest in the way an institution functions.

The first chapter provides a historical account of the influence of psychoanalysis within psychiatry, and by association its place in the treatment of patients in institutions, the majority of whom experience psychotic illness. Its historical roots attest to the contribution psychoanalysis has made to theoretical development and practice in this area. Prior to deinstitutionalisation the most common treatment venue was the psychiatric hospital. Nowadays treatment is spread through hospitals, clinics, community services, and outpatient programs. The current treatment strategies of psychiatry are elucidated: their strengths as well as their limitations. Psychoanalytic and psychiatric approaches reveal similarities and particular differences.

The second chapter unfolds the different ways psychoanalysis approaches the structure and treatment of psychosis, and how the subject, the patient, is conceived. This is based on the conceptual models around which the clinician's knowledge is organised. Within psychoanalysis there are many different theoretical schools and approaches, particularly regarding the treatment of psychosis. Although such variety complicates the matter, it also adds a richness that can open up space for collaboration and diversification. The theoretical orientation places priority on the works of Freud and Lacan and this is evidenced in the discussion.

The third chapter considers key developments in the history of European psychoanalysis in its institutional application with emphasis on the contribution of Freud and pioneer psychoanalysts in the treatment of psychosis. The first and second-generation psychoanalysts had a significant influence on the evolution of the treatment of psychosis and institutional care that changed psychiatric practice and asylum treatment for decades. The psychiatrists from the Burghölzli Clinic in Switzerland formed the nucleus of a small group that fought for the recognition of psychoanalysis and for the opportunity to apply it in institutional practice. The application of the psychoanalytic method to these settings required adaptations from Freud's original technique. This chapter traces those developments, highlights the discoveries and identifies events that shaped its evolution.

Chapter four introduces the nature of institutions through the lens of psychoanalysis in considering the structure, organisation and group dynamics of an institution. This includes exposing the dominant culture of the psychiatric facility and its services as a social system with view to exploring how psychoanalysis can influence institutional practice. It is only in revealing the nature of institutions, studying them and their effects, including the consequences of particular types of management, and experimenting with alternatives, that other possibilities can be envisaged.

The intention of chapter five is to bring to light some of the fundamental principles that guide the application of psychoanalysis to the treatment of psychosis in psychiatric institutions. Various institutional models anchored in psychoanalysis are identified and they provide a framework for understanding and explaining certain institution. Of interest is the institutional field model developed by members of the Italian Psychoanalytical Society. In this chapter, the works of two well known pioneer hospitals in the United States that are oriented to psychoanalysis are studied: the Menninger Clinic and the Austen Riggs Center. Both institutions have functioned as psychiatric hospitals for over eighty years and were influenced by psychoanalysis for at least sixty of those years. Institutions that use psychoanalysis to guide the treatment of psychosis reveal a number of similar characteristics, regardless of their theoretical orientation.

Chapter six focuses almost exclusively on Chestnut Lodge hospital in the United States and the practice of individual psychoanalytically oriented psychotherapy for all patients admitted there. Chestnut Lodge provided a stable container for a prolonged inpatient stay that initiated, maintained, and sustained the therapeutic process. The historical links are central to an understanding of the significance of Chestnut Lodge in the work of Harry Stack Sullivan, Frieda Fromm-Reichmann, and others who developed interpersonal psychotherapy, and the rich legacy they passed on to the field in the treatment of psychosis in institutions. Of significance is the 1954 research of Stanton and Schwartz who undertook a socio-psychoanalytic study of one of the female wards at Chestnut Lodge. The study investigated the social setting of the hospital and concerned itself principally with the frequency that unrecognised forces influenced the behaviour of both patient and staff.

Chapter seven addresses the Lacanian psychoanalytic approach to psychosis and presents a number of institutions that work from a Lacanian orientation. The structure of psychosis needs to be understood before engaging in the question of the analytic treatment, both individual and institutional. Accordingly approaches to the theory and practice of psychoanalysis are discussed. The central concern of institutions considered in this chapter is the technical and theoretical problems encountered in the application of psychoanalytic treatment to the psychoses resulting in alternative approaches to traditional psychiatric care.

Chapter eight explores the therapeutic community model and its contribution to modern institutional psychiatry with its antecedents in pedagogy, psychoanalysis, and social medicine. The main aim of this chapter is to trace the psychoanalytic and social links within institutional psychiatry during a time of change in mental health care systems. Since the Second World War the therapeutic community model has had a significant impact on the practice of institutional psychiatry with particular attention directed towards the staff and the organisation as a whole. Examples of institutions that functioned as therapeutic communities are presented and studied here with particular reference to their origins and theoretical orientation.

The emphasis of Chapter nine is psychoanalytic treatment with psychotic children and adolescents and their residential care. The impact of psychoanalytic theory in the establishment and operation of institutions for the treatment, care and education of psychotic children and adolescents is demonstrated by the specific institutions. A largely experimental approach to the treatment of children inspired the work of many successful clinicians. It is therefore important to be inclusive of different views, approaches and modifications to the analytic method until the efficacy of their use is better understood.

The final chapter concludes the book bringing together the insights that have been generated through the process of investigating institutions that reference psychoanalysis and deliberating on the outcomes. A number of institutional models are discussed, including themes and recommendations that have arisen from the work.

INTRODUCTION

The psychoanalytic approach to patients with psychosis is generally not well understood in contemporary psychiatry and yet therapy based on psychoanalysis permeates most psychological approaches. There is significant consensus that the psychoanalytic treatment of psychosis is different in its application to that of neurosis and that it is dependent on each person's unique presentation. Psychoanalytic theory provides a foundational model for thinking about mental illness, including informed and ethical approaches to the practice of working with and treating patients. Meta-analytic evidence of psychological treatments for people with schizophrenia strongly supports the use of individual psychoanalytically informed therapy (Gottdiener, 2004; Gottdiener & Haslam, 2002, 2003). Some studies conclude that psychoanalytic therapy is an effective treatment for schizophrenia but only if it is conducted by experienced therapists (Alanen, Räkköläinen, Rasimus, Laakso, & Kaljonen, 1985; Karon & Vandenbos, 1981). Others show no particular difference between therapeutic approaches to the treatment of patients with psychotic illness (Gunderson, et al., 1984; McGlashan, 1984; Wallerstein, 2000). However, completed analytic treatments were invariably associated with greater benefits, longer treatments had better outcomes and intensive psychoanalytic treatment was generally more effective than psychoanalytic psychotherapy (Kächele, 2001).

The psychoanalytic and institutional treatment of patients with psychotic illnesses are inclusive of psychiatric practices and its definition and classification of mental disorders that are key issues for mental health services. Psychosis is generally experienced by patients on a very broad continuum and is frequently episodic in nature. The treatment may or may not incorporate a support network or team approach, such as liaison with a psychiatrist, a mental health team, the family or even a hospital service. Psychiatric patients these days are managed in a range of outpatient and community based mental health services. The best treatment setting is dependent on the particular person, their level of disturbance, the severity of symptoms and the level of risk. In many cases a psychotic patient, especially if they have schizophrenia, is likely to be exposed to institutional treatment, in one form or other, during the lifetime of his or her illness (McGorry, 2004). As a result, the institutional context is indispensable in the treatment of patients with a high degree of risk. This is because patients who are potentially unsafe need a complex range of supports that include protection, containment, skilled personnel, and tools that go beyond the range of a single treatment approach. No single theory can account for the complexity of psychotic phenomena so a wide range of approaches may be appropriate.

Traditionally, psychoanalysis has been defined as a method of inquiry, which leads to observations that result in a body of theory, and the practical application of those theories that is the analytic treatment. Freud (1923a, p. 235) described psychoanalysis as the name of:

> [...] a procedure for the investigation of mental processes which are almost inaccessible in any other way, of a method (based upon that investigation) for the treatment of neurotic disorders and of a collection of psychological information obtained along those lines, which is gradually being accumulated into a new scientific discipline.

Psychoanalysis originated from Freud's clinical neurology practice in Vienna. He explained psychoanalysis as depth-psychology; a psychology of unconscious mental life that was called upon "[...] to provide psychiatry with an indispensable groundwork and to free it from its present limitations" (Freud, 1923a, p. 251). He saw that the future would give birth to a scientific psychiatry, to which psychoanalysis would serve as an introduction. At first the early practitioners of psychoanalysis had no way of knowing just which patients were treatable with the analytic method and which ones would require special changes or parameters. Some analysts significantly modified their praxis so that more problematic psychopathology could be available to treatment; others treated psychosis without much alteration to the method at all.

Psychoanalysis in institutions

An institution can be an organisation founded for a specific purpose or it can be an establishment consisting of a building or buildings that function to promote some cause. It can also be a psychiatric hospital, mental hospital or mental asylum for the containment and treatment of mentally incompetent or unbalanced persons (The Oxford English Dictionary, 1989). A psychiatric or mental hospital is a specialised hospital based facility that provides inpatient care and long stay residential services for people with severe mental disorders (World Health Organisation, 2011). Mental asylums were essential to the evolution of psychiatry as they provided a universal platform for education, research, and practice throughout the world. The development of the modern psychiatric hospital is the story of the rise of institutional psychiatry from which it evolved, eventually replacing the older mental hospitals and lunatic asylums. Clinical practice in the public sphere of a mental health service is unquestionably connected to its institutional context. In a hospital, group processes are organised socially with varying degrees of structuralisation in which both the patient and the staff participate.

The relocation of inpatient psychiatry to general hospitals as part of deinstitutionalisation was an attempt to normalise and de-stigmatise mental illness, and at the same time reduce the isolation of psychiatry from medicine. However, there is more to dealing with the problems associated with institutions than simply changing the institution's physical structure and location. In contemporary times rather than a psychotherapeutic model of care the balance has shifted towards a more mediated approach, limiting the therapeutic potential of inpatient and outpatient psychiatric services. "Current-day psychiatric treatment of severely disturbed populations tends to focus on the biological, behavioral, and social dimensions of rehabilitation" (Felix & Wine, 2001, p. 17). In the existing mental health system of case management, the lack of direct practice models has created a conceptual vacuum that has been filled with bureaucratic attempts to define the kind of work that is done with psychotic patients. Too little knowledge about the needs of the seriously mentally ill has found its way into practice. This conceptual vacuum is evident in the neglect of the complex psychodynamic and interpersonal aspects of the treatment and rehabilitation of psychiatrically disabled individuals.

Psychoanalysis provides perhaps the most compelling argument for continuity of care in community settings in the preservation of a consistent therapeutic relationship with a clinician to ensure the patient engages in ongoing treatment, which is foundational to continuity of care and better outcomes. Psychoanalysts tend to be cautious about predicted outcomes of analytic treatment, basing their approach on the uniqueness of the subject in front of them with the transference as the central feature of the treatment and therefore the greatest predictor of outcome. This knowledge can help inform the design of treatment settings, the management of the transference, the handling of transitions from hospital to home, approaches to community care and outreach, and other practical treatment decisions. Problems in the individual treatment of psychosis can frequently be understood in terms of the transference and this is where an analyst's level of experience and training come to the fore.

The psychoanalytic approach to the subject involves adopting a certain position on the part of the analyst towards the patient otherwise psychosis can be exacerbated setting up the conditions for failure in the treatment. The setting for the treatment of psychosis is the same as for neurosis, that is, in the consulting room and, if possible, on the couch but this is dependent on the particular person and their level of disturbance. The nature of the treatment is determined by circumstances such as, the severity of symptoms and the level of risk that may or may not require a support network in the form of a team that could comprise liaison with a psychiatrist, a community mental health team, the family or even a hospital service. It is very likely that an individual diagnosed with a psychotic illness will, from time to time over the course of his or her life, need an environment that is predominantly containing. "Our own experience leads us to believe that, during his therapeutic journey, the psychotic patient may need two or more interlocutors and structures, each separate but complementary and closely interdependent" (Vigorelli, 1998, p. 39). Ultimately, psychoanalytic effects do not depend on the setting but on the discourse and the installation of the symbolic coordinates by an analyst whose quality as an analyst does not depend on the location of the consulting room nor the nature of the patient but on the experience being engaged in.

Individual psychoanalytic treatment is thought to be effective, in conjunction with a continuum of interventions and resources that contribute to the treatment of psychosis. The disruptive effects of acute psychotic symptoms can compromise individual psychoanalytic treatment so certain institutions, such as Le Courtil, La Borde, and others have adopted a model that de-emphasises the importance of individual psychoanalysis that is conducted away from the institution's influence. However, Chestnut Lodge, Austen Riggs Center, GIFRIC and the Cassel Hospital are institutions that maintained the patient's individual psychoanalytic treatment as a central feature of the institutional treatment. Psychoanalytic theory and practice have been adapted in certain institutions in the form of a therapeutic milieu, group work, creative workshops, and family therapy, and for staff there are clinical seminars and case conferences, in addition to supervision.

Approaches to psychosis

In Australia, psychotic disorders represent a major public health challenge. A high burden of ill-health and disability is experienced by people with psychotic disorders throughout their lifetime and only a minority gain an optimal level of functioning and wellbeing that is commensurate with a good quality of life. Eugene Bleuler (1950) described psychosis as a generic psychiatric term indicating a disordered mental state where the person's relation to reality is disturbed. Psychosis is used as an umbrella term, employed as an initial diagnosis to preclude a potentially misleading early diagnosis becoming fixed. Diagnostic categories are concepts that provide a useful framework for organising and explaining the complexity of clinical experience in order to make predictions about outcomes and to guide decisions about the general direction of the treatment. In Australia and other countries, there are currently two widely established systems that classify mental disorders by listing categories of disorder and providing standardised criteria for an array of diagnoses. The first system is the ICD-10, part of the *International Classification of Diseases* (World Health Organisation, 2005). The second is the recently released fifth version of the *Diagnostic and Statistical Manual of Mental Disorders* (DSM-V) (American Psychiatric

Association, 2013). *The Diagnostic and Statistical Manual of Mental Disorders* is a handbook originally used for diagnosing mental disorders in the United States but is now used all over the world. It is a reference manual that provides descriptions of diagnostic categories in order to enable clinicians and investigators to diagnose, communicate about, study, and treat people with various mental disorders. The weakness of the *Diagnostic and Statistical Manual* is that it takes a developmental approach to mental disorder. It locates the disorder on the plane of deficit or malfunction emphasising what is absent, whereas a psychoanalyst's focus is located on what is phenomenologically observable and a production of the subject. The convenience of a nomenclature that has become more important than gaining an understanding of the person can be seen in the modern representation of psychiatric diagnosis that serves to enhance an increasingly positivist, biomedical model.

Psychiatry views psychosis is an impairment of mental functioning where there are fundamental disturbances in the person's thinking, perception, and emotional responses that can be manifest in delusions, hallucinations, confusion, and impaired memory (American Psychiatric Association, 2013). Schizophrenia is the most serious form of psychosis and is differentiated from other psychotic disorders by the absence of identifiable causative factors, the longer duration of disturbance, minimal mood disorder and the presence of other psychotic symptoms in addition to delusions. Approximately one in every one hundred people will experience schizophrenia at some stage in their lives. "Schizophrenia is a disease of the brain that is expressed clinically as a disease of the mind [...] a disease of neural connectivity caused by multiple factors that affect brain development" (Andreasen, 1999, p. 645). The current model of the cause of schizophrenia is linked to that used to understand cancer, i.e., that schizophrenia probably occurs as a consequence of multiple dynamics, which include some combination of inherited genetic factors and external factors that affect the regulation and expression of genes responsible for brain function or that injure the brain directly.

The Lacanian practice of psychoanalysis is based on the work of Jacques Lacan, a French psychiatrist and psychoanalyst who is best known for recommending a return to the teaching of Sigmund Freud. Lacan's re-examination of Freud's work brought him into dialogue with other academic disciplines such as linguistics, mathematics, anthropology, and philosophy, and important intellectual movements of the time such as structuralism, phenomenology, and surrealism. Lacan (2004a) proposed that the unconscious is structured like a language that can be read and deciphered, and that this deciphering takes the subject towards what is most real in his or her life. Lacan had more experience than Freud in the area of the psychoses having written his 1932 doctoral thesis on a case of "self-punishing" paranoia and he would readily take psychotic patients into analytic treatment. Lacan was well known for the regular seminars he gave at *Hôpital Sainte-Anne* in Paris from 1953 until 1964 (and elsewhere until 1981) where he often presented cases of psychosis and interviewed hospitalised psychiatric patients during his seminars. In his third seminar 1955–1956, Lacan (2002a) spent an entire year studying the question of psychosis.

In the psychoanalytic treatment of psychosis two issues need specific attention: they are the logic of the treatment and the handling of the transference (Lacan, 2002a; Lacan, 2004a). The work of the treatment with psychosis occurs in the creation of a dialogue that slowly brings the patient to a way of simply formulating questions about his or her life in such a way that is not overwhelming. The aim is to establish contact with the subject and this is achieved by carefully creating a climate in which their identification with the analyst is fostered without provoking a negative transference. This approach is psychoanalytic even if the analytic work is with a psychotic person and if it is applied in an institutional setting. This is because it is a psychoanalyst who is drawing from psychoanalytic theory and experience, and applying it appropriately. Psychoanalysts do not begin with the premise that the patient is suffering from some sort of illness, nor is it held that an analysis will lead to the end of suffering. Psychoanalysis is unique in that it places the burden of defining oneself on the side of the patient, the subject. The subject cannot be reduced to a list of symptoms or as a target for statistics. What psychoanalysts deal with is the subject and each one is unique.

As in psychiatry, establishing a diagnosis is crucial for a psychoanalyst to determine their general approach to the patient and serves as a guide for specific kinds of interventions. Based on the work of Sigmund Freud and Jacques Lacan, a diagnosis involves three structures: neurosis, psychosis, and perversion. Lacan (2002a) maintained that a diagnosis was required so that the psychotic phenomena in each case could be understood in terms of the patient's structure, and that an accurate diagnosis required the structural mapping of the subject's position. Under the structural umbrella of psychosis psychoanalysis includes the

Freudian classifications of schizophrenia, melancholia, paranoia, and autism.

Schizophrenia is the most frequently represented and recognised of the psychotic disorders and psychoanalysis is in general agreement with the *Diagnostic and Statistical Manual of Mental Disorder's* (APA, 2013) description of the symptoms of schizophrenia. These are delusions and hallucinations, speech and thought disturbance, blunted, impoverished or incongruent affective responses, distorted representation of sex and the body, and the absence of desire and general inertia regarding life. Symptoms are the subject's attempts to manage the confusion that results from the collapse of his or her world, manifest in fragmentation of the imaginary representation of his or her body.

Melancholia is characterised by self-loathing, delusional feelings of worthlessness, sleep disturbance, loss of drive function, suicidal ideation, and lack of energy or motivation. "The shadow of the object fell upon the ego and the latter could henceforth be judged by a special agency as though it were an object, a forsaken object" (Freud, 1917e, p. 249). Originally described by Freud as the narcissistic neurosis *par excellence*, melancholia is the outcome of a struggle between the ego and the superego (Abraham, 1949b). Melancholia is associated with the subject's complete identification with the lack in the Other and the absence of the desire of the Other leaving nothing except death (Lacanian concepts are discussed further in Chapters two and seven). Manic episodes are a potential manifestation in melancholia, consistent with Bipolar Affective Disorder.

Paranoia is differentiated from schizophrenia by the delusional production that is the subject's attempt to rectify the disintegration of their world as the result of the invasion of libido to which the subject is defenceless. Freud (1911c) used the case of Daniel Paul Schreber as the prototype of his work on paranoia, as presented in Chapter two.

Autism is considered to be a disorder of childhood that includes aloofness and the inability to relate to others, a profound disturbance in language, for example, echolalia, literalness, and mechanical repetition. The presentation of autism reveals an absence of the Other in how the body and the world is represented.

Conventional community outpatient settings often fail to provide a holding environment that allows the individual to transition to a more autonomous position at their own pace. Nor do these services offer a consistent containing function that assists the person to cope with times when they experience overwhelming anxiety. The patient's objective reality is often intertwined with an internal reality that defends against powerful anxieties of psychotic fragmentation, significantly interfering with their ability to determine a course of action or make a decision. In such cases, the patient's psychotic symptoms can impede their ability to participate in the analytic treatment, at least until they can represent themselves better. In applying a psychoanalytic perspective to the treatment of people suffering from severe mental illness, the goal is to facilitate a trusting and safe alliance so that the patient's most compelling needs are met. Winnicott (1960) considered a secure holding environment to be essential and Bion's (1967, 1955) concept of the container-contained is of significance here as well. The best outcome is for the patient's continuing engagement in a working transference relationship because it has both therapeutic and protective value. It is, therefore in the patient's best interest to continue in the treatment with as little disruption as possible but with the support of a team, which may mean inpatient or community treatment. The characteristic problems associated with this disorder also need consideration; such as relapse, poor compliance with medication, poverty, homelessness, unemployment, drug and alcohol abuse, crime, breakdown in family relations and social life (The National Institute for Health and Clinical Excellence, 2010). It is generally agreed that the best way of managing the treatment of psychosis is a combination of approaches that address the uniqueness of the individual's presentation.

The Maudsley Hospital.
S.W. '13.

CHAPTER ONE

Psychiatry and the influence of psychoanalysis

The history of psychiatry includes the history of psychoanalysis; its historical roots attest to the contribution psychoanalysis has made to theoretical development and practice in these areas. Coming from separate origins, psychoanalysis and psychiatry were linked by their medical backgrounds and so managed to form an alliance, each providing something the other needed. Psychoanalysis offered psychiatry a dynamic understanding of psychopathology and the possibility of a therapeutic treatment; psychiatry offered psychoanalysis the respectability and status of the medical profession and the opportunity to infiltrate a major area of mental healthcare. For psychoanalysis, the relationship with psychiatry was influential in its foray into the treatment of psychotic patients and consequently their institutional care. This was because psychoanalysis oriented the physician toward the patient in a completely different way by opening a door to understanding the patient and the meaning of what the patient said. Nevertheless, psychoanalysis struggled to gain full recognition in psychiatry and it was thanks to the work of a small group of pioneer psychiatrist psychoanalysts that a psychoanalytic praxis with psychotic patients was established in psychiatric institutions. This eminent group had significant influence on leadership in psychiatry for several generations. In the present day, psychiatry and psychoanalysis have branched out and now embrace other traditions and disciplines. Psychiatry regained its status as a branch of medicine when it retired from psychoanalytically based theories and moved towards scientific indications where care is designed for clusters of similar type patient presentations. As a consequence, the social context was side-stepped and relegated to a secondary place that tended to overlook the role that poverty, isolation, prison, social segregation, stigma, racial and gender based discrimination, violence, and the abuse and neglect of children play in the experience of psychosis.

Prior to deinstitutionalisation the most common treatment venue for a psychotic patient was a psychiatric hospital, now treatment is offered in general hospitals, clinics, community services, and outpatient programs. Change is inevitable but in the rush to close institutions there was a failure to acknowledge all the functions that an institution provided, and policy makers underestimated the challenges that the community care of vulnerable people with complex problems would create. It was not the mental hospitals of the past that were the problem but more likely the way they were governed that was the issue. Although psychiatric and the various psychoanalytic approaches present very different conceptual fields, they are not necessarily exclusive of one another. Psychoanalysis has had to adapt and diversify in its application to practice with regard to psychiatric and institutional environments.

A historical perspective of psychoanalysis in psychiatry

The man who created psychoanalysis, saw psychiatry as a descriptive and classificatory science whose orientation was directed towards the somatic rather than the psychological, and was thus unable to provide explanations for the phenomena it observed (Freud, 1923a). Freud's intention was that psychoanalysis influence psychiatric practice with asylum patients, and it was for this reason that he was very keen for Eugene Bleuler and the psychiatrists of the Burghölzli clinic in Zurich, Switzerland to join his cause. This was because their presence would serve to legitimise his work in the face of criticism and opposition (Freud, 1914d). The Psychiatric University Hospital Burghölzli in Zurich opened in 1870 marking the beginning of the modern era in Swiss psychiatry. Eugene Bleuler, the director of the Burghölzli after August Forel, said that when it came to the treatment of schizophrenia they were forced to "grope in the dark" as they had no idea how to successfully treat the disease (Bleuler, 1950).

Bleuler's views on the moral treatment of insanity were in line with those of Philippe Pinel's one hundred years earlier, that the most appropriate approach was through the asylum regimen of education, reasoning, and persuasion. The aims of any recommended treatment at the Burghölzli were to contain and alleviate the patient's acute agitation, and to teach the patient to re-establish contact with reality. To this end staff were encouraged to make repeated attempts to gain access to the patient. It was important that the patient's routine was structured and their time utilised properly. In Bleuler's experience though, most forms of therapy had little effect. The systematic re-education of thinking, suggestive therapy or hypnosis, and the reward system of proven correctives (the precursor to behaviour modification) did not produce genuine change; it only taught patients to adapt their behaviour to the expected norm. Bleuler insisted on the principal rule that no patient would ever be completely given up on (Bleuler, 1950, p. 482).

Emil Kraepelin was a contemporary of Freud's, often referred to as the father of modern psychiatry. He was an institutional psychiatrist who dealt with predominantly psychotic patients. Whilst he and Freud were born in the same year and had much in common, their thinking was poles apart. In 1883 Kraepelin developed the first scientific system of classification for mental illnesses in his *Compendium der Psychiatrie* where he promoted a pluralistic approach to psychiatry. Researching the psychopathology of hundreds of patient case studies, Kraepelin proposed two broad categories of psychosis: Dementia Praecox (Schizophrenia) and Manic Depressive Psychosis (Bipolar Affective Disorder). He selected the term "dementia praecox" to describe the early mental decline that was followed by a deteriorating course (Kraepelin, 2002). Kraepelin insisted that dementia praecox was a single entity disease and although Bleuler was very much influenced by him, he identified primary symptoms that occurred in every case in the group of schizophrenias. Based on his expanded notion of dementia praecox Bleuler pushed for a name change to "schizophrenia" because the splitting of different psychical functions was one of its most prominent characteristics:

> By the term "dementia praecox" or "schizophrenia" we designate a group of psychoses whose course is at times chronic, at times marked by intermittent attacks, and which can stop or retrograde

> at any stage […]. The disease is characterised by a specific type of alteration of thinking, feeling and relation to the external world which appears nowhere else in this particular fashion. (Bleuler, 1950, pp. 8–9)

Bleuler described the core pathology of schizophrenia as a primary associative disturbance, blunted affect as reflected in indifference and unresponsiveness; autism described as the predilection for fantasy and detachment from the outside world, and ambivalence, which is the tendency to endow the most diverse "psychisms" with both a positive and negative indicator at the same time. Bleuler visited each patient at the Burghölzli every day, even if it was only for a minute or so. This was quite an achievement considering that the population was around 200 inpatients in 1900 and over 500 by 1910 (Palmai & Blackwell, 1966). One of Bleuler's contributions to the management of schizophrenia was his observation that prolonged confinement in an institution was deleterious to the patient and he advocated early discharge as soon as acute symptoms were resolved. He also created the beginnings of community care by organising a rehabilitation and follow up service for patients after discharge.

The principles underlying Kraepelin's approach bases its practice on scientific knowledge that is empirical, verifiable, and reproducible, so he afforded psychoanalysis no place at the German Institute for Psychiatric Research in Munich on the grounds that it was unscientific:

> We meet everywhere the characteristic fundamental features of the Freudian trend of investigation, the representation of arbitrary assumptions and conjectures as assured facts, which are used without hesitation for the building up of always new castles in the air ever towering higher, and the tendency to generalization beyond measure from single observations […]. As I am accustomed to walk on the sure foundation of direct experience, my Philistine conscience of natural science stumbles at every step on objections, considerations, and doubts, over which the likely soaring tower of imagination of Freud's disciples carries them without difficulty. (Kraepelin, 2002, p. 250)

Prior to World War One the new doctrine of psychoanalysis spread through Europe to the United States, bringing new hope for the treatment of asylum patients with a priority on the patient's subjective experience. The awareness that psychotic symptoms could be meaningful had an important humanising effect on asylum psychiatry even though it did not initially have a direct influence on the treatment. This early interest from asylum psychiatrists came from the support psychoanalysis could provide as a framework for understanding symptoms and their pathogenesis.

The dissemination of psychoanalysis

In the beginning, Freud (1924f) was only able to elaborate and test his therapeutic method on the severest cases, mainly those patients who had tried everything else without success, and had spent a long time in sanatoria. He believed that the psychoanalytic study of the neuroses was the only preparation for gaining an understanding of the psychoses, and yet, it is well known that Freud was cautious about recommending the use of the psychoanalytic method with psychotic patients believing them to be inaccessible and in need of an alternate therapy (Freud, 1905a). He thought that patients who were psychotic were unable to work in the transference, preventing the development of a working alliance because they withdrew their libido from people and things in the external world (Freud, 1914c). Nevertheless, Freud was very supportive of those analysts, such as Ernst Simmel and Max Eitingon, who took on the exploratory work of applying psychoanalytic theory in psychiatric clinics and institutions. He also encouraged the work of psychiatrists such as, Paul Federn, Sandor Ferenczi, Gustav Bychowski, and Wilhelm Reich, who treated patients with a higher degree of mental disturbance. Abraham, Federn, Jung, and Simmel have all written about the supervision and advice Freud gave them in their clinical endeavours with psychosis, especially those psychiatrists from the Burghölzli (Abraham, 1949a; Federn, 1953; Jung, 1960; Simmel, 1929).

The developments in Europe did not go unnoticed in America and as early as 1906 James J. Putnam, a professor of neurology at Harvard University, wrote a paper on the use of psychotherapy at the Massachusetts General Hospital with specific reference to Freud's theories of psychoanalysis (Putnam, 1906). Putnam adapted what he called a simple form of psychoanalysis as an experiment in the treatment of neurological cases where most of the patients were diagnosed with hysteria; naturally it failed (Taylor, 1988). Putnam and some of his colleagues appropriated

Freud's language and certain conceptual formulations, but their underlying framework was uniquely American in its pragmatism and in the eclectic way theories were appropriated. In the first two decades of the twentieth century, psychoanalytic approaches were assiduously undertaken in the treatment of psychosis by Abraham Brill, Adolph Meyer, and Edward Kempf. Psychoanalysis started to dominate in the United States, especially after the Second World War when it slowly became better represented in the American university, psychiatric, and cultural circles, by the 1960s a psychoanalytic orientation was well-established in leading psychiatric institutions where virtually every university professor of psychiatry was psychoanalytically trained (Kernberg, 1997). The Ego-Psychology approach is derived from the work of Anna Freud, and was represented by Hartmann, Kris, Loewenstein, Rapaport, Erikson, and later on by Jacobson and Mahler. From the 1940s the Interpersonalist approach to psychoanalysis shaped the development of the neo-analytic view in the United States. Although it did not constitute a unified theory, Interpersonal Psychotherapy is significant for its institutional origins and the efforts that psychiatrists, such as Harry Stack Sullivan and Frieda Fromm-Reichmann, made to find a method derived from psychoanalysis that could be used for inpatient psychiatric treatment.

Many of the European psychoanalysts, intellectuals, and cultural figures who fled Germany and Austria principally to America and England before, during and after the Second World War assumed psychoanalytic leadership roles and exerted considerable influence on the direction of American psychoanalysis. But what they found was a version of psychoanalysis that was disconnected from its cultural and political roots ending up sterile and prescriptive. The European émigrés were left-wing intellectuals born around the turn of the century and, as second-generation psychoanalysts, they thought of psychoanalysis as a cause that would help make sense of a disjointed world. The American practice of psychoanalysis that these European psychoanalysts joined was rigidly medicalised and so, for the ensuing decade, the principal problem became that of lay analysis. This was because only medically qualified candidates were accepted for psychoanalytic training. A number of the European emigrant psychoanalysts were either not physicians or their European medical qualifications were not recognised in the United States. Consequently, a significant division developed between orthodox European analysts, on the one hand, and contemporary medically qualified American analysts on the other.

The first psychoanalytic training institute was established in Berlin in 1923 based on the three pillars of psychoanalytic formation: a didactic or instructional analysis, theoretical courses and the practice of controlled analyses. Although Brill strove to safeguard what he regarded to be the core ideas of Freudian psychoanalysis, he opposed Freud's judgment about who might practice it. Freud argued that some psychological training and an open human approach were more important in a psychoanalyst's training than a medical education (Freud, 1926e). But Brill (1934) was determined that psychiatrists alone should practice Freud's controversial new science. This opposition to lay analysis is significant because of its enduring institutional effects. Brill's politics of exclusion meant that other mental health disciplines in the United States could not receive psychoanalytic training. This position contributed to the success of the American Psychoanalytic Association (APA) in centralising its control over psychoanalysis, making it the exclusive property of psychiatry (Richards, 1999).

Freud founded the IPA in 1910; today it is a worldwide umbrella organisation and the world's largest regulatory body for psychoanalysts. In the United States of the 1920s and 1930s the IPA served as a gatekeeper to keep certain types of people out of the field. Much of the history of psychoanalysis in the United States was concerned with preserving the assumption of an uncontaminated version of psychoanalysis that belonged to certain analysts in local institutes of the International Psychoanalytic Association (IPA) (Kirsner, 1998). Freud dreaded the American tendency of trying to turn psychoanalysis into "a mere house-maid of psychiatry" (Ernest Jones, 1957, p. 323). He tried to reason with them as follows:

> The resolution passed by our American colleagues against lay analysts, based as it essentially is upon practical reasons, appears to me nevertheless to be unpractical; for it cannot affect any of the factors, which govern the situation. It is more or less equivalent to an attempt at repression [...] would it not be more expedient to recognize the fact of their existence by offering them opportunities for training? (Freud, 1926e, p. 258)

After several decades the close association between psychoanalysis and psychiatry in North America started to change in the 1970s and the pendulum started to swing in a different direction. By the 1980s and early 1990s psychiatry was engaging more with the neurosciences and psychopharmacology, as well as social and community models.

Except for Ernest Jones's founding of the British Psychoanalytical Society in 1919, psychiatry in the United Kingdom was largely removed from the developments in Europe and America, especially the evolution of psychoanalysis between the wars. By the early 1930s Melanie Klein established herself in London and just prior to the onset of the Second World War Anna Freud and her father escaped from Vienna to London. Anna Freud and Melanie Klein uncomfortably became members of the same society. The central dispute between them was on a child's ability to establish a transference relationship in analytic treatment. Klein openly criticised Anna Freud's work on child analysis. Klein (1963) used play therapy and interpretive techniques that could be equated with an adult's free associative speech and this meant that in her view children could be analysed. She observed that children expressed their fantasies and anxieties in their play and that children's play substituted as a framework for the ego's attempts to defend itself from instinctual conflicts in order to work them out.

During the war these two women clashed, and heated debates occurred within the British Psychoanalytical Society that resulted in a profound schism in the psychoanalytic community. This was resolved through a series of wartime discussions that resulted in the permanent division of British psychoanalysis. As a consequence, the original British Society and the Kleinians became the British School and those behind Anna Freud became the Freudians. Those non-aligned object relations theorists who did not take sides in the debates, went on to promote their own unique contributions to psychoanalytic theory; they became known as "the Middle School" or "Independents". Hence, the term "object relations" has been used in reference to different formulations, generally categorised as either the American School or the British School. After the death of Anna Freud, the Freudians became known as the Contemporary Freudian group (Pines, 1999b). Many American psychoanalysts, more closely aligned with Freudian Ego Psychology, rejected Kleinian and Object Relations theory, and in turn the British School generally disapproved of the Ego Psychology movement. This resulted in different technical approaches in the practice of psychoanalysis that tended to create factions. The Post-Kleinians, Herbert Rosenfeld, Hanna Segal, and Wilfred Bion, were noteworthy for their work with psychosis.

The Second World War had a deep impact on British psychiatry with the expansion of academic departments of psychiatry and some psychoanalytic appointments within them; prominent examples were the Maudsley Hospital and Tavistock Clinic in London. The work of a number of psychoanalysts involved in the Northfield experiments led to the development of group psychotherapy and the therapeutic community model that had a significant influence on psychiatric services in England that lasted for decades. On the other hand, there was hostility to even a diluted version of Freudian psychoanalysis on the part of mainstream institutional psychiatry in Britain. So it was not until the 1970s that psychoanalytic ideas were formally incorporated into the training of psychiatrists there. The modern discipline of psychiatry grew from the belief that mental illness could be treated and that the institution could have a therapeutic function. With the development of psychotropic drugs in the 1950s there was an increasing move away from institutional care towards the integration of psychiatric treatment within the general health sector.

Institutional psychiatry

In the past, mental hospitals were set up as separate institutions with funding and administration independent from those of general health care. They represented a part of the culture of mental health care that was more than the residential requirement it fulfilled: it included a complex set of functions such as the availability of medical care, the rendering of respite for a patient's family and the provision of a social network for the patient. Equally, in designing these institutions little attention was paid to the impact the institution might have on patients who were incarcerated there or on the staff who had to work there. The accommodating structure and routines of an institution can produce a narrowing or reduction in an individual's critical judgment and reasoning. This is revealed in a slowed reaction to change that hinders the person's ability to adapt to new circumstances. Institutionalisation can be described as a human being's loss of subjectivity; it represents the application of inflexible systems of control in the treatment of vulnerable people that lead to the stripping away of whole areas of identity. Franco Basaglia described institutionalisation as:

> The loss of a scheme, the loss of the future, the state of being in the power of others without being able to direct oneself, and having

> one's day tuned and organised on an impersonal rhythm, dictated only by organizational demands that—such as they are—cannot take into account the single individual and particular circumstances: this is institutionalisation. (Basaglia, 1964, p. 1)

Institutionalism, while closely associated with institutionalisation, is the consequence of prolonged residence in a closed community and the impact of factors, such as, social pressure, susceptibility to those pressures and the length of exposure to them (Wing & Brown, 1970). Goffman (2007) saw institutionalism as a disease entity that was fostered in a mental hospital and was an intrinsic part of that institution regardless of staffing and accommodations. Long stay patients in psychiatric hospitals who had been inpatients for years or even decades were observed to be apathetic, self-neglecting, and isolated; descriptions that had long been ascribed to the negative symptoms of schizophrenia (Peele, Luisada, Lucas, Rudisell, & Taylor, 1977). The effects of an institutional environment on patient outcomes are particularly complex and long-term outcome studies have demonstrated that psychotic disorders, such as schizophrenia, have a much more heterogeneous outcome than had previously been understood (Harding, 2003; Harding, Brooks, Ashikaga, & Breier, 1987). Many of the long stay hospital patients who were researched made substantial improvements over the years post-release without any psychiatric treatment.

Of the problems present in state run psychiatric hospitals many were found to be endemic to all institutions and organisations, even those that were influenced by psychoanalysis. It is this fact that is important to consider here because one would think that psychoanalysis could offer some understanding for the problem of institutions. The Stanton and Schwartz 1954 study at Chestnut Lodge in the United States highlighted the complexity of the interpersonal relationships between those who reside in and those who are employed by the hospital, and the deep effects they have on each other's adjustment and on the course of the patient's treatment. Further to this, Barrabee's 1951 research at the Boston Psychopathic Hospital in the United States revealed that even under favourable circumstances large portions of a hospital's social organisation were dominated by tradition and inertia, together with a preoccupation with bureaucratic and administrative processes. Added to this were staff attitudes of indifference manifest in their opposition to patients receiving any form of therapy. The concentration of large numbers of people in a hospital inevitably leads to poor communication between levels of authority for both patients and staff. Augment these issues with an impersonal administration and an inflexible bureaucracy that dominates in order to maintain control. Belknap's conclusion was that modern concepts of psychiatry are unworkable in a centralised mental hospital that is used as a convenient dumping ground for people with complex problems.

Deinstitutionalisation

The deinstitutionalisation of psychiatric services connotes an event that started in the United States, Canada, and Great Britain during the 1960s and 1970s when psychiatric hospitals were closing down and their inpatients released into the community. Deinstitutionalisation was first and foremost the affirmation of a renewed therapeutic intention in psychiatry that theoretically took responsibility for restoring the rights of citizenship to the disenfranchised. This included encouraging patients' self-respect and sense of identity, and the general assumption that mental patients do have the capacity to assume responsibility for their own actions. A persuasive argument based on principles of social justice and moral grounds, as well as a powerful critique of the efficacy of segregated and congregated care, drove the release of patients from institutions (Green, 2003). Mental health reformers emphasised the horrors endemic in the Victorian asylums to which earlier generations consigned the insane, and this has helped to legitimise the notion that any change represented an improvement over what had gone before (Scull, 1989). At the time the asylums were shutting down, it was felt that chronic schizophrenia was the result of institutionalisation and that effective community care would obviate the need for inpatient beds (Lucas, 1985). The biggest problem, according to Fuller-Torrey (1997), was the naive sense on the part of some in the civil-rights movement that patients with mental illness did not have much wrong with them leading to the idea that mental hospitals could be emptied *en masse*. The stability and structure of institutions together with their inherent continuity of care were rarely thought to be of any value, given that it was their very existence, in the most repressive forms that drove the closure of institutions in the first place.

The progressive closure of long stay psychiatric hospitals, the co-location of psychiatric units within general hospitals and the increased provision of community based services resulted in the mainstreaming of health services for people with mental illness (Sealy & Whitehead, 2004).

Now psychiatric units are part of a system of psychiatric care whose focus is situated in the community where an in-patient stay is viewed as transitory. The result has been a reduction in hospital beds for people with mental illness, a shorter average duration of inpatient treatment due to the early discharge policy and the provision of resources to community-oriented services (Harvey & Fielding, 2003). Although homelessness among the chronically mentally ill is closely linked with deinstitutionalisation, it is not the result of deinstitutionalisation, as such, but of the way deinstitutionalisation was carried out.

The lack of planning for structured living arrangements and for adequate treatment and rehabilitative services in the community has led to many unforeseen consequences such as homelessness, the tendency for many chronic patients to drift from place to place, and the entry of those with mental illness into the criminal justice system. The closure of institutions, policies of non-institutionalisation plus early discharge policies have led to the breakdown of service delivery with significant and increased demands for low cost housing, general health services, family support, and specialist clinical services. The period following deinstitutionalisation saw many people being accommodated in semi-institutional settings such as boarding houses, residential group homes and hostels that are smaller than the traditional asylums but the same in other respects (Green, 2003; Robinson, 2003). Governments and policy makers also assumed that most of the functions previously carried out by institutions would be taken over by families, neighbourhoods, public services and community agencies. Another reason why deinstitutionalisation faltered in its early days was that many mental health professionals in the community were ill prepared and poorly trained for dealing with the release of seriously mentally ill patients from psychiatric hospitals, where they had been incarcerated for prolonged lengths of time.

The psychiatric hospital fulfilled the function of asylum for the individual patients need for safety and security and this was lost in deinstitutionalisation together with the beneficial aspects of asylum care. Moving the care of the mentally ill away from institutions to the community has led to their over representation in general hospital emergency departments (Singh & Castle, 2007). This happens when social structures are viewed simplistically with little regard for the consequences that may follow when cultural change is imposed abruptly and thoughtlessly. A wider culture of managerialism has developed in the National Health Service (NHS) in the United Kingdom where the emphasis has shifted away from the needs of the patient and closer to administrative control (Winship, 2000). The dominant frame has become the enumeration and control of risk, and no longer the transformative potential of humanity:

> Until the art of running them [psychiatric hospitals] is appreciated and implemented they are probably better closed, the public inconvenienced, and the taxpayer obliged to pay three or four times as much for a less effective service fragmented into units in general hospitals, day care centres, and hostels, run by an administrative miasma in which committees, quarrels, and professional self indulgence command more time than patients. (Barton, 1972, p. 505)

In the context of the institutional treatment of psychotic patients, psychiatry is in a process of change. Although deinstitutionalisation towards "a psychiatry-without-walls" was meant to offer the opportunity for re-integration of mentally ill people, the outcome has led rather to a new era of fragmentation and social exclusion (Winship, 2000). In modern times a direct and dynamic relationship exists between asylums, prisons, laws related to vagrancy, homelessness, and societies response to difference. The services an institution provided that were an entrenched and established part of our health care system for the chronically mentally ill disappeared and were never replaced. After thirty years, it is unclear if our mental health system has developed any service models that suitably reflect the needs of the community. Some of the problems for those with a mental illness could be addressed by building smaller mental hospitals with an open ward and rehabilitation facilities; providing employment or occupation, building more halfway homes, quarter way homes, day care centres, sheltered workshops; providing housing facilities; establishing special courts that deal with cases that pertain to the mentally ills on a preferential basis and passing laws to protect the rights of the mentally ill (Sheth, 2009).

Psychiatric treatment

Psychiatry is the branch of medicine that deals with the diagnosis, treatment, and prevention of mental disorders (The Royal Australian and New Zealand College of Psychiatrists, 2010). The last century has seen significant developments in the various treatment approaches to psychosis. The medical model in psychiatry classifies symptoms or behaviours under a disease construct based on a Kraepelinian approach where the individual is applied with a label and placed in a category. A patient admitted into psychiatry is exposed to a treatment service and is subjected to an array of options that cater to the psychopathological manifestations of that person's disorder. Treatments based on the medical model, are inclined to emphasise symptom management and reduction using medical interventions that are primarily pharmaceutical. The appearance of a biologically based medical approach in the 1960s and the escalating use of psychotropic drugs caused a radical transformation in psychiatric treatment. Accepted diagnostic standards of mental disorders also changed due to pressures from insurance companies, pharmaceutical companies, and political lobby groups. The psychiatric treatment of psychotic disorders has three main components: medication to relieve symptoms and prevent relapse; education and psychosocial interventions to help patients and families cope with the illness; and rehabilitation to help patients reintegrate into the community (World Health Organisation, 1998). Integrated early intervention services developed in Australia aim to provide assertive case management, medication, psychological therapy, family and group therapy, and vocational interventions (Gleeson & McGorry, 2004). The mainstreaming of mental health services associated with deinstitutionalisation includes the co-location of psychiatric units within general hospitals. The result has been a reduction in psychiatric hospital beds, a shorter average duration of inpatient treatment owing to early discharge policies and the proposed allocation of more resources to community-oriented mental health services (Harvey & Fielding, 2003).

Patients with chronic schizophrenia are the group who historically received inpatient care in long-term state psychiatric hospitals and who continue to consume the bulk of expenditures associated with the treatment of mental disorders. These days the majority of hospitalisations for this group of people are brief with inpatient care extending to merely cover the period of symptom exacerbation that could not safely be contained in a less restrictive setting (Bloch & Singh, 2001). The term "revolving door" describes this subpopulation of chronically mentally ill patients who are frequently readmitted to psychiatric units (Garrido & Saraiva, 2012). Patients with inadequate support networks, lower levels of education, challenging social environments and poor compliance to medications do not remain well for long. The most consistent predictor of relapse is the number of previous hospitalisations. Considering the social burden and the pressure on inpatient services caused by revolving door patients, it is important to understand the factors that may contribute to this phenomenon. Research has shown that the most severely disturbed patients may be discharged as failures at the very moment they are becoming accessible to therapeutic treatment (Rosser, Birch, Bond, Denford, & Schachter, 1987). It was thought that this group would probably benefit from longer inpatient treatment than was needed for less disturbed patients. A small group of patients with unremitting psychotic symptoms are served by relapse prevention and recovery care programs designed to provide a bridge between short term intensive residential rehabilitation and recovery support prior to returning home (Olfson & Glick, 1993). Most patients on discharge from hospital return to live with relatives who are usually the primary care givers. Families have to cope with disability, abnormal behaviour, welfare arrangements, medication, attendance at day programs or outpatient clinics, and have to make arrangements for appropriate action in the case of relapse. Their needs are often not taken into account and yet they are the backbone of a patient's support system (Wing, 1981). Other patients without family support go to a solo existence in boarding houses and special accommodation facilities or, like many others, are homeless or in jail.

Psychiatric medications are licensed psychotropic or psychoactive drugs prescribed by a medical practitioner in a psychiatric setting and are given to exert an effect on the individual's mental state. The targeting of a specific psychopharmacological treatment for schizophrenia started in the second half of the twentieth century with the introduction of neuroleptics, discovered by three French psychiatrists, Delay, Deniker, and Harl, in 1952 (Lehmann & Ban, 1997). Neuroleptic drugs, also referred to as antipsychotics, ataractics or major tranquilisers, are the preferred form of treatment in psychiatry for most psychotic disorders. In addition, mood stabilising drugs, antidepressant drugs, and electroconvulsive therapy (ECT) are used in the treatment of mood disorder that is related to psychoses and used as an adjunct to neuroleptic drugs (Copolov, 2003). The past twenty years has seen the arrival of atypical or second-generation neuroleptics that have largely replaced traditional agents as a first line drug therapy in the treatment of psychosis. Advances in psychopharmacology have produced drugs that have greater efficacy in the treatment of positive and negative symptoms associated with schizophrenia, and have some effectiveness in the prevention of relapse or symptom exacerbation after an acute psychotic episode (Fenton, Blyler, & Heinssen, 1997). These neuroleptics are seen as therapeutically more effective with very few extrapyramidal symptoms, but there are still concerning side effects, (Gardner & Teehan, 2011; Hasnaina, et al., 2008; The National Institute of Mental Health, 2008). Adopting practices that involve using neuroleptics in a selective manner are recommended because this would dramatically increase recovery rates, avert the consequences of chronic side effects and decrease the percentage of patients who become chronically ill (Whitaker, 2004).

In the clinical treatment setting, the patient's acceptance or rejection of psychotropic medication is considered to be the single greatest determinant of treatment outcome (Jarrett, Bowers, & Simpson, 2008). Inpatient admissions aim to maximise treatment adherence through education to enhance the patient's compliance in taking neuroleptic medications, because a lack of compliance is associated with a higher relapse rate. Research (Fenton, et al., 1997; Mitchell & Selmes, 2007) shows that treatment compliance or, more accurately the patient's adherence to taking medication, is linked to the degree of concordance between clinician and patient in the therapeutic alliance. It follows, in that case, that a dualist (biological and psychological) approach to the treatment would be most beneficial for the patient. Psychological therapies for psychosis are indispensable because in the first instance, while neuroleptic medications have been the mainstay of psychiatric treatment and show considerable benefits, they do not necessarily guarantee a good outcome being only partially effective in approximately forty per cent of cases (Garety, 2003; McGorry, 2004). The second reason is that adherence to neuroleptic medication is frequently poor with up to a seventy per cent non-compliance rate, and even in the case of long-term use of neuroleptic medication a substantial proportion of patients will relapse anyway. And finally, medication typically has no impact on a wide range of other areas an individual may have difficulty with. Neuroleptics offer only partial control over the full range of psychotic symptoms and their consequences. Whilst this is laudable, many people with psychosis, even if appropriately medicated, do not return to proper social functioning and remain seriously impaired in the areas of relationships, living conditions, and vocation (Singh & Castle, 2007). These and other issues, such as stressors that are the consequence of traumatic life events, hostile environments, psychoactive drugs, alcohol abuse or prolonged social isolation that affect both the cognitive and emotional processes of these vulnerable individuals, are all problems beyond can be offered with psychotropic medication.

In Australia and elsewhere, the treatment of patients with chronic psychiatric disorders, such as schizophrenia and severe bipolar affective disorder, is arranged through targets and interventions. For example, patients with psychosis who experience social and emotional deficits are directed towards interventions such as of counselling, group activity programs, and case management to access rehabilitation services (Keks, Altson, Sacks, Hustig, & Tanaghow, 2003). Psychiatric treatment is available from community psychiatric services that consist of: twenty-four-hour crisis assessment and treatment, consultation and continuing care, intensive assertive case management that provides individual management plans, and community care units that provide residential accommodation and long term, intensive rehabilitation. Many of the traditional functions of institutions have been packaged into an assortment of supported housing programs, community residential services, and locally based treatment, care and support programs. Hospital in the home, day procedures, early discharge programs, new psychotropic drug regimes, and coordinated home care packages have all been designed to keep people out of costly hospitals and institutions.

The case management model is an example of the packaging of care as a response to the problems of matching available resources with the needs of those with a mental illness. In spite of reported improvements in compliance with treatment, there is an absence of evidence to support improvements in the patients mental state, social functioning and quality of life (Green, 2003). Today psychiatry places priority on the sciences and in particular the neurosciences in the field of public mental health where objectives, rules, and evaluation criteria place less value on the requirements of a clinical practice based on the uniqueness of an individual patient's presentation. Fifty years after the advent of neuroleptic and antidepressant medications, and several decades after deinstitutionalisation, the basic aetiology, the fundamental pathophysiology, and the definitive treatment for disorders such as schizophrenia, bipolar disorder, and depression are still elusive (Drake, Green, Mueser, & Goldman, 2003). Consequently, the treatment of psychotic disorders continues to challenge and preoccupy psychiatry, psychoanalysis, and other mental health professions. This chapter provides a background for considering the current psychiatric treatment for patients with psychosis and their care in an attempt to open a space from which a dialogue can proceed about other possibilities and alternate contributions to the field. Psychiatry provides the benefits of progress derived from advances in the neurosciences and pharmacology; psychoanalysis offers psychiatry a singular approach to mental illness. An approach to the treatment of psychosis does not have to be an either-or dichotomy but a respectful working together on ways that provide the patient with the best options.

Sheppard & Enoch Pratt Hospital

CHAPTER TWO

Psychoanalytic approaches to the treatment of psychosis

This chapter discusses the various ways psychoanalysis approaches the treatment of psychosis and how the subject, the psychotic patient, is conceived, and it offers a theoretical foundation for understanding the work of psychoanalysis in institutional psychiatric treatment. In the first decades of the last century, Freud and his early followers were discovering how best to treat various types of patients. It took some years before a standard technique would take shape and be accepted by the majority of practicing analysts. The evidence of Freud's observations was documented in his case histories through which he revealed the process of his discoveries. Fundamentally, psychoanalysis is a practice of speech that involves two partners: the analyst and the analysand. An analysis is the treatment based on the discursive relationship between this couple and how the analyst directs it. Consequently, psychoanalysis is a language experience that obtains its effects through words and encourages each subject to produce his or her own singularity. At the very least, in the area of psychosis the experienced practitioner must retain the capacity to be steady and competent despite provocation, anxiety, and the pressure to transgress boundaries. There are numerous theoretical approaches to psychoanalytic praxis in the areas of psychosis and they vary as much as the theories do.

This cross-pollination of alternate theories and approaches to analytic practice is important for psychoanalytic inquiry, research, and development. However the problem of different definitions and meanings for psychoanalytic concepts demands an explanation and an assessment of their helpfulness before they are delivered to a patient. So we need to wade through the fundamentals of how to think about this phenomenon that is the treatment.

Freud's theoretical developments on psychosis

A distinction between psychosis and neurosis can be found in Freud's (1894a) early writings on paranoia in *Draft H* of his correspondence with Fliess (Masson, 1985). In *Draft K* Freud (1896b) continued his work on paranoia and the failure of defence with the return of the repressed in a distorted form. He identified the determining element in paranoia as the mechanism of projection that involves the refusal or withholding of belief. He was essentially concerned with clarifying the notion of defence in hallucinatory confusion, paranoia, and hysterical psychosis. Freud separated actual neurosis that is related to somatic conditions from psychoneurosis as related to mental conflicts. The main clinical distinction drawn between the psychoneuroses was transference neuroses (hysteria and obsessional neurosis) and narcissistic neurosis (schizophrenia, paranoia, melancholia). In the transference neurosis the subject has a quantity of libido striving to be transferred on to extraneous objects; whereas the narcissistic disorders are characterised by a withdrawal of the libido from objects (Freud, 1923a). Later Freud separated schizophrenia into a separate category of psychosis. He tried to show the defence against sexuality that is activated in certain psychoses, but it was his theory of narcissism that came to occupy a central place in his understanding of psychosis, although his different notions of narcissism are inconsistent.

Freud (1924b) thought that neurosis was the result of a conflict between the ego and its id, whereas psychosis was the outcome of a disturbance in relations between the ego and the external world. Usually, the external world governs the ego by perceptions that are continually renewable, and by the store of memories of earlier perceptions. The ego autocratically creates a new external and internal world, constructed in accordance with the id's wishful impulses. The motive for this dissociation from the external world is an intolerable frustration that comes from reality. The first step in psychosis is the dragging of the ego away from reality, and the second is the attempt to make good the damage done and re-establish the subject's relations to reality (Freud, 1924e). The genesis of psychosis is in the creation of a new reality as an attempt at reparation. The transforming of reality is carried out on the memory traces, ideas, and judgements that were previously derived from reality and represented in the mind. After the initial flight into psychosis, there is a phase where the piece of reality that was rejected is actively remodelled or replaced, and attempts are made to substitute it with something else. Thus a new reality is created which does not raise the same objections as the old one and so the process of remodelling produces perceptions that correspond to the new reality in the form of psychotic symptoms, such as delusions and hallucinations.

The case of Schreber

Freud's analysis of a case history, derived from the writings of *Senatspräsident* Daniel Paul Schreber (*Memoirs of my Nervous Illness*) became the cornerstone of the development of his theory of paranoia. Since Freud published this case over one hundred years ago the psychoanalytic community has referred to it extensively. Schreber started writing his memoirs in 1903 whilst confined in Sonnenstein Asylum near Dresden in Germany having kept notes during the previous seven years of his incarceration believing that his documented experiences would be of future use to science and religion (Schreber, 2000). It is helpful to pay attention to the initial sequences of a psychosis while it is crystallising even though it can take years to emerge because this enquiry can help us to understand the nature of psychosis and its triggering (Leader, 2011). Schreber functioned adequately in life maintaining a successful career as a presiding judge before he suffered three successive psychotic breakdowns. His first breakdown occurred in 1884 and was triggered by the rejection of his candidature application for the Reichstag. This episode was manifest in predominantly hypochondriacal and depressive symptoms from which he recovered after six months and returned to his regular life. Schreber's second far more serious episode occurred eight years after the initial onset. It is this second episode that is of most interest here because it was during this time that Schreber wrote his memoirs. Schreber's final episode was precipitated by his wife suffering a stroke followed by the death of his mother that led to a final inpatient admission that culminated in his death in 1911.

The second episode was triggered by his wife giving birth to a still born child after the repeated failure of the couple to have children (Freud, 1911c). Also, at around the same time, Schreber was appointed *Senatspräsident* (Chief Magistrate) presiding over an appeals court in Dresden and he found that the work load was too heavy for him (Schreber, 2000). Both these problems confronted Schreber with something he could not symbolise. This second illness began after a dream where Schreber's thought that the original illness had returned and on another occasion while in bed he had an idea that struck him as peculiar:

> It was the idea that it really must be rather pleasant to be a woman succumbing to intercourse. This idea was so foreign to my whole nature [...]. (Schreber, 2000, p. 63)

This impression preoccupied Schreber and became central to his delusion formation but at the height of his illness he was convinced of the imminence of a great catastrophe that would lead to the end of the world (Schreber, 2000). Following an initial stay at the University Psychiatric hospital at Leipzig, Schreber was transferred to Sonnenstein Asylum for a further eight years before he was released.

The original ideas of the imagined pleasure of a woman submitting to intercourse and the conviction of a great catastrophe happening to the world took hold as the basis for a florid and devastating psychosis. Schreber developed many ideas in an attempt to understand what was happening to him and advanced various theories to explain his anticipation of the end of the world, such as pestilence, disease, earthquake or glaciation due to the sun's withdrawal. He blamed Dr Flechsig, his doctor at Leipzig, for a devastating epidemic. In order to prevent the end of the world and the destruction of mankind Schreber believed that God, in accordance with the order of the world, had chosen him to be unmanned and transformed into a woman as a solution for the renewal of the human race. The signs of his unmanning went on for years in the form of divine miracles that were enacted on Schreber filling his body with nerves of voluptuousness. God demanded continual enjoyment through nerve contact with Schreber without his consent. For years Schreber thought that he was on another planet as God had an intimate connection with celestial bodies, in particular the regulation of the sun. Schreber was under the influence of terrifying and grandiose visions and experienced auditory hallucinations telling him that he was the last person left alive and that those around him were "fleeting-improvised men" in human shape created by a divine miracle (Schreber, 2000, p. 85).

Schreber was certain that Dr Flechsig was the main source of his suffering and accused him of "soul murder" (in German *Seelenmor*) (Schreber, 2000, p. 54). Schreber believed that Dr Flechsig had fraudulently gained access to divine rays in order to take possession of his soul and sexually misuse his body once he had been transformed into a woman. It was to avoid this fate that Schreber was driven to attempt suicide on a number of occasions. Schreber's delusions of soul murder produced a hole in the order of the world. Freud hypothesised three distinguishing factors that mark paranoia: the homosexual wish, the mechanism of repression and the mechanism of symptom formation with the return of the repressed in the form of a delusion (Freud, 1911c). The process of recovery occurs via the mechanism of projection that undoes the work of repression and brings back the libido. Freud saw the prognosis in paranoia as more favourable than in paraphrenia (schizophrenia) because of the paranoiac's capacity for reconstruction.

Delusion formation

A delusional system is a means for the patient to hold their world together and "[...] is found applied like a patch over the place where originally a rent had appeared in the ego's relation to the external world" (Freud, 1924b, p. 151). Freud spoke of psychosis in terms of a disturbance between the ego and the external world where a delusion covers the hole in the ego's relation with external reality in an attempt at a cure or reconstruction (Freud, 1924b). Schreber's delusional explanations produced a form of stabilisation, although he felt that he had been profoundly changed. Following Freud, Lacan (2004a, p. 178) stated: "the problem is not that of the loss of reality, but of the mainspring of what takes its place". Here Lacan was emphasising the hole or gap in the psychotic subject's relation to the world and the nature of the patch that is applied over the hole. Delusions and hallucinations are usually of a distressing nature and are bound up with the generation of anxiety, "a sign that the whole process of remodelling is carried through against forces which oppose it violently" (Freud, 1924e, p. 185). Freud identified two moments in the onset of Schreber's psychosis: the first moment corresponded to the withdrawal of love from the world around him followed by the subjective experience of catastrophe, i.e., the end of the world. The second moment corresponded to Schreber's spontaneous attempt at recovery when, in the face of a profound internal change, psychotic symptoms emerged. The external threat was countered by the delusion regarding Schreber's bond with God that allowed Schreber to rebuild the world. "The delusional formation, which we take to be the pathological product, is in reality an attempt at recovery, a process of reconstruction" (Freud, 1911c, p. 71). The end of the world is a projection of the internal catastrophe and delusions are the work of rebuilding the world again.

The formula that is repeated in Schreber's delusion is based on meaning that no longer refers to anything; language (the code) fails to produce meaning (the message). Schreber is introduced to a new language of divine rays and nerves; these are codes and messages that he tries to interpret and reinterpret. This is his attempt to find a solution to the enigma with which he is faced. An excess of drive in the form of jouissance often accompanies the onset of psychosis; this jouissance invades the subject appearing as something traumatic and alien that resembles the end of the world. It is this jouissance or excessive libidinal enjoyment that produces extreme anxiety and terror. The production of a delusion is an attempt to symbolise this unspeakable real that cannot be symbolised. The real is defined by Lacan (1977) as the impossible; it is that which has not yet been articulated, such as traumatic events that have never been talked about or signified. The real introduces a hole in the symbolic order of language that demands to be filled in some way. Schreber was pushed towards the Other (God) to seek the signifiers that might name the traumatic real that was invading him. Schreber's relation was to a bizarre and irregular Other whose interest in him was mysterious and obscure, and most of all malevolent and perverse.

In his seminar on psychosis, Lacan (2002a) considered delusion formation in the context of the trend towards feminisation using the example of Schreber's idea that it would be pleasant to be a woman succumbing to intercourse. This was a prelude to his later unmanning by God as part of the process of transforming him into a woman so that he would be fertilised by God in order to repopulate the world. At this point Schreber reached a degree of delusional stabilisation when he assumed the very important position of becoming God's woman in order to save the world (Lacan, 2002a). Lacan (2009) took this further with his theory of "the-push-to-the-woman" described in his seminar *L'étourdit*, as the Other forcing something foreign into the subject, producing an invasion that has no sense. Lacan's theory shows the masculine universal for the missing Name-of-the-Father in Schreber's failed attempts at fatherhood and his nomination as presiding judge that were followed by a fantasy that it would be pleasant to be a woman succumbing to intercourse. The appeal to the foreclosed Name-of-the-Father was followed by an effect of the push-to-the-woman that involved the ongoing confrontation with the demands of a tyrannical God who was transforming Schreber's body into that of a woman.

Ultimately, Schreber developed the ability to seal over the frank expression of his psychosis and, except for some mannerisms, was socially agreeable. Evidence of his success can be seen in the production of an autobiographical account of his illness, which reveals his intelligence and superior reasoning, interspersed with overt manifestations of psychosis and his convincing petition to the court that led to his release from the asylum (Schreber, 2000).

A Lacanian formulation

Lacanian psychoanalysis regards psychosis as a structure that is formed around the time when a child is negotiating the Oedipus complex and as a consequence of the child's triangular relation with his or her parents. Lacan revised Freud's version of the Oedipus complex elaborating the paternal metaphor or Name-of-the-Father as the symbolic function that provides structure, boundaries, authority, and reality. Lacan theorised that the mechanism of foreclosure was what actually constituted psychosis. This term was introduced by Freud in German as *Verwerfung* and was later renamed in French by Lacan as *foreclusion*, translated in English as foreclosure (Lacan, 2002a). It is the radical rejection from reality of the signifier of the paternal function, the Name-of-the-Father, making it impossible for the subject to realise the signifier "father" at the symbolic level of language (Lacan, 2004b). The Name-of-the-Father is a fundamental signifier that permits signification in relation to the symbolic world of speech and language. Human beings have no real idea of what the father actually is because fatherhood is claimed when the father gives the child the signifier of his name.

In psychosis the three structural moments of the subject's Oedipal history fail to be organised (Rodríguez, 1987, p. 133). In the first moment the mother represents the absolute Other as she is the primary object of desire for the child and the child is in the position of being the mother's phallic object. Lacan distinguishes between the organ of the penis and the phallus as a signifier of the desire of the other; it is also a signifier of lack and sexual difference, and of lost jouissance that implies castration. In the second Oedipal moment, an injunction is introduced via the father; this is not a reference to the presence or absence of a real father but to the father's symbolic function. What is required is the introduction of the primordial signifier that brings symbolic castration in the form of the prohibition of incest, which presents the subject with a new orientation to sexual desire. The father functions as the one who comes as a limit between the mother and the child, initiating the child into the wider world of culture and social reality. This is the mediating structure of the paternal metaphor, the Name-of-the-Father. In the third moment the child's desire is reoriented and his or her orientation to the phallus is apparently normalised permitting access to the symbolic world, allowing the child to emerge as a separate entity in his or her own right.

The presence or absence of the mediating structure of the Name-of-the-Father has an implied connection with the mother's unconscious acceptance of the father; it is the castration of the mother, in the form of her lack that opens up the possibility of desire for the child, which conveys subjectivity. In psychosis the subject does not have a mediating structure that protects in his or her relation with the mother. It is the maternal figure who lays the ground work for the failure in the paternal function, leaving the child open to her "fantasmatic capture" (Lacan, 1990a, p. 7). The inadequacy of the instillation of the Name-of-the-Father produces a chain reaction of failures in symbolisation. The foreclosure of the Name-of-the-Father, the paternal metaphor, and the corresponding lack in the imaginary of any phallic meaning, produces fragmentation in the psychotic subject's experience of his or her body. It is around the lack of this essential signifier that the psychotic subject makes attempts at repair that then cause a chain reaction, as revealed in the dispersion and fragmentation that happens in psychosis:

> For psychosis to be triggered, the Name-of-the-Father—*verworfen*, foreclosed, that is, never having come to the place of the Other—must

> be summoned to that place in symbolic opposition to the subject. It is the lack of the Name-of-the-Father in that place which, by the hole that it opens up in the signified, sets off a cascade of reworkings of the signifier from which the growing disaster of the imaginary proceeds, until the level is reached at which signifier and signified stabilize in a delusional metaphor. (Lacan, 2002a, p. 481)

For psychosis to emerge the subject has to have inherited a psychotic structure and have the Name-of-the-Father called into symbolic opposition to the subject. Something specific has to happen that draws attention to a hole that exists due to foreclosure of the Name-of-the-Father that places the subject in an impossible position that then becomes catastrophic, as in the case of Schreber. When these conditions are present psychosis is triggered and the latent psychosis is manifest in positive psychotic symptoms. Lacan situated Schreber's psychosis in terms of foreclosure because the Name-of-the-Father failed for Schreber (Lacan, 2002a). Schreber became convinced that, for his own satisfaction, God was demanding femaleness from him. Schreber was confronted with a hole that had always existed. His delusions were the result of his inability to deal with what was required of him as a man, a judge, a father, and a subject. At the point at which the Name-of-the-Father is summoned "[…] a pure and simple hole may thus answer in the Other; due to the lack of the metaphoric effect, this hole will give rise to a corresponding hole in the place of phallic signification" (Lacan, 2004b, pp. 465–466).

Strategies in the treatment of psychosis

A question prior to any possible treatment of psychosis was identified by Lacan as the handling of the transference (Lacan, 2004b). The transference is the subject's relationship to the analyst as it develops in the analytic treatment. In establishing a working transference relationship with a psychotic subject the analyst is likely to be more active in the promotion of discourse. An alternative discourse is gradually produced as the direct result of a sustained transferencial relationship and through the creation of a dialogue that constitutes a point of contact between the individual and the world outside. Thus a bridge is carefully built between the individual and reality via the creation of an alternate discourse, which allows delusional certainty to be questioned or discarded later when no longer relevant. This demands imagination and creativity on the part of the analyst in discovering a means of expression and use of language that establishes points of contact in the subject's discourse that gives access to the construction of his or her identity.

The use of interpretation in the treatment of psychosis is usually ineffective and can even be provocative because the interpretation plays on a double sense that makes the subject work at deciphering its meaning. Herbert Rosenfeld, whose patient experienced the analyst's interpretations as intrusive and persecutory, illustrates this:

> My patient felt that whenever I made an interpretation, I put myself, containing his sadistic omnipotent self, into his mind, and he felt this so concretely that he sometimes threatened to inform the police about what I was doing to him. (1988b, p. 192)

To question the subject about the ambiguity of the meaning of a specific word they have used will probably cause perplexity or have no effect at all but it could also trigger a psychotic response. This is why it is important to refrain from imposing signifiers onto someone experiencing psychosis or by insisting that they speak, as this can be as experienced as overwhelming:

> It sometimes happens that we take prepsychotics into analysis, and we know what that produces—it produces psychotics. The question of the contraindications of analysis would not arise if we didn't all recall some particular case in our practice, or in the practice of our colleagues, where a full-blown psychosis [...] is triggered during the first analytic sessions in which things heat up a bit [...]. (Lacan, 2002a, p. 251)

It is possible for the transference to function as a prosthetic device, a kind of substitute Name-of-the-Father that stands in for what is missing as a result of foreclosure in psychosis. The work of analysis is the reintegration into the symbolic of something of the paternal function and this facilitates the subject's admission into language. In this way the psychoanalytic treatment functions like an artificial support structure that can contribute to the reduction of psychotic symptoms and crisis. The analyst facilitates the steady integration of the subject into discourse; this means the making of social bonds that are compatible with the limitations of the human world and in the subjects own body.

There is no formula for the treatment of psychosis although there are indications and contraindications that, in each individual case, have to be rethought and reinvented. The analyst follows the psychotic subject's lead and is witness to the subject's speech. In this was the analyst gives evidence of the subject's existence behind the words, thus naming what the subject is trying to do or not do. The secretarial function has an organising effect. The analyst presents a space where the subject may be able to place his or her testimony. In this way, the subject makes a plea to the analyst for help to contain, organise, and manage his or her disruptive world. In adopting a position of trying to understand the subject's productions the analyst encourages them to link these productions with other experiences in their history.

The analyst's desire is the driving force of the analytic process in the Lacanian approach as it keeps the analysand working. "The true and final mainspring of what constitutes transference is the expectation of this being's advent in relation to what I call 'the analyst's desire'" (Lacan, 2004a, p. 716). What the analyst has to give is what he or she has, and what he or she has is their desire. The difference with desire between an analyst and analysand is that with the analyst it is an experienced desire (Lacan, 1992). Rather than identification, the analyst desires the analysand's own unique truth emerge in the treatment, a truth that is absolutely different to that of the analysts desire (Lacan, 1977). Lacan was concerned about developing the clinical practice of psychoanalysis with the topic of "the desire of the analyst" as central because ethics are implicated in the way the patient structures his or her desire through the transference in the analysis. The psychoanalytic treatment of psychosis is based on the place where the patient's demand encounters the analyst's desire, and this is central to installing the transference and bringing the subject into the analytic process. The analyst's desire is responsible for the stability of the treatment's direction and the reshaping of the subject's position with regard to the Other's demand in psychosis. The analyst refuses to occupy a pre-established position in the work by decentralising his or her role in the relationship. Psychoanalysis has to be critical of its practice in order to acquire knowledge and remain ethical because it is the desire of the analyst that ultimately operates in psychoanalysis.

Stabilisation

Stabilisation is a place of symptomatic construction where the psychotic subject seems, for a while, to be in a state of remission. As Freud (1924e) said, in psychosis there is an active phase of remodelling where hallucinations and delusions are produced as attempts at reparation. Delusional construction is a spontaneous attempt at recovery or reconstruction with the creation of a new, albeit fragile, reality that is temporary and tenuous because any unanticipated encounter could trigger a psychotic response. So a delusional metaphor is a precarious stabilisation that results in an unstable psychical organisation manifest in perplexity, states of agitation, catatonic withdrawal, and the collapse of symbolic and social functions (Gallano, 2002). Delusional production can, however reconcile a subject to a common meaning or allow them to gain some distance from senseless signs and intrusive phenomena that are constantly aimed at them from an Other that invades their body and their mind. The uncertain logic that informs this production also provides the basis for a therapeutic approach that evolves as two logical moments in the form of stabilisation and suppletion.

Freud (1924b) described a delusional system as a means for the patient to hold their world together like a patch applied over the hole in the ego's relation to reality and the external world. The rejected piece of reality constantly forces itself upon the mind as attempts are made to replace or substitute it with something else that is a new reality. This concept of Freud's is the antecedent to Lacan's idea of psychotic suppletion, which is the tentative constitution of a new partner-symptom for the subject where the reconstituted symptom makes use of certain elements of the subject's delusional construction. Lacan (2002a, p. 203) illustrated what was lacking in the symbolic of those subjects with psychosis:

> Not every stool has four legs. There are some that stand upright on three […]. It's possible that at the outset the stool doesn't have enough legs, but that up to a certain point it will nevertheless stand up, when the subject, at a certain crossroads of his biographical history, is confronted by this lack that has always existed.

Suppletion (*suppleance*) is an umbrella term given to phenomena that have a stabilising function; they cover up, repair or stand-in for what is missing at the level of the symbolic in such a way that the triggering-off of psychosis does not take place. The phase of construction of a suppletion is a compensatory activity that involves the creation or invention of a device that enables the subject to connect with the real world in a manner that is not persecutory or destructive. "The psychotic subject, on lacking a phantasy to frame reality, can transform it by creating something not already existing in the world. He can become an inventor" (Gallano, 2002, p. 2). Such a process is based on the principle that the disintegration of the subject's relation to discourse requires a reconstruction, rather than a process of rectification or correction. For the psychotic subject this requires re-establishing the broken links of the signifying chain:

> The construction of a more elaborated delusional metaphor perhaps will take place, spontaneously, within or outside of any analytic cure. This construction then would be considered as the preliminary work or as the principle work, but the aim of the cure will go farther, putting in question the delusional knowledge until perhaps the subject constructs what Lacan called a *suppleance*, a substitute for the Name-of-the-Father. (Haarscher, 2001, p. 8)

These suppletions can be imaginary in the form of identifications leading to the formation of a new ego; they can be symbolic through, for example writing and fine art, or real via psychosomatic phenomena. The strategy for the construction of a suppletion is provided by the work of psychotic writers, artists, scientists, and others who have been able to create or invent a relatively stable world for themselves. It is thought that analysts can learn a lot from the production of writers such as James Joyce, Antonin Artaud, Fernando Pessoa, the mathematician Georg Cantor, and many others who have been able to either keep their psychosis at bay or co-exist with it by producing a prosthetic device that allows them to find some peace, to be useful to others and to have the opportunity of living in a constructive and socialised way (Rodríguez, 2005).

Lacan mapped a fourth order he called the symptom (*symptôme* in French) or "sinthome". The sinthome is used to articulate a psychic stabilisation that holds the structure together; it is centred on the body events in the moment of knotting and the point at which it is possible for the subject to knot the Real, the Symbolic, and the Imaginary.

A sinthome is a real suppletion that connects the symbolic and the real without passing through the imaginary. This allows a realisation of the subject, in an efficient enough way to provide a partial repair of the Name-of-the-Father as the failed father. The aim of the treatment is to help the psychotic subject construct a sinthome, which is a connection between the symptom and fantasy that produces a new identification. It is the construction by means of the transference of a new mode of discourse specific to that particular subject, through which they are able to reconstruct a position in the world within discourse. Every subject has the potential to construct something like a suppletion a prosthetic device or inventive compensation but not every subject will necessarily succeed. When a suppletion does succeed, clinical experience demonstrates its efficacy for a substantial proportion of psychotic subjects in psychoanalytic treatment.

The sinthome is a concept introduced by Lacan (2015) in his *Seminar XXIII, Joyce and the Sinthome*, which examines the writings of James Joyce. Lacan tried to demonstrate, in the case of Joyce, that in spite of his having a psychotic structure his writing achieved the function of the Name-of-the-Father. This meant that Joyce was able to bind the three orders and fend off a psychotic breakdown, something rarely achieved by psychoanalysis. The seminar gives an original meaning to the symptom in psychoanalysis by producing a new differential axis to the Borromean knot. Lacan saw psychosis in terms of the Borromean knot where the three rings (Real, Symbolic, and Imaginary) of the knot serve to secure the integrity of the entire structure. In psychosis, the symbolic ring is not necessarily missing, but rather it is the overall structure that is lacking in the interdependence of the three rings leading to a loss in structural integrity. The clinical objective of the treatment may be to create a fourth ring or order to prop up the structure since it is impossible to otherwise patch a fundamental defect in the symbolic.

Object relations and post-Kleinian theory

Object relations theory is an organised explanation of personality development and the evolution of psychopathology based on the creation of internalised mental representations of interpersonal relationships (Fairbairn, 1963). It is a set of theories that hypothesise the development of an individual's identity through relationships that are primarily intrapsychic, interpersonal and group experiences. In general,

Kleinian theory states that all adults retain psychotic processes that involve a constant struggle to cope with paranoid anxiety and depressive anxiety. For that reason Kleinians do not make a distinction between the diagnoses, applying the same treatment approach to neurotics and psychotics, adults and children (Klein, 1935, 1946, 1963). The goal of Kleinian therapy is to overcome the schizoid phase by means of a therapeutic alliance with the healthier aspects of the split ego and in the development of the capacity to tolerate ambivalence and so to enter the depressive position.

An understanding of the psychoanalytic treatment of psychotic states of mind started with Melanie Klein's (1946) claim that psychotic disorders could be understood through the structural psychic processes of the paranoid and schizoid positions. Klein considered that the paranoid-schizoid position and thus the origins of schizophrenia were established in the early mental life of an infant. She shaped the idea of the paranoid-schizoid phase as the first step of ego development in the context of an ego-object relationship. During this first phase the death instinct produces anxiety of annihilation and the infant copes with this by distancing him or herself from the destructiveness by splitting both the ego and the object into separate, manageable good and bad entities. The bad aspects or bad ego-object complexes are split off and expelled via projective identification resulting in a partial denial of reality. Klein believed that schizophrenia, paranoid psychosis, and schizoid personality were the outcomes of a failure to adequately overcome certain mechanisms and defences that characterise the paranoid-schizoid positions (Klein, 1946, p. 110).

The 1950s were significant in the development of Kleinian theory and practice because Klein's ideas about psychotic anxieties and defences were being tested with psychotic patients to see if that population could be analysed without changing the essentials of the psychoanalytic method. The post-Kleinians investigated and applied Klein's theories and in so doing addressed Freud's therapeutic pessimism regarding the psychoses. They also found confirmation of Klein's ideas on projective identification, the early persecutory super-ego, the pain of depressive anxiety and the retreat from it using the manic defences. This group of analysts approached the treatment of psychosis using the classical method with only minor changes. There was no alteration in the analyst's attitude in the treatment of psychosis; negative and positive productions in the transference were interpreted and they relied almost exclusively on interpretations to deal with serious language and thought disorder. The post-Kleinians encountered the frequent triggering of psychosis, impasses in the treatment, lack of containment and issues associated with projective identification. The insistence on the centrality of interpretations in the treatment had an effect on the prevalence of the triggering of psychotic episodes. Bion, Segal, and Rosenfeld all agreed on the viability of the psychoanalytic method in treating psychosis and found substantiation of Klein's views that the fixation point for schizophrenia was in the paranoid-schizoid position.

Wilfred Bion was possibly the most influential of Klein's followers. He is well known for his work on groups but the inroads he made into the understanding of psychosis and a theory of thinking have probably been the most profound of the contributions he made to psychoanalysis (Bion, 1955, 1962, 2007). His work is very complex as many of Bion's insights came from his work with schizophrenia and these observations led him to significantly re-conceptualise Klein's original thinking of projective identification. He called attention to the works of Freud and Klein that he saw as vital to understanding the analytic treatment of psychosis, which he described as "psychotic analysis" (Bion, 1955; Bion, 1957). Bion tended to see the nature of psychosis as a structural problem; the intrusion into a sane personality of an increasingly large psychotic part. Thus, one or other part, the sane or the psychotic, can take over and be in charge of the overt personality at different times.

Bion saw the psychotic person's experience as the result of a failure of the mother to contain her infant's fear of dying, perhaps as a consequence of her being psychotic or depressed. In this situation, all of the infant's anxiety is projected into the mother and instead of being contained and modified by her, the fears are returned to the child in a heightened form. Bion felt that one of the central tasks of the psychoanalyst was to contain the psychotic patient's anxiety without being destroyed and that this process relied on the use of projective identification. Consequently, the patient projects intolerable anxiety onto the analyst who in turn contains and gives the experience back in a more manageable form. Thus taking over the role of the environment-mother that first failed the child. Bion's (1955) concept of the "container-contained" was to have significance not only for Kleinian thinking but also for psychoanalytic theory in general.

Bion suggested modifying the classical psychoanalytic approach for psychosis by using counter-transference rather than associations of the patient as the basis for interpretations. In line with a Kleinian approach, he conducted the analytic treatment of a patient who was psychotic the same way he would a neurotic patient, on the couch interpreting associations with frequent sessions. He thought that the psychotic patient was fixed in the paranoid-schizoid position and that these patients used projective identification where words are taken as things or as split off parts of themselves and forced onto the analyst. Bion felt that the patient was afraid of becoming more normal because then he or she would have to become aware of being insane. He claimed to have successfully treated psychotic patients to the point where they were able to work and support themselves.

The evolution of Bion's work began with his early papers on schizophrenia in the 1950s that were the basis of the elaboration of a more sophisticated theory of thinking he developed later (Bion, 1955, 1962). Bion's theory of thinking is based on the conjecture that pure thoughts exist long before there is a mind to think them. According to his theory, thoughts are evoked from passivity into disruptive energies by the sense organ of consciousness, which is stimulated by events in the external or internal world. "Alpha function" refers to perceptual experiences that are converted into a form that can be registered in the unconscious. "Beta elements" are sensory or emotional experiences that are metabolised by the process of thought and whatever is incapable of being metabolised is evacuated by means of projective identification or hallucinations. The thinking apparatus evolves in response to the pressure of thoughts and this begins when the infant projects his uncontainable discomfort and anxiety into the mother who acts as a container for the child's fears thus assisting the child to develop the ability to make meaning out of raw unprocessed data. For Bion the task of analysis in psychosis was for the patient to internalise the containing alpha function provided by the analyst in his or her capacity to receive beta elements evacuated via projective identification.

Another of the pioneers in the psychoanalytic treatment of psychotics was Herbert Rosenfeld whose psychoanalytic cases were among the first records of adult psychotic patients being treated by a purely psychoanalytic method relying only on interpretation. Rosenfeld emphasised the importance in an analysis of distinguishing between the psychotic and non-psychotic aspects of the patient's personality. In particular, he highlighted the role of projective identification in the psychotic part of the personality as a substitute for repression leading to destructive attacks on the ego (Rosenfeld, 1957). His most famous case was that of Mildred who was diagnosed with schizophrenia and was in analysis with Rosenfeld for several years from 1944 (Rosenfeld, 1947).

Hanna Segal made history in 1950 when she treated a hospitalised patient named Edward who was diagnosed with schizophrenia. She acknowledged the increasing number of analysts who modified their technique in the treatment of psychosis and described her position as an analyst who interprets with only minor deviations from strict analytic technique. An early appearance of Segal's (1957) concept of "symbolic equation" took place in connection with this patient who was unable to make a distinction between symbols and the objects that they symbolised. For him, "being like something" was the same as "being something". Symbols were equivalent to the things being symbolised (Segal, 1950, p. 271). After a brief stay in a military hospital Edward was transferred to a nursing home where Segal commenced psychoanalytic treatment with him for five hours per week visiting him there each day. Edward was mostly silent except for some over excitement in the beginning. Segal reports that although Edward started talking to her, she meant no more to him than a piece of furniture. Segal interpreted Edward's feelings bringing them into the transference and connecting them with his phantasies and delusions. Edward described her interpretations as literally "castration". By the end of the first year of his analysis all of Edward's delusions had seemingly disappeared, he was in touch with reality and leading a relatively normal life. In the ensuing years his analysis contained him by preventing several potential breakdowns. Edward ended his analysis after four years and went on to complete his studies, work, marry, and have a family.

Object relations theorists do not make a significant diagnostic distinction between schizophrenia, mania, paranoia, and other forms of psychosis except as examples of the failure to adequately overcome the paranoid-schizoid position. In general, Kleinian theory states that all adults retain psychotic processes that involve a constant struggle to cope with paranoid anxiety and depressive anxiety. For that reason object relations clinicians apply the same treatment approach to neurotics and psychotics, adults and children. This represents a fundamental difference with Lacanian theoretical approaches to the treatment of psychosis because an approach to the patient that is required in the establishment of the transference with neurotics can be quite destructive in the relationship with psychotics. Another question is the accuracy of diagnoses between differing psychoanalytic schools of thought providing much ongoing contradiction and discussion. This is why Colette Soler's (1991) critique of the analytic treatment of Marion Milner's patient, Susan, is of particular interest. Soler questions the lack of evidence to back up the diagnosis of schizophrenia that Milner and apparently Winnicott gave to this patient. Soler draws attention to the difficulty with object relations diagnoses that locate a nucleus of psychotic anxiety at the heart of neurosis as a remnant of a normal paranoid–schizoid phase of development. The failure to differentiate at the structural level in object relation's theory means that little attention is paid to the phenomenology that may assist in discrimination between diagnostic categories.

Ego psychology

Ego psychology is a school of post-Freudian psychoanalysis that developed in the United States in the years following the Second World War. It was derived from Freud's second topography, Anna Freud's work on the ego and its defences, and child psychology. Ego psychology focuses on ways of strengthening the defence mechanisms of the conscious mind rather than the unconscious motivation of an individual's actions, as in classical psychoanalysis (Kernberg, 1997). It is based on an elaboration of Freud's structural model of the mind, which focuses on the function of the ego in its mediating role between the conflicting demands of the instinctual id, the moralistic superego, and external reality. Ego psychology has dominated North American psychoanalysis and it is this position of dominance that enabled ego psychology to put itself forward as the inheritor of Freudian psychoanalysis.

Ego psychology is most closely associated with Heinz Hartmann and his collaborators Ernst Kris and Rudolph Loewenstein, also David Rapaport, Erik Erikson, and later on by Edith Jacobson and Margaret Mahler (Kernberg, 1997). Hartmann (1950) undertook a fundamental revision of Freud's structural theory arguing that the healthy ego includes a sphere of autonomous ego functions that are independent of mental conflict. The aim of psychoanalytic treatment, according to Hartmann, was to expand the conflict free sphere of ego functioning that would result in an adaptation to a more effective mutual regulation of the ego. The ego is a substructure of personality that organises and controls perception and it tests reality (Hartmann, 1950, p. 75). It also serves as a protective barrier against excessive external and, in a somewhat different sense, internal stimuli.

Patients with schizophrenia were said to be afflicted with severe ego disturbances. Rudolph Loewenstein (1958) said that in such cases considerable variations or even modifications of the analytic technique were necessary. The analyst, in order to achieve what is termed a "restructurization" of the subject's ego, had to abandon the usual stance of neutrality and replace it with an attitude of presence. To not do this "is to deprive the patient of a possible cure for the sake of guarding the 'gold of analysis' from being alloyed" (Loewenstein, 1958, p. 240). Here he is referring to Freud's Budapest speech (Freud, 1919a). Loewenstein was Jacques Lacan's training analyst and interestingly, for much of his professional life, Lacan disputed ego-psychology's claim to being the true heir to the Freudian legacy, indicating a conflict between the two men. In the view of ego psychology the analyst's role is to become an ally of the healthy ego forces in their struggle to dominate instincts and drives. In order for a patient to strengthen his or her autonomous ego they are expected to identify with the ego of the psychoanalyst. Hence, the analyst needs to develop a strong ego. Lacan (1991) repudiated this position criticising the ego psychologist's conception of a healthy part of the ego and other concepts, such as adaptation and the autonomous ego. Lacan concluded that an analysis had failed if it ended with the analysand identifying with the analyst because the aim of an analysis is quite the opposite.

Interpersonal psychotherapy

Interpersonal psychotherapy comprises different approaches to theory and practice held together by underlying assumptions and premises of a relational model advocated by members of the William Alanson White Institute. The group were strongly influenced by the psychoanalytic work of Sándor Ferenczi who emphasised the mutuality of the relationship between patient and analyst. The Interpersonalist method contradicted drive theory and the sexual foundation of classical Freudian psychoanalysis proposing that there was an under-representation of a social and cultural context in the Freudian approach:

> Psychoanalytic formulations are extremely individualistic, in the sense that they are largely Prof. Freud's opinions about his experience with his patients, in the formation of which opinions—as in the great part of all psychiatric opinions—the social and cultural aspects of the thinker's opinion-formation have mostly been ignored. (Sullivan, 1931b, p. 523)

Instead the interpersonalists favoured the interactive, experiential dimension where human motivation is said to be embedded in relational and self-esteem needs: the experience of satisfaction gives way to the experience of security, the pleasure principle is replaced by psychological motives, such as curiosity and the search for meaning, and the Oedipus complex is rejected in favour of a much wider concept of self-realisation in an acculturating social environment (Leonoff, 1996). The perceived phallocentric theory of Freud was rejected and supplanted with a socio-psychological perspective that stressed the effects of culture, attitudes, and social organisation on sexual behaviour and the sexual aspect of identity.

The members of the White Institute came together to deliberate on ideas concerning the interpersonal and psychosocial aspects of communication. They all knew each other and/or had worked together at Chestnut Lodge Sanatorium. This group formed an alliance based on respect for freedom of thought, a humanistic concern in their commitment to psychoanalysis as a response to human suffering, a proactive political stance toward redefining social structures and an abiding interest in interactions between individuals and their interpersonal environment (Lionells, 2002). Harry Stack Sullivan was called upon to provide a conceptual centre for the Institute and many of his theories were incorporated into the Interpersonalist tradition (Leonoff, 1996). Frieda Fromm-Reichmann and others were recruited to form the core faculty of the Institute. Proponents of the interpersonal model have published extensive case histories of psychotic patients who were treated in four or five times weekly therapy, mostly in a hospital setting. The White Institute was created as an independent non-profit centre, governed by a Board of Trustees selected from an informed lay community and it was among the first institutes to establish a low cost clinic for psychoanalytic treatment. It explored new territory in psychoanalytic theory and praxis, breaking away in the middle of last century in protest to the constriction of mainstream American psychoanalytic thought.

Fundamental to the routine psychotherapeutic treatment of psychosis is the building of an enduring, positive relationship with the patient.

Other approaches

Fundamental to the routine psychotherapeutic treatment of psychosis is the building of an enduring, positive relationship with the patient. The following approaches to the work with psychosis show a variety of proven techniques, interventions, and theories derived from psychoanalysis that broaden the field significantly. The research of Karon and Vandenbos (1981) presents a modified psychoanalytic approach to the treatment of schizophrenia that claims to have successful outcomes. Fundamental to Karon's view is that every symptom and every verbalisation from the patient has meaning. Equally, the patient's associations have meaning whether they are immediately understandable or not and transference reactions are inevitable and at the core of what occurs in the treatment. Delusions are understood primarily as (a) transference to the world at large (b) defences against pseudo-homosexual anxiety (c) concepts and meanings are idiosyncratic to a particular family and (d) an attempt to make sense out of one's world and life despite strange experiences and symptoms (Karon & Vandenbos, 1981).

Otto F. Kernberg and Heinz Kohut are two theorists who have focused on the observation of patients with narcissistic and borderline psychopathology. However, their perspectives concerning the causes, structure, and treatment of these disorders are considerably different. Kernberg is most widely known for his psychoanalytic theories on borderline personality organisation and narcissistic pathology (Kernberg, 1975; Kernberg, et al., 1989a). His work has been central in integrating post-war ego psychology with Kleinian object relations (Kernberg, 1973). Kohut (1971) developed his Self Psychology theory with influences from ego psychology, object relations theory, and humanistic psychology. Kohut theorised that the central pathology in narcissistic behaviour and personality disorders was the defective or weakened condition of the self, and that the goal of therapy was the rehabilitation of this structure (Kohut & Wolf, 1978). Both Kernberg and Kohut contend that narcissism is somewhere between neurosis and psychosis. Kohut regards narcissism as an essential function of the ego whereas Kernberg sees borderline phenomenon on the verge of psychosis and in this respect he identifies narcissism with schizoid phenomena. Kernberg and Kohut regard the analytic process and the role of the analyst in quite different terms. Specifically, Kohut advocates the analyst's position within the treatment as one where a full narcissistic transference should be encouraged. The analyst should be able to present an empathetic style that reflects the narcissist's self experience so that a cohesive healthy self can eventually emerge. Kernberg considers the analyst's main function is to foster a more integrated object relation by examining and elucidating the narcissist's basic aggression. The role of the analyst should be neutral rather than supportive in order to modify the narcissist's pathological structure.

The main contribution of Gisela Pankow in the treatment of psychosis was the redefinition of Lacan's concept of foreclosure as a defence mechanism that directly implicates the body image, and her use of non-traditional analytic techniques, such as drawing, painting, clay modelling, and family interviews (Pankow, 1974, 1985). Pankow was a neuropsychiatrist and psychoanalyst practicing in Paris whose area of interest was the analysis of patients with psychosis. In formulating her theory and method of "dynamic structurization" Pankow (1985) synthesised the ideas of Sigmund Freud, Ernst Kretschmer, and the existential thinkers. She developed her conception of an "image of the body" drawing from Françoise Dolto's (1973) idea of the unconscious body image. According to Pankow (1974) the body image serves two symbolic functions: The first ensures the recognition of spatial and formal structure, incorporating a dialectic of inside and outside, and part and whole. The second involves the content and meaning of that structure. Thus the body image is the basis of the ego and its relation to the other. Pankow thought that the structurization of the body image would repair the limits of the body-ego.

Another example of an approach based predominantly on Sigmund Freud and Jacques Lacan's psychoanalytic theory is ego-structuring psychotherapy, elaborated by Palle Villemoes and others (De Waelhens & Ver Eecke, 2001). Ver Eecke (2002) promotes Villemoes method that he says follows the work of Gisela Pankow, Piera Aulagnier, Vergote, and others from the University of Leuvin in Belgium. Villemoes worked in public psychiatric hospitals in Sweden and Denmark as a psychiatrist and psychoanalyst, developing ego-structuring psychotherapy over many years. Ego-structuring psychotherapy is a personality developing method conducted in the later stages of a patient's hospitalisation. In describing the world to the patient, the therapist's words help the patient to structure their sensory experiences and in time to become a structuring agent. The therapist provides language in its structuring capability, and the first linguistic connection the patient makes is between object-representations in the "belonging to" aspect, that allows the patient to become part of the scenery or surroundings. In the treatment Villemoes used words to label objects or representations and then linked them together via a linguistic connection. He adopted "a picture book" way of looking at the world where he and the patient would meet (sometimes escorted from the inpatient unit by a nurse) twice a week in the same place at the same time for about twenty minutes and this routine would continue for up to six months. Eventually signs that the patient is engaging in language appear and this implies a shift from imaginary to symbolic identification.

In the 1980s a number of research projects were established in Scandinavia that facilitated the development and integration of psychotherapy for the psychoses in mental health services in Norway (Ugelstad, Haugsgjerd), Sweden (Cullberg, Levander, Sandin), and Finland (Räkköläinen, Siirala). In Turku, Finland Yrjö Alanen initiated a wide-ranging approach to the treatment of schizophrenia that evolved over decades of experience that he spent working as a psychiatrist, family researcher and psychoanalytic therapist. Alanen developed the need adapted approach for the treatment of psychosis. This is based on a flexible and integrated way of incorporating individual psychoanalytically informed therapy adapted to the needs of the individual, including family therapy and pharmacotherapy (Alanen, 1997a). Representatives from medicine, nursing, and social work form a specialist psychosis team trained in one of the main psychotherapeutic modalities adapted for psychosis. Supervisory activities and multi-professional training programs for both individual and family therapy are considered essential to developing therapists' capacities to an adequate level.

The Open dialogue approach of Jaakko Seikkula grew out of and is compatible with the need adapted approach of Alanen and colleagues (Seikkula & Olson, 2003). Open dialogue is a family therapy and social network approach aimed at treating psychotic patients in their homes. As identified with previous models, it integrates different methods of treatment in order to form a single treatment process. During the treatment process the patient may be exposed to many different therapeutic modalities, such as family therapy, psychoanalytically based individual therapy, group therapy, occupational therapy, and pharmacological therapy. This is according to the patient's changing needs which emerge in the meetings with the case specific team, the patient, and the family (Seikkula, et al., 2006).

Open dialogue is a psychotherapeutic approach based on semiotic theory that focuses on constructing a joint dialogue between the participants in a treatment who meet in order to generate a new understanding of the circumstances related to the actual crisis. The need adapted and open dialogue approaches have achieved significant treatment outcomes by reducing hospitalisation rates, lowering the use of medication, and helping patients and families get through a crisis (Cullberg, et al., 2002).

Schloss Tegel Sanitorium.

CHAPTER THREE

The origin of psychoanalysis in institutions

This chapter introduces key developments in the history of psychiatric institutions in Europe in the decades prior to the Second World War and how psychoanalysis entered the field of treating people with psychosis in and out of institutions. The first and second generation pioneers of psychoanalysis in the era of Freud were psychiatrists who had a significant influence on the evolution of the treatment of psychosis and institutional care, heralding changes to psychiatric practice and asylum treatment. The application of the psychoanalytic method to these settings required that they adapt Freud's original technique and think about the institution in a different way. The history of asylums is associated with social and scientific attitudes towards mental health and patients with mental illness, both of which have changed greatly over the past century. Although the first half of the twentieth century saw some attempts to humanise institutions with the introduction of non-restraint policies and an increase in psychological understanding of the treatment of mental illness, it was not until the 1950s after the Second World War that there was the rediscovery of the beginnings of a humane and egalitarian model of care.

The early psychoanalysts in institutions

There was a period of general enthusiasm about psychoanalysis during the first and second decades of the twentieth century. The Zürich psychiatrists from the Burghölzli Clinic in Switzerland formed the nucleus of a small band who were fighting for the recognition of psychoanalysis and for the opportunity to learn the new art and to apply it in asylum practice. These psychiatrists trained to become psychoanalysts and were the closest associates of Sigmund Freud: Carl Jung, Max Eitingon, Karl Abraham, Adolf Meyer, Abraham Brill, Emil Oberholzer, and Ludwig Binswanger all disseminated psychoanalytic teachings throughout Europe and America. "I have repeatedly and gratefully acknowledged the efforts of the Zürich Psychiatric School in the spreading of psychoanalysis, especially those of Bleuler and Jung, and I do not hesitate to do the same today, even under such changed circumstances" (Freud, 1914d, p. 26). But it was through Eugene Bleuler the Burghölzli's director that psychiatry became the first field to which psychoanalysis was applied (Freud, 1924f). Bleuler's 1911 *Dementia Praecox or the Group of Schizophrenias* expressed an optimistic tone and inspired others, especially those in Freud's circle, to try new methods in the treatment of formerly untreatable patients with schizophrenia. Bleuler was fascinated by Freud's work and introduced psychoanalysis to Jung and the other doctors at the Burghölzli (Falzeder & Haynal, 2002). Although Bleuler distanced himself from the organisational side of psychoanalysis and rejected those aspects of psychoanalytic theory that were not clinically verifiable, he did accept psychoanalytic theories that were borne out by his personal experience and his clinical experience as a psychiatrist. Even though Bleuler opened the doors of international scientific discourse to Freud and to psychoanalysis, he was caught in the middle and struggled against the disapproval of established psychiatry, particularly the views of Emil Kraepelin.

Carl Jung (1960) was senior staff physician at the Burghölzli from 1900 to 1909 and he encouraged the medical staff there to abandon the anatomical explanation for serious mental illness, such as schizophrenia in favour of an understanding of the psychical disorder. He thought that psychoanalytic theory could help physicians understand the psychotic symptoms associated with schizophrenia. An investigation of the patient's history made the symptoms understandable in the context of an unusual emotional reaction to particular emotional problems, and pathological ideas that dominated the patient when psychotic were derived from the most important questions that dominated them when they were well. Jung's work developed in two ways: on the one hand, he used association tests and on the other, he became interested in the imagination, ideas, dreams, and bizarre fantasies of his schizophrenic patients, convinced that they were meaningful. Jung insisted on the role played by complexes in schizophrenia, which would split from conscious control and completely swallow the ego producing psychotic symptomatology. He called his therapeutic method depth psychology because it provided a possibility for the patient to experience the unassimilated archetypes as something meaningful in a personal or cultural context.

On the strength of his research into schizophrenia, Jung published *The Psychogenesis of Dementia Praecox* in 1907 and it was this work that impressed Freud's, prompting an invitation for Jung to visit:

> Jung employed with success the analytic method of interpretation in the strangest and most obscure phenomena of dementia praecox, the origin of which appeared quite clear when correlated with the life and interests of the patient. From that time on it became impossible for the psychiatrists to ignore psychoanalysis. (Freud, 1914d, p. 28)

Jung's objection to the psychogenesis of severe schizophrenia was the poor prognosis, the incurability of the condition and the ultimate dementia and yet he treated his psychotic patients as if they were psychogenic and could be cured by psychological means. Experience told him that the overwhelming majority of cases were psychologically determined (Jung, 1960). Jung reported that after successful treatments he was told that the patient was never schizophrenic in the first place, indicating that because the treatment had been successful the patient must not have had schizophrenia. For him this revealed a discouraging prejudice whereby the very diagnosis meant that psychiatrists and psychoanalysts alike found the patient to be untreatable. Jung insightfully advised caution when the diagnosis was unclear in relation to latent psychosis and the triggering of a psychotic break by analysing the subject as though he or she were neurotic without making some adjustments. Many patients he treated never saw the inside of a hospital but were able to be treated with psychoanalysis in private practice. He concluded there were two aspects of schizophrenia, the biological and the psychological, and that successful treatment was possible for particular patients.

For seven years while Jung was still at the Burghölzli he was closely involved in the psychoanalytic movement and much of the correspondence between he and Freud centred on clinical cases of dementia praecox. Jung saw the circumstances between he and Freud as diametrically opposed because of Freud's lack of experience in applying psychoanalysis to the difficult work conditions at the Burghölzli where he dealt "[…] mostly with uneducated insane patients, and on top of that with the uncommonly tricky material of dementia praecox" (Jung, 1906, p. 1). Jung saw that his scientific premises were totally different from Freud's and even towards the end of their relationship, still claimed that Freud did not understand him. Ultimately there was too fundamental a difference between them and they fell out with each other. Nevertheless, Jung holds the place as the first to lead psychoanalysis towards the field of psychosis.

Karl Abraham was also a central figure in the early history of psychoanalysis. He was a dedicated teacher and mentor to an influential group of analysts that include Ernst Simmel and Melanie Klein. Abraham took a leading role in the orientation of the training institute attached to the Berlin Poliklinik, which involved the selection, training, and supervision of suitable analyst candidates. He founded the Berlin Psychoanalytic Society in 1910 and was actively involved as its president until his premature death in 1925. Abraham worked with severe mental illness as a psychiatrist at the Burghölzli and other asylums. He was interested in the study of manic depressive psychosis and psychotic despair as the result of a traumatic loss, and treated these patients analytically with some successes (Abraham, 1949a). It is difficult to interpret some of the claims of success that were made by pioneer analysts about their treatment of apparently psychotic patients because a universally accepted approach to psychiatric diagnosis was not in place before the Second World War. Abraham identified schizophrenic renunciation as the result of regression to an early narcissistic infantile fixation, and melancholia as a similar regression to an early oral stage. He collaborated with Freud confirming and deepening the understanding of melancholia and manic-depressive illness that led to Freud's (1917a) later paper on "Mourning and melancholia". Abraham found that during the analytic treatment of many cases of melancholia in an institution, in addition to private practice that evidence of progress and change could be seen in patients, under the following conditions: the patient's capacity for transference increased after a piece of analytic work was achieved, the patient's negative attitude and irritability towards people eased, they were able to direct their libido in a relatively normal way, the effects of a punishing super-ego lessened and in the formation of transitory neurotic symptoms, which indicated a different object choice (Abraham, 1949b).

Freud's contribution

Freud was not a hospital psychiatrist (alienist) and he had little to no exposure to asylum patients. Nevertheless, he wanted to know about and understand the mystery of psychosis; he also wanted to achieve a therapeutic effect although he was not confident of his skills with psychotic patients. An investigation of Freud's notes shows that he did accept psychotic patients into analytic treatment as long as they were not acutely psychotic (May, 2008). He restricted the patients he saw to those with isolated, circumscribed delusions and not with full-blown psychotic symptoms or acute suicidal ideation. In the treatment approach to delusional patients, he recommended waiting until the delusions faded before he started the analysis proper. Freud concluded that the psychotic process was an adjustment; something that should not be too greatly disturbed or interfered with (Freud, 1940a [1938]). He admitted in a letter to Simmel his unfamiliarity with schizophrenia which accounted for his hesitancy in treating such cases (Deri & Brunswick, 1964, p. 103). Although, even when he was not successful in curing a case he considered the outcome of the analysis in terms of its scientific value and therapeutic helpfulness. In a communication to Abraham, Freud spoke of two cases of melancholia he had successfully treated, and in one there was no relapse ten years post-treatment (Abraham, 1949a). Federn (1953) referred to the advice Freud gave him about the therapeutic triggering of psychosis that could be successfully treated, Freud said, if there was a thorough understanding of the narcissistic mechanisms involved and if the treatment was conducted with the support of a psychoanalytic clinic. Freud's correspondence about the case of A.B provides interesting information about his private thoughts and fears that are familiar to many analysts who treat psychosis. Freud's analysis of A.B is not a story of the application of an objectively definable, reproducible procedure; it was a process of interaction and connection between two people that defies technical description (Lynn, 1993). The cases of A.B and others with psychosis who were treated by Freud are discussed in more detail elsewhere (Mackie, 2011).

Freud (1925d) reflected that the history of psychoanalysis fell into two phases: in the first he stood alone and did all the work by himself and in the second phase he shared psychoanalysis with others, his students, analysands, colleagues, and collaborators. As psychoanalysis grew in importance Freud found he had less control over it, especially as he was drawing towards the end of his own life but there were a few discoveries where he claimed a prominent role. They were in the sphere of narcissism, the theory of the instincts, and the application of psychoanalysis to the psychoses. "Since then analysts have never relaxed their efforts to come to an understanding of the psychoses. Especially since it has been possible to work with the concept of narcissism, they have managed, now in this place and now in that, to get a glimpse beyond the wall" (Freud, 1925d, p. 61). It was not Freud but some of the analysts who followed him who transformed his recommendations about the treatment of psychosis into commandments. The process of reinterpretation of Freud's work has gradually created strictures that were contradicted in Freud's own practice.

In his address to the Budapest Congress towards the end of World War One Freud spoke of the social obligation that psychoanalysis be made freely available to all, acknowledging that this would mean adapting and modifying the psychoanalytic method for it to be applied outside of the standard practice. He said (Freud, 1919a, p. 167) it was probable that, as a consequence, this would:

> [...] compel us to alloy the pure gold of analysis freely with the copper of direct suggestion [...]. But, whatever form this psychotherapy for the people may take, whatever the elements out of which it is compounded, its most effective and most important ingredients will assuredly remain those borrowed from strict and untendentious psycho-analysis.

Freud was protective of the analytic method but he had to relinquish his rights over its application so that it could be made available for the common good of the people. Several years later, having become reconciled to this, he referred to the comment about alloying the gold of analysis saying in a letter to Pfister that "gold never occurs in nature without an admixture of silver and copper" (Freud, 1926, p. 105).

Large-scale application of psychoanalysis

Europe found itself in a state of upheaval after World War One. Austria was proclaimed a republic from 1918 to 1934 and Red Vienna became the shining example of a socialist future with the introduction of major social reforms. The Weimar era (1919–1933) in Germany followed the post-war revolution from which, as in Austria, a republic emerged. The Weimar Republic was marked by explosive social, cultural, and intellectual productivity based on the doctrine of radical functionalism. Functionalism is about the interdependent sections of society working together to fulfil the functions necessary for the survival of society through social order, consensus, and social integration. Radical functionalism centres on the structures, modes of domination, deprivation, and contradictions that exist in society and is committed to overthrowing those social structures. This new paradigm introduced an understanding of psychoanalysis that was rooted in humanism, political activism and the empowerment of disenfranchised people in society. Berlin and Vienna became the heart of a progressive, civilised, and politically aware society that also fostered the rise of Nazism. Freud, in a series of politically charged statements, expressed the ruling zeitgeist of the years between the wars revealing his allegiance to the progressive urban energy of "Red Vienna". Analysts of the time were known as political revisionists for whom psychoanalysis represented human liberation, social empowerment, and freedom from bourgeois convention.

From 1920 psychoanalysis was made available to outpatients and inpatients alike when pioneer psychoanalysts, Max Eitingon and Ernst Simmel inspired by Freud's Budapest speech and drawing from their experiences with war neurosis, founded the first public psychoanalytic clinic and training school in Berlin. The Berlin Poliklinik and its companion inpatient service, the Schloss Tegel Sanatorium pioneered psychoanalytic treatment and training methodologies. This was probably the most productive period in the record of psychoanalysis with psychoanalytic treatment being offered as a service within public mental health, and the example of the Berlin Poliklinik became a springboard for the spread of free clinics throughout Europe. Treatment decisions were based on the urgency of the case, the patient's motivation for analysis and their responsiveness to the treatment, rather than their social class or ability to pay. The clinic was a non-profit private charity funded by a variety of sources: patient fees, private donations, and donations from the Berlin Society. Analysts in training were analysed free of charge in exchange for their service in the clinic and every analyst treated at least one patient free in their private practice freeing up more space at the clinic (Danto, 2005). Their funding strategies, research activities, and approaches to clinical problems, like the length of a session and duration of treatment, tell the story of a dynamic and innovative psychoanalytic institute.

In 1922 Paul Federn, Eduard Hitschmann, and Helene Deutsch established the Vienna Ambulatorium, which was co-directed by Hitschmann and Wilhelm Reich (Fine, 1979). The clinic developed in parallel with a government assistance scheme for children and families, and grew to include a training institute and a child guidance centre. These were the only institutions on the continent to make psychoanalytic treatment accessible to patients of all ages and social classes, ranging in occupational status from professional to unemployed at no cost or according to a sliding scale. Although government funding was a wished for financial boon it created a bind because the bureaucratic strings attached to the funding interfered with the flexibility and freedom of how analysts could govern the institution and limited the ways in which they could interpret psychoanalytic principles (Danto, 1998). Treating all people regardless of their ability to pay was an ethos consistent with the ideology of Red Vienna, as these social democrat analysts bridged the gap between Viennese society, mental health services, and the psychoanalytic community. The Berlin Poliklinik, the Vienna Ambulatorium and other free clinics, such as the London Clinic of Psycho-Analysis and Ferenczi's clinic in Budapest, were born out of this enlightened period where at least one fifth of the work of these first and second generation analysts went to indigent city residents.

Wilhelm Reich, an avid Marxist, was interested in taking psychoanalysis at the Ambulatorium in the direction of social reform. He sought to treat the more difficult patients, in particular those labelled psychopath, antisocial, criminal and destructive, and patients with "rageful tendencies" who made attempts at suicide (Fine, 1979). In the latter part of the 1920s Reich and Gustav Bychowski, another recruit from the Burghölzli, progressed to the treatment of psychosis, in particular schizophrenia. Reich advocated greater therapist activity in order to reach certain patients and break down their resistances to analysis, which was a precursor to the later development of character analysis (Reich, 1972). In his approach Reich would point out to patients their character flaws aiming to shake up the defences of resistant patients by screaming and shouting at them in order to draw them out of their shells. Bychowski seemed to balance Reich by using less forceful methods. Reich become known for challenging traditional assumptions and for his fanatical ideas that ultimately led to his being discredited. A supporter of Reich, John Rosen, later established a sanatorium near Philadelphia in the United States where he applied his Direct Analysis to the treatment of patients with schizophrenia. The method involved long hours of loud, forceful, and even vulgar interpretations to the patient's speech as a kind of shock therapy. The aim was to wake patients up so they could be more open but on follow up all his patients had relapsed (Stone, 1999). Rosen followed the same fate as Reich; he had his license to practice medicine revoked and criminal charges were laid against him.

Heinz Hartman and Paul Schilder advanced a shared psychoanalytic and biological approach to the treatment of psychiatric disorders. They opened a special experimental department attached to the Vienna Ambulatorium for the treatment of psychosis and borderline cases (Danto, 2005). Subsequently Hartmann immigrated to America, Schilder did the same and then Eduard Bibring took over enhancing the department with a more radical fundamentalist philosophy. Patients were intensively assessed and observed regarding their suitability before any course of treatment was decided. The aim of the treatment for psychotic patients was to allay their anxiety with a modified analytic approach: sessions were shorter, only forty-five minutes in length; the patient and analyst would meet less frequently, perhaps only three times per week; and the chair was used more often than the couch.

The interwar years saw enormous hardship and political unrest in Hungary with the collapse of the Austro-Hungarian Monarchy, the declaration of an independent republic followed by rebellion and further invasion. For these reasons, it was not until 1930, after much wrangling with the authorities that the first free psychoanalytic clinic was opened in Budapest by the Ministry of Public Welfare (Swerdloff, 2002). Sandor Ferenczi was the Budapest Clinic's first director, albeit briefly, followed by Michael Balint who was driven out by the Nazis in 1938 and immigrated to England. Balint facilitated people paying only nominal fees for analytic treatment and those who could not pay were subsidised by private benefactors, including candidates wanting a training analysis. Balint believed that anyone who wanted help should not be denied it, so the clinic was very busy and carried more patients in treatment than both psychoanalytic clinics in Vienna and Berlin.

Psychoanalysis in sanatoria

Sanatoria or private treatment centres were common throughout Europe and the United States during the nineteenth century until the 1930s. They were often referred to as rest homes, cure hotels and, in Germany and Austria, treatment centres. There is a distinction between a sanitarium, a health resort or spa, and sanatorium, which is a treatment facility such as a clinic, hospital or asylum. Sanatoria were medical facilities, usually located in a quiet isolated rural area, for the rehabilitation of chronic illness, typically tuberculosis or psychiatric illness. Therapy involved a combined regimen of diet and exercise, plus rest and recuperation. In central Europe they used techniques specifically referred to as psychotherapy that was generally thought to have originated with the Nancy school of hypnotism in France. The technique of "positive persuasion" was introduced by the Bernese psychiatrist Paul Dubois that involved the disciplined ordering of patients' lives in the clinic through psychic influencing, approximating a nascent form of psychoanalysis (Shorter, 1990, p. 193).

Gradually psychoanalysis found its way into the clinical practices of sanatoria. Georg Groddeck combined Freud's psychoanalytic principles with his own original somatic theories at his sanatorium at Baden-Baden that he founded in 1900 and where he treated medical patients for thirty years (Avila, 2003). He is noted for his work in psychosomatic medicine and dedicated himself to chronically ill patients who came to him as a last resort. Through observation of the symptoms and complaints of his patients, Groddeck gradually formed the idea that the processes of every illness had a symbolic dimension. He considered disease as a form of language and symptoms as different ways for unconscious needs to express themselves. In this way he became alert to the strong womb fantasies and maternal transferences of his hospitalised patients. In the treatment of the organic patient, Groddeck found psychoanalysis a powerful way to reveal the unconscious, to remove resistances and to liberate healing forces. He was the first to propose a way of applying psychoanalysis to the study of the body.

Frieda Fromm-Reichmann worked for four years as a psychoanalyst at a health spa at *Weisser Hirsch* (White Stag) near Dresden where psychosomatic illnesses were treated with systematic relaxation and psychotherapy (Hornstein, 2000). Later, she set up her own sanatorium, a kind of therapeutic community based on Orthodox Jewish principles, where she personally analysed all the residents, including the housekeeper, the cook, and her future husband Eric Fromm. For several years in the mid-1920s about a dozen people, a few of them psychotic, lived communally in her large house in Heidelberg, Germany before she immigrated to the United States in 1935 and started her work at Chestnut Lodge.

In Switzerland, Carl Jung and Marguerite Sechaheye both treated psychotic patients in their private practices but if necessary their patients were lodged at a nearby sanatorium from where they could attend daily consultations with their analysts. In the case of more severe relapses the patient was placed in an asylum (such as the Burghölzli) and returned to the sanatorium and their usual sessions once they were settled.

Paul Federn avoided the clinics and sanatoria around Vienna as he considered them completely unsuitable. As an alternative he treated psychotic patients at home or occasionally arranged with the patient's relatives to set up separate households or a foster home with a guardian or nurse (Federn, 1943b).

Schloss Tegel Sanatorium

The first official psychoanalytic institution was the Schloss Tegel Sanatorium, a Renaissance manor house dating back to 1558, located near Lake Tegel on the outskirts of Berlin in Germany. In 1927 its director, Ernst Simmel, opened the clinic as the inpatient service associated with the Berlin Poliklinik. Simmel became acquainted with the successful use of a combination of psychoanalysis and hypnosis on soldiers during the First World War and his paper on the successful treatment of combat veterans brought him to Freud's attention (Simmel, 1921). The patients who were admitted to Schloss Tegel were diagnosed generally as severe neurosis, some with psychosis, severe character disorder, drug and alcohol addiction, and those with chronic organic problems (Deri & Brunswick, 1964). Simmel was interested in the psychogenic origin of certain types of organic dysfunction and wanted to demonstrate a psychotherapeutic approach to their treatment (Warburg, 1932). He also had a particular interest in schizophrenia having written his dissertation on the psychogenic theory of the origin of dementia praecox. Simmel wanted to treat psychosis at Tegel but they were only able to take on cases of schizophrenia and paranoia where the disease was in its early stages and where the patients had retained considerable contact with the object-world (Simmel, 1929). This was because the original plan to include a locked ward at Tegel was blocked by the landlord, as it would have lowered the land value. Although disappointed by this, Simmel arranged to use the locked ward of a nearby psychiatric hospital if his psychotic patients needed it.

Clinically, the sanatorium provided a total therapeutic milieu where patients were treated with respect according to the values of social justice. Simmel's activities were permeated with the socialist principles and he believed that all people had the right to free psychoanalytic treatment. But a sanatorium that provides free treatment is very expensive to run without the support of the state. Tegel was subsidised by large Viennese and Berlin Companies as a private charity together with funds donated by the Berlin Psychoanalytic Society. Nonetheless Tegel was always in economic difficulty. The sanatorium accommodated twenty-five to thirty patients and at its peak there was a ratio of one analyst to every eight patients. Simmel and two chief physicians, who were analysts from Vienna, supervised the staff on the general principles of psychoanalysis and the nature of the transference with particular patients. The staff comprised analytically trained medical assistants or trainee analysts and nurses, in addition to a matron and domestic staff. The novelty of the treatment approach in conjunction with the diversity and difficulty of the nature of the patients drew many trainee psychoanalysts to gain work experience at Tegel.

The special law of the sanatorium was that the patient's mental attitude to life on the outside was reflected in his life inside the institution. The analytic treatment was thought to be more productive if the patient was isolated from his former environment and allowed to develop an attachment to the institution, especially in the first few days. The institution was designed to intensify the patient's frustration by closing off all avenues of resistance so that they were left with their own original infantile reality. The way the milieu was arranged helped patients make the most of their psychoanalytic hours on the couch by extending the therapeutic time to the whole twenty-four hours of the day. This was achieved by allowing transference relations to develop which would in turn be interpreted and corrective responses applied by sanatorium staff. The psychoanalytic clinic included the clinic as a whole, "[…] as a kind of extension of the analyst's personality or as the archetype of the family in general" (Simmel, 1929, p. 79). The matron represented the mother, the physician/analyst the father, and the other patients and sometimes nurses and attendants stood in for the siblings. Simmel paid close attention to the feedback from staff, who he described as his extra sense organ, with regard to conflicts that were projected onto the staff by patients in the transference. This idea is linked to the radical functionalist beliefs of a society that is compared to a living organism, in that both a society and an organism are made up of interdependent working parts (organs) and systems that must function together in order for the greater body to function:

> Every morning the physicians and the nursing staff meet in the consulting-room. The sisters and attendants tell what they have noticed about their patients outside the analytic sessions of the previous day. The analysts then give directions for the coming day. The attendants are continually given explanations both of the general principles of psycho-analysis and of the special transference-situation of the individual patients. We insist that, while being as tactful as possible, they must not give in to the patients, but must refer them again and again to the physician who is treating them and must themselves refuse to take any personal offence. The attendants' observations as well as those which we ourselves are able to make of the patients' behaviour outside analysis, by night and day, are brought into the analysis itself when the right moment comes. It is true that this is contrary to customary analytic procedure, but, as I said, a psycho-analytic clinic has its own law. (Simmel, 1929, p. 79)

The environment functioned like a crutch or a prosthesis until the patient was able to get back on his or her feet again and enter the world again. Simmel contended that the protective milieu of the sanatorium provided the patient with a new reality that functioned as a symbol of the mother's womb. This was reflected in powerful intrauterine and infantile fantasies as demonstrated in patients' attitudes and dream life. Simmel recognised the maternal identification of many patients as an integral part of the corrective analytic experience at the sanatorium.

"The genius loci of the psycho-analytic clinic, the house which takes into its protection and care, sick people in their torment, which binds their anxiety but also inevitably stirs it up again at times, is ... the symbol for the mother herself" (Simmel, 1929, p. 87).

Over time the minimal budget allocated for the running of Tegel forced them to employ low cost personnel and inexperienced analysts who required training and supervision from the already overworked Simmel. Anna Freud was a frequent visitor at Tegel either accompanying her father on one of his visits or to give seminars on child analysis. She commented in a letter to her friend Eva Rosenfeld, the matron at Tegel, about staffing at Tegel saying that the numerous therapeutic conflicts could be responsible for impeding solid patient care (Danto, 2005, p. 238). She spoke of the burnout staff must experience with the work load involved in caring for such difficult patients and the question of how much pure and how much applied psychoanalysis a patient needed or could stand. Associated with this was her concern about the patient's capacity to tolerate the amount of anxiety that the treatment provoked. Only seasoned analysts could assess this and she believed that having inexperienced analysts in charge could be disastrous. Simmel and those close to him anticipated a time when they could introduce a more serious Marxist approach to sanatorium treatment that combined personal insight-oriented analysis and what they called community organising, a precursor to the therapeutic community model developed later in the 1940s. However, Schloss Tegel was never a financially viable project, especially in the economically unstable inter-war years. The sanatorium was declared bankrupt in 1929 and struggled on until finally it closed its doors in 1931 after operating for only four years. In its brief life Schloss Tegel satisfied Simmel's vision of applying psychoanalysis to inpatients. It also served as a model for other North American psychiatric institutions such as the Menninger Clinic in Topeka, Kansas, Austen Riggs in Massachusetts, and Chestnut Lodge in Maryland.

Bellevue Sanatorium

Ludwig Binswanger was another early adherent of psychoanalysis and one of the first European psychiatrists to introduce psychoanalysis into the sanatorium context. He came under the influence of Bleuler and Jung at the Burghölzli, accompanying Jung on his first visit to Freud in 1907. From this time Freud and Binswanger developed a lasting correspondence. In a letter dated January 30th 1911, Freud indicated the need for modifications to the analytic method in its institutional application:

> I must protest in retrospect against the notion that by assigning to you the task of introducing psychoanalysis into medical practice I was trying to bar you from scientific work, as you seem to assume in your proudly modest way. On the contrary, we look to you for many more contributions [...]. I merely tried to convey to you that our method needed certain modifications for institutional application, and these no one could evaluate better than you. (Freud, 1911, p. 59)

Binswanger took over the directorship of the Bellevue Sanatorium in Kreuzlingen on Lake Constance, Switzerland from his father in 1911 and it kept going until 1980. At the time wealthy and well-educated patients and their family members came to Bellevue from all over Europe. Freud sent many of his more intractable patients to Bellevue for inpatient care and encouraged Binswanger in the application of psychoanalysis there. However, by the 1920s Binswanger had become dissatisfied with what he saw as the scientific orientation of psychoanalysis, so he applied a modified psychoanalytic model that included a phenomenological and existential dimension, much to Freud's displeasure (Lanzoni, 2003).

Existential analysis or *Daseinsanalyse* owed its origin to Binswanger's striving to gain a new understanding of the concerns of psychiatry, psychopathology and psychotherapy on the basis of the analysis of existence (Binswanger, 1958–1959). Binswanger claimed that phenomenological intuition and empathy could provide access to understanding the psychotic person holistically. A significant contribution of Binswanger's was to systematically emphasise the importance of finding out what a patient meant by a symptom; it was the underlying specific meaning that was to be explored and never guessed at or imposed on the patient. The existential encounter was a means to enhance the therapeutic efficacy of other treatments rather than as a method in its own right. This encounter formed the basis for Binswanger's active treatment methods of influencing, encouraging and even forcing patients to conform to the patterns and rules of asylum community life.

Binswanger saw therapy as the individual's experience of a mutual working out of a healthier perspective and he used the institution's resources to create an atmosphere of openness and tolerance of deviant behaviour (Hoffman, 2002). This was because he believed that an essential prerequisite for inner change to occur was that patients could feel secure in their being accepted for who they are. Binswanger's model of transference was its use as a tool to renounce isolation through submission to authority rather than working through the parental relationships. Issues of authority and control were a constant problem at Bellevue in the shaping of patients' behaviour to come in line with communal norms and what was deemed appropriate social behaviour. The management of difficult and disruptive behaviour, often in the context of psychosis, was an everyday challenge with the use of authoritative physical and social interventions in an open and trusting milieu.

Binswanger's concept of *Tragung* was found useful in the context of psychotherapy for patients with chronic schizophrenia, described as "the act of carrying, sustaining or bearing" (Rostek, 2003). It is a term for the position that is necessary to support therapeutic transferences and counter-transferences that allows them to be possible, endurable and resolvable. Despite the rudimentary nature of Binswanger's early work on existential analysis, it provided a clinical model for a more direct relationship with patients and has been influential in existential psychiatry.

Variations to the psychoanalytic method

The most outstanding feature of the pioneers was their desire towards the psychoanalytic treatment of psychosis and the position they took regarding its application outside of the standard method. The analyst had to be willing to endure and persevere in the treatment with psychotic patients, communicating the belief that a successful treatment could be possible and that the patient would not be given up on or lost hope with. These analysts challenged Freud and the official doctrine of psychoanalysis at the time, risking rejection and ostracism in order to do what they felt was right.

Federn's analytic technique

Paul Federn was one of Freud's early disciples, outside of those at the Burghölzli, who worked analytically with psychotic patients from the beginning. He believed that certain of these patients were accessible to analytic treatment and could form a transference relationship but that generally the transference would be an unstable one (Federn, 1943b). He built on Freud's notion of libido withdrawal and the concept of ego boundaries that he thought were an important part of the ego but deviated substantially from Freud's conceptualisation of schizophrenia. He postulated instead that the ego lacked enough narcissistic cathexis to occupy boundaries completely and as a consequence was unsafe and became overrun by the unconscious, which obscured reality resulting in delusions and hallucinations (Federn, 1953). He concluded that psychosis was an illness of the ego itself, not a conflict between ego and reality, that was weakly cathected and could be strengthened with analytic therapy, his original model of ego psychology. It is important to distinguish between Federn's ego psychology model and that of Heinz Hartmann, although they used the same terminology, Federn and Hartmann addressed very different issues. Federn's ego is worked up from the concept of the ego as Freud (1914c) used it in his "On narcissism", whereas Hartmann's ego is conceptualised in terms of its functions, as formulated later by Freud (1923b) in *The Ego and the Id*.

In Federn's ego psychology the task of therapy was to establish appropriate ego boundaries and to help defence mechanisms re-repress id impulses in order to maintain the integrity of the patient's personality. Federn emphasised the importance of an accurate and early diagnosis before analytic treatment began and supported the aim of Freud's trial analysis to ascertain if the patient could potentially be psychotic or have a latent psychosis (Federn, 1953, p. 125). He did not recommend the same analytic approach as practiced with the neurotic because psychoanalysts who treated psychotics like neurotics had poor outcomes. Federn's restricted technique in the analytic treatment of psychosis was based on the classical method but in homeopathic dosage where the patient received only small amounts. He also recommended abandoning the use of free association and the analysis of the positive transference because without it psychotic patients cannot be treated. He said that:

> Transference-neurosis quickly develops into transference psychosis; the analyst becomes a persecutor who is introduced in all kinds of delusional and hallucinated constructions [...]. This development is dangerous and may make further work impossible [...].

> Responsibility toward the patient forbids the analyst to make him more psychotic. (Federn, 1943c, p. 477)

Federn maintained that the transference should be positive so as to protect against increasing regression and if the transference should become negative he recommended the treatment be suspended or that the patient continue with another analyst. Federn stressed the need for flexibility in dealing with psychotic patients who should be able to attend sessions at other than customary times, especially when they were disturbed. Keeping them waiting overly long or failing to keep an appointment could be precarious, consequently psychotic patients should be carefully prepared for interruptions and absences in the treatment. Federn also preferred that psychotic patients not lie on the couch as they may not cope with the reality confusion it created (Federn, 1953). For a treatment to be successful the patient would need someone in their life, either a family member or friend who was interested in their welfare and was able to take care of them by providing assistance, if they needed it. For Federn, the psychoanalytic treatment of psychosis was not possible unless there was a helper who could protect the patient when the transference to the psychoanalyst became uncertain. This could be a family member or friend, a trained nurse or social worker. He also endorsed the analyst seeking expert supervision for their analytic work. Federn escaped from Austria in 1938 like many other analysts of the time and immigrated to America, settling in New York.

Schwing's motherliness

Paul Federn frequently incorporated a trained female nurse or social worker to work alongside him with hospitalised patients and without this skilled assistance he predicted that the treatment was not possible (Bachmann, Resch, & Mundt, 2003). Gertrud Schwing was a nurse who studied psychoanalysis in Vienna from 1935 to 1938 when she worked with Paul Federn and Istvan Hollös treating psychotic inpatients at Otto Pötzl's Psychiatric and Neurological Clinic attached to the University of Vienna (Federn, 1943a). Federn advocated the psychoanalytic training of lay analysts, especially nurses, and pushed for the bylaws of the Vienna Psychoanalytic Training Institute to be stretched so that Schwing could pursue psychoanalytic training in spite of her lack of a university degree (Federn, 1943a; Schwing, 1954).

Schwing and Federn often worked with patients together. For Schwing motherliness (in German *Mütterlichkeit*) or a motherly nature was a prerequisite attitude towards the patient with schizophrenia. In her opinion motherliness is sublimated from the original mother function and is reflected in a women's natural capacity to devote herself to others. The logic is that severe illness goes back to a long chain of disappointments in early childhood and "these primal conflicts are most intimately connected with the mother" (Schwing, 1954, p. 49). Accordingly, the experience of motherliness in the treatment was said to provide the patient with what they were deprived of in infancy. In this way she helped patients to give up their narcissistic autism, enter a reparative object relationship with a mother substitute and so master the Oedipus complex. The therapist nurtured a positive transference towards the psychotic patient and this was accomplished by giving the patient undivided attention and gratifying their early infantile orality with gifts such as food (Schwing, 1954). Through motherliness the patient was thought to be more accessible to and capable of the transference; the male analyst provided the link to the father thus completing the Oedipal situation. Schwing found that this parental arrangement was useful because it prevented regressions during temporary absences, it made it easier to revive and resolve infantile conflicts, and finally, it shared the burden between two analysts.

Schwing was interested in the provision of care that was underpinned by dynamic understanding and genuine humaneness towards the most hopeless cases of mental illness. She identified the need to penetrate the desolate loneliness of schizophrenia and for the therapist to reach out to patients she believed had a desperate longing to make contact with the outside world. Schwing warned against preventing patients from performing bizarre rituals or odd mannerisms, if they caused no harm to the patient or others. She believed such behaviour satisfied a need for them and they should be left alone (Brody & Redlich, 1952). She thought that negative and persecutory attitudes were caused by hospital staff who constantly interfered with or thwarted the patient. A hopeful attitude about recovery was encouraged, in an approach of reaching out to patients and allowing them to set the pace. Schwing was responsive to patients when they were accessible to interacting with her but she also respected their wish for her to leave them alone. She did not give up on any patient and quietly kept up her regular visits to them waiting for them to eventually respond to her.

Ferenczi's mutual analysis

Sandor Ferenczi pioneered an alternative to the orthodox Freudian method in the analytic treatment of more difficult cases, for example character disorders, psychosis and trauma. He was an independent thinker who developed a clinical style of psychoanalysis based on a democratic form of mutual analysis where he introduced a more active method. Through his revised analytic technique he aimed to break through the patient's primal repression and go deeper in the analysis using manifestations from the past. Analysts of the era, including Freud, referred cases to Ferenczi that were rejected by others as too difficult, and he maintained patients in treatment for as long as they were willing to come. Ferenczi did not reject anyone because they were too disturbed; for him no one was unanalysable and he never lost hope in a patient's capacity for change. He believed that it was the analyst's job to fit the method to the patient, not to fit the individual to the method (Rachman, 1998). His clinical success was said to come from his therapeutic responsiveness, the mutuality he introduced to the analytic situation and to the emotional encounter with the patient in the here and now relationship that unfolded.

Ferenczi (1931) studied the analyst's personal qualities in the relationship with a patient and identified that the main role to take in fostering the transference was that of a good parental figure. To aid the treatment of difficult cases Ferenczi used relaxation and the nurturing kindness of a tender mother transference to heal the split in the underdeveloped portion of the patient's ego (Rachman, 1998, p. 68). Ferenczi introduced what he called elasticity or flexibility to the psychoanalytic technique with traumatised patients where the analyst was empathic, responsive, and interpersonally engaged. Ferenczi's technique involved indulging the patient's wishes and impulses and so he gave up all consideration for his own convenience by prolonging sessions until the patient was emotionally ready to finish. Freud (1919a) stated that the gratification of all wants and requests is not productive, as a certain degree of frustration ought to be maintained to ensure that the patient continues to work in the treatment. Too much literal gratification of a patient's immediate needs fostered dependency and Ferenczi's technique was considered excessively indulgent, reflecting his own inability to set limits.

Ferenczi was aware that his approaches contained infringements of Freud's injunctions about technique but he convinced himself that:

> [...] Freud's "Recommendations" were really intended only as warnings for beginners and were designed to protect them from the most glaring blunders and failures; his precepts contained, however, almost no positive instructions, and considerable scope was left for the exercise of the analyst's own judgment, provided that he was clear about the metapsychological consequences of his procedure. (Ferenczi, 1930, pp. 433–434)

Ferenczi did go too far and was severely criticised for not practicing the proper method of analysis, to the point that his work was censored. On the one hand, the early psychoanalysts called for complete honesty and public discussion in matters of analytic technique, on the other hand, practically none of them wrote about what they actually did with patients in their own practice (Falzeder, 2004). There was an unwritten law about the correct practice of analysis, even if nobody knew what that actually was. Freud was uncertain about how his followers were interpreting and practicing his technique, and would have them checked up on and censured if there were irregularities. This defensiveness caused many divisions within the psychoanalytic community and left others cautious, especially those analysts who treated more difficult cases and experimented with the technique. When Freud withdrew his support Ferenczi found himself isolated without the benefit of mentorship and supervision of his clinical work.

Although Jacques Lacan (2002c) criticised certain aspects of Ferenczi's work especially the developmental stages, he did recognise that Ferenczi's ideas on the development of the sense of reality, on the origin of the subject and countertransference had influenced his own theories in numerous ways (Eros, 2003). It was not only Ferenczi's nonconformist theories that Lacan admired, the active therapy and other innovative techniques were, in some respects, forerunners of the variable length of sessions with which Lacan was to experiment several decades later (Barzilai, 1997).

Sechehaye's symbolic realisation

Like other psychoanalysts who treated psychotic patients at the time, Marguerite Sechehaye (1956a) gave precedence to the maternal relationship in the treatment. She was a Swiss psychologist who was analysed by Raymond de Saussure and later presented lectures at the Burghölzli Clinic on her unique method of psychotherapy. Sechehaye's work proceeded from discoveries she made in the psychoanalytic treatment of a young girl with schizophrenia called Renée. The treatment began in 1930 and continued for around ten years in the background of many psychiatric hospital admissions (Sechehaye, 1951b). Sechaheye would eventually adopt Renée, who went on to become a psychoanalyst herself.

Sechehaye described symbolic realisation as the process of reconstruction of the psychotic patient's ego through the production of a symbol. The therapy was directed at the needs and frustrations that the patient experienced in early childhood with the aim of satisfying those needs on the pre-symbolic level. The method sought to modify harsh reality and replace it with another that was more tolerable. In the process of creating a new imago for Renée on which she could start to construct a differentiated ego, Sechehaye identified the need to firstly establish a relation between the ego and its symbol. She realised that the primary link in this process was located in the mother-analyst relation as the source of symbolic satisfaction. Thus, she interpreted the satisfaction of Renée's intense need for mother-feeding as the only way she could be freed from the grasp of her punitive super-ego (Sechehaye, 1951a, p. 101). The analyst fostered the mechanisms of projection and imitation, and the libidinal tendencies drawn from maternal love were nurtured in the treatment in an effort to neutralise the self-destructive urges.

In order for analyst and patient to understand each other, Sechehaye learned to speak Renée's language and use her signs. Sechehaye gave Renée a soft toy monkey that became the first symbol of Renée's self, thus establishing the symbol formation approach in the treatment. Later, a baby doll was introduced that she called Ezekiel and Renée would observe the analyst she called Mama, affectionately taking care of and feeding the doll:

> Taking courage one day when Ezekiel was in Mama's arms, I pushed the head forward on her bosom to test whether I had the

> right to live. At this, Mama pressed him to her breast and let him nurse. This she did regularly several times a day so that I awaited the moment in fear of her forgetting. But Mama did not forget and I dared to live. (Sechehaye, 1951a, p. 81)

The analyst fed an apple, representing the mother's breast, to Renée at a time when Renée was starving herself, thus saving her life. Sechehaye commented that the apples she fed Renée were not necessarily a symbol of the mother's milk but a magical pre-symbolic participation "[...] in which a unity exists between the satisfying object (e.g. the mother's breast) and its symbol (in Renée case, apples)" (Laplanche & Pontalis, 1988, p. 441).

Throughout much of her treatment, Renée would feel unbearably guilty for being alive and was haunted by "the System", her punishing delusional superego that wanted to reduce her to nothing. The analyst's position was one of sitting beside the patient, taking sides against the punishing System (Sechehaye, 1951b). Only the consistent maternal support for her eating could induce in Renée the right to live, but it was a battle that often brought her into severe conflict with the System. On occasion, the conflict would precipitate acts of self-harm and suicide attempts that resulted in numerous and prolonged inpatient hospitalisations. Sechehaye explained that if the patient with schizophrenia suffered maternal abandonment in infancy, then the mother-transference would become the means for compensating for that suffering and for the first time the patient feels loved, satisfied and secure. The patient is able to relive the trauma but only at the level where it is corrected and adjusted by the therapist to a weaker state of the psychotic ego. "This graft-transference is experienced by the schizophrenic in a very intense and dramatic way, because it is lived as pre-symbolic-magic participation" (Sechehaye, 1956b, p. 273). The regressed patient can develop an integrated sense of identity and tolerance for aspects of external reality.

In Sechehaye's view, to work with psychosis the analyst's disposition should be robust, they should be intuitive and have the capacity to foster a maternal character in his or her approach (Sechehaye, 1956a). She entered into contact with patients at the level of their regression, which provided them with the gratification of personal growth and instinctual needs. No less important was the ability to respond to pre-symbolic expressions by which the patient's regressive needs can seek satisfaction and compensation. Sechaheye promoted the realisation of the subject's reality through the construction of a symbol that meant that the analyst had to be creative and imaginative in his or her approach to the treatment. This can also be seen with children in the use of play therapy to create a dialogue and so a way for symbolisation, as demonstrated in Melanie Klein's work with children.

The legacy of psychoanalysis

For the most part the early analysts were psychiatrists, many having trained at the Burghölzli Clinic in Zurich where Freud's psychoanalysis introduced a psychological point of view that was fundamentally different. Psychoanalysis was in its infancy prior to the Great War and at a standstill while the war raged with many analysts serving in the military. The treatment of soldiers with psychoanalytic methods during and after that war launched psychoanalysis as a treatment for more serious mental illnesses. But it was the interwar years that were the most exciting for psychoanalysis, when it was in its prime and analysts were filled with enthusiasm about its potential for social good. Up until the early 1930s, German psychoanalysis and specifically the Berlin Psychoanalytic Institute was a model for how psychoanalysis might be practiced and developed in an advanced society. It was explicitly social reformist in attitude and approach in the way it adopted a program of developing psychoanalysis so that it could be of benefit to all people as outpatients and inpatients in sanatoria at low cost.

Yet, within a remarkably short time after the accession of the Nazis to power all this vanished. The National Socialists became very powerful and targeted psychoanalysis for annihilation. They set about destroying its institutional foundations and persecuting and expelling its psychoanalysts. After 1933 the Berlin Institute was Aryanised and Freud's works were publicly burned; Simmel was arrested and later fled to the United States as did Federn, and Eitingon immigrated to Palestine (Danto, 1999). In 1936, the Ministry of Culture announced that psychoanalysis would be allowed to continue if the Berlin Psychoanalytic Institute would join with other branches of psychotherapy under Göring's leadership with a commitment to developing a new German psychotherapy. It was to be based on a non-Freudian, pro-Nazi, anti-Semitic core where the reading of Hitler's *Mein Kampf* was an obligatory part of the training (Frosh, 2003). Thus, the epicentre of psychoanalysis was relocated from Vienna and Berlin to New York and London as refugee and Jewish analysts fled Nazism. Sigmund Freud moved to London in 1938 just prior to the onset of war and died the following year.

SW. '13
St Elizabeths W.A.

CHAPTER FOUR

Group organisation and the social system

This chapter introduces some of the approaches to thinking about institutions and organisations: their structures and their contexts as well as the dynamics around which they are organised. An institution is an organisation that provides a system by which it can be regulated. Institutions provide the structure for social order and cooperation that direct and make rules governing people's behaviour. "The term 'institution' can be defined as the coming together of separate parts in the service for a common task and the structure that arises as a consequence of this process" (Obholzer, 1986, p. 201). It is only by exploring the general conceptualisation of an institution, its effects, its mistakes and the consequences of particular types of management and alternatives, that other possibilities can be brought forth. The institutions under scrutiny in this book are psychiatric or mental health institutions. As social systems they influence institutional practice and psychoanalysis is used as a lens through which this can be interpreted. This chapter is directed towards a psychoanalytic understanding of the nature of human beings in groups and how this knowledge can be applied to the service structures that treat psychotic patients in our society. Drawing on a range of psychoanalytic theories and practices, certain ongoing problems that are inherent in institutions are identified in order to make sense of why they occur, and how to plan ways forward for human beings who work and are treated within these structures. There is no doubt that human beings have significant effects on one another and that group phenomena is complex and multidimensional. The inexplicable instability of groups that become negative and destructive, with seemingly little provocation, to such an extent that they threaten the group's viability, needs to be considered especially in the context of psychiatric institutions. The relationship between the individual and larger organisational systems is central to that understanding.

Organisational consultancy has become popular in the corporate world and this is due to an increasing awareness of the need for healthier organisations. A healthy organisation has effective leadership; it is grounded in openness to new ideas, transparency in its actions, a clarity of purpose, realistic expectations, values that are overt, the ability to tolerate uncertainty and the capacity to learn from mistakes. However the poorly funded areas of public mental health remain neglected. Underfunding is the most common complaint in public mental health and the reason why a model of choice is not implemented or is implemented only partially or in an inadequate way.

Psychoanalysis applied in institutions

A psychiatric institution approaches the patient's treatment according to the psychiatric medical model that typically runs with an agenda of curing the patient of his or her symptoms. This implies an external body that decides what the problem is, what the cure will be and how long it ought to take. The agenda of this kind of market place places pressure on everyone to find answers quickly so that the patient can be cured and discharged so that a bed can be made available for another patient. The revolving door policy is based on the frequency with which a patient comes back to be "re-cured", again. In contrast and of greater interest here, are those institutions that apply a psychoanalytic understanding to the treatment of patients in their conceptualisation of the institution as a whole. A psychiatric facility that is psychoanalytically informed uses the theories of psychoanalysis to inform the organisation in its governance, its training and supervision of staff, as well as in the treatment of patients.

There are many variations to how psychoanalysis can be applied in an institution. For example, a psychiatric unit in a general hospital may be influenced by psychoanalysis in the treatment of its patients or a psychoanalyst may be consulted about particular cases in the supervision of staff. But this level of involvement has little or no effect on how the facility is managed nor does it affect how major decisions are made in an institution. Some institutions are distinguished by their use of psychoanalysis in the conception of the whole organisation. The more sophisticated forms of social rehabilitation in the therapeutic community model use living-together opportunities as treatment tools that enrich the whole hospital milieu. Investigations of the impact of institutional dynamics on the treatment process has led to the formation of integrated therapeutic strategies that focus on the dimensions of individual psychodynamics, the interactional and social processes, in addition to the large group and institutional dynamics.

Institutions where the work is strictly based on psychoanalytic principles offer another illustration. Le Courtil in Belgium references the work of Freud and Lacan in how to integrate the analytic work according to its function so that the whole institution is able to work towards the treatment of the patient. As a result, the treatment of psychosis is a variation of the classical analytic treatment that avoids the pitfalls associated with conducting prescriptive forms of psychoanalysis and maintains flexibility in what the institution offers. The aim is to insert analytic discourse at the very heart of the institution with the intention of disrupting the development of institutional ideals. Clinicians who work with psychotic patients can acquire a deeper understanding of psychosis if they have a desire to work with these patients, if the hospital milieu is interested in psychoanalysis and if there is ample opportunity for supervision and discussion (Jackson, 1995). Hinshelwood describes the relevance of the psychoanalyst in an institution as:

> [...] firstly to be a marginalised representative of a split-off aspect of the human response to suffering patients; secondly, to have some real understanding of the meaning of this marginalisation for the institution. This capacity to search for understanding, for meaning, is partly what we would mean by "containing". In an individual psychoanalysis the role is to be unconsciously used by the patient, whilst consciously struggling to appreciate what that use is and does for the patient. Likewise, we can think of an institution as having a need for a container of those aspects of the human response to suffering which lead to specially intense anxiety. (Hinshelwood, 1994, p. 289)

Psychoanalysts have to find different ways of dealing with the position they are required to adopt within an institution based on a particular kind of response derived from his or her own psychoanalytic formation, and this is their unique contribution to an institution.

Applied psychoanalysis is a body of open-ended continually evolving applications of the psychoanalytic method. "The task of applied psychoanalysis is to discover the specific effects of the unconscious in a given field and the necessary transpositions of the general method when applied specifically to this field" (Anzieu, 1984, p. 2). It is the extension of the work of psychoanalysis into an institution where the opening of a psychoanalytic space within the institutional collective can generate a questioning of the theories around the diverse phenomenology of psychosis and allows for an elaboration of the logic of the structural differences. In the Founding Act of the Freudian School of Paris in 1964, Lacan (1990b) constituted three sections that provide a foundational model for the practice, research and the ongoing systematic investigation of psychoanalysis.

The first section of pure psychoanalysis is the practice and training of psychoanalysts, including the internal criticism of this practice, training, and supervision (Lacan, 1990b, p. 98). Lacan wanted psychoanalysts to be selected on the basis of the examination of analysands relation to their unconscious and to psychoanalysis with their own testimony as analysands through "the Pass" as a starting point, and with the analysis itself as their research (Lacan, 1995, p. 1). In the procedure of "the Pass" the candidate has to give testimony of the passage of their analytic formation to a cartel. The principle of "the Pass" emphasises the particularity of the transmission of knowledge of the analytic experience and the singularities of desire.

The second section is that of applied psychoanalysis that is of greatest interest here as it involves the fields of the therapies and clinical psychiatry, including everyone who contributes to the clinical work in an institution. Lacan spoke of this section as follows:

> To which will be admitted medical groups, whether or not they be composed of psychoanalysed subjects, to the extent that they are capable of contributing to the psychoanalytic experience; through the criticism of its indications in its results; through the testing of the categorical terms and structures that I have introduced as sustaining the undeviating course of Freudian praxis, that in clinical examinations, in nosographical definitions, in the very positing of therapeutic projects. (Lacan, 1990a, p. 99)

Lacan's model concerning applied psychoanalysis refers to the concepts and principles of psychoanalysis that orient the practice of psychoanalysis within the broader field of an institutional framework. It involves going beyond just the clinic to include other functions, such as the medical domain and therapeutics, the research of psychoanalytic concepts in the clinic by way of a critique of the results of the analytic experience. The psychoanalysts working in institutions maintain the knotting that holds the place of psychoanalysis there. To conceive of a place for psychoanalysis in institutions requires a consideration of the history of psychoanalysis in institutions and the nature of group dynamics. Thus, following Lacan's lead we will return to Freud and the work of the pioneers to obtain a perspective on how psychoanalysis developed its theories of group function.

The third section of the Founding Act is for taking inventory of the Freudian Field and is responsible for summarising and critically examining its publications.

Group organisation—Freud and Bion

Sigmund Freud's curiosity about group organisation led him to study the specific role played by the unconscious in communal life. The father complex stands at the conceptual heart of Freud's (1912–1913) *Totem and Taboo* as it suggests a historical explanation of the original primitive grouping of humanity, the "primal horde". This mythical group was headed by a father, a violent authority figure, who forbade any incestuous acting-out among his sons. He was the law and only he was allowed to enjoy the women, as this father was exempt from the incest taboo. The myth says that in order to gain their sexual freedom the sons eventually murdered and devoured their father. However, they were not liberated by this act and instead became identified with their castrating father holding more strongly his prohibition of incest. They discovered the symbolic paternity of the father and thus the work of their mourning was that of remorse, ambivalence, and guilt (Freud, 1912–1913). The result of the murder of the primal horde father by his sons was the establishment of a pact essential for the institution of the law prohibiting incest. In *Totem and Taboo* Freud extended the scope of his theories to hypothesise on the arrangements of early human societies, locating the beginnings of the Oedipus complex at the origins of human society. Freud expanded the idea of ambivalence towards parental figures to include the relationship of citizens to those in authority. He discovered the basis for his work on group psychology in the genesis of institutions in *Totem and Taboo*.

The libidinal dynamics that constitute such groups were elaborated later in *Group Psychology and the Analysis of the Ego* (Freud, 1921c). Here Freud emphasised the unconscious mechanisms that characterise group function and institutional life, as in the church and the army, in his attempt to understand the human destructiveness he witnessed in World War One. For Freud group psychology was concerned with the individual as a member of a race, a nation, a caste, a profession, an institution, or as a component part of a crowd of people organised into a group at some time for some particular purpose. Under special conditions, when continuity is severed or there is a breach of some kind, the social instinct, otherwise known as herd instinct or group mind, is activated and this arouses a profound alteration in mental activity. The intense emotional ties that Freud observed in groups explain the characteristics of "[...] the lack of independence and initiative in their members, the similarity in the reactions of all of them, their reduction, so to speak, to the level of group individuals" (Freud, 1921c, p. 118). The group as a whole shows some of its features in "[...] the weakness of intellectual ability, the lack of emotional restraint, the incapacity for moderation and delay, the inclination to exceed every limit in the expression of emotion and to work it off completely in the form of action" (Freud, 1921c, p. 118). Freud concluded that this showed a picture of a regression in mental activity to an earlier level of primitive thinking.

Freud recognised the tendency for individuals to project their narcissism onto a group and to hold onto differences between groups for narcissistic and destructive reasons. He described the group ideal as the state of mind of individuals in groups who denigrate another group in order to uphold a sense of superiority about their own group, to which they are narcissistically identified (Freud, 1921c). He questioned why a certain group mentality, which led to destructiveness, could be so acceptable to individuals who would otherwise question such acts. He postulated that the group ideal often seemed to resonate with the ego ideal of an individual, so that a heightened value of one's own group was reflected in a heightened value of oneself, in a narcissistic way. Instead of working through the narcissism of the ego ideal, the group ideal is recruited to maintain the narcissistic state of mind. This situation has detrimental effects on an individual's psychic functioning; group members lose the capacity to think for themselves or make informed judgments, seeming unable to take personal responsibility for their own thoughts and actions. In his later works, Freud analysed the psychical processes involved in the transition from studying isolated individuals to the social group. The primary conflict in *Civilization and its Discontents* (Freud, 1930a) comes from the individual's instinctual push towards freedom and civilisation's contrary social system that demands conformity and instinctual repression.

Recognising the destructive potential of a group provides the opportunity to intervene and to disrupt aggression or harness it so that potentially it can be transformed into something therapeutic. Wilfred Bion was guided by his previous familiarity with leaderless groups and his brief experience on the training wing at Hollymoor Military Hospital when he developed his idea of group therapy as a planned experience that could lead to cooperative activity in a group. Bion was convinced that change in soldiers' morale could be brought about through the study of their own behaviour and through their experience as a member of an effective group. He wanted groups and individuals to reflect on the processes in which they were caught up and to develop rational solutions to the problems that arose.

The application of psychoanalytic theory to groups unfolded in England during the Second World War at the Military Neurosis Centre at Hollymoor Military Hospital in Northfield, Birmingham. Two treatment trials, known as the Northfield experiments, were conducted between 1942 and 1948 and brought together a group of talented and influential psychoanalysts. Models of group psychotherapy and sociotherapy were developed in the treatment of soldiers suffering mostly from neurotic disorders. Jacques Lacan became interested in the first of the Northfield Experiments in the context of Wilfred Bion and John Rickman's 1943 paper "Intra-group tensions in therapy, their study as the task of the group". Hence in 1945 Lacan embarked on a five week study tour to explore what was happening in British psychiatry as a consequence of the war (Lacan, 2000). Bion's analytic work with groups, in particular the group as a site for the emergence of the subject, influenced Lacan's idea of the cartel as a work group. This interest fostered the theoretical development of the relation of the individual to the group, where each member would have to deal with their existence in the group (Forrester, 1987; Parker, 2005).

Bion was appointed director of the Training Wing at Northfield towards the end of 1942 when he and Rickman instituted a disciplined program of daily parades for the soldier-patients with a period of time each day spent in group discussion (Bion & Rickman, 1943). The group discussion provided the men with an opportunity "[…] to step outside their framework and look upon its working with the detachment of spectators" (Bion, 1961, p. 16). The first Northfield experiment gave the initiative of the group to the men so long as they abided by these rules:

> (1) Every man must do one hour's physical training daily unless a medical certificate excused him. (2) Every man must be a member of one or more groups—the groups designed to study handicrafts, Army correspondence courses, carpentry, map-reading, sand-tabling, etc. (3) Any man could form a fresh group if he wanted to do so, either because no group existed for his particular activity or because, for some reason or other, he was not able to join an existing similar group. (4) A man feeling unable to attend his group would have to go to the rest room. (5) The rest room would be in charge of a nursing orderly, and must be kept quiet for reading, writing, or games such as draughts. (Bion, 1959, p. 16)

Lacan thought that Bion's position as the group's leader produced even more of a hold on the group than the psychoanalyst had on the individual patient in analysis. Bion organised the situation, says Lacan, "[…] so as to force the group to become aware of the difficulties of its existence as a group, and then to render it more and more transparent to itself, to the point where each of its members may be able to judge adequately the progress of the whole" (Lacan, 2000, p. 17). Each time the group got into trouble and demanded an intervention from Bion he took the position of feigned inertia by not responding, so leaving the group to find its own solution. Very quickly a new group spirit developed in the ranks that became the basis for the principles of group treatment. Lacan was fascinated by the experiment saying that it was "[…] pregnant with a birth of sorts that is a new outlook opening upon the world" (Lacan, 2000, p. 19).

Part of the research at Northfield involved the constitution of leaderless groups or teams with no pre-established authority where the men were given a task they had to accomplish through mutual collaboration. An example of this was a group task using a rope to cross a river, which required ingenuity in the use of the rope and its retrieval. The difficulties the men experienced called for constructive imagination, the capacity for improvisation, foresight, and a sense of productivity. Each subject's capacity as a leader emerged; especially in the ways they were able to subordinate a concern for looking good to the common objective of the unity of the group. This kind of group mental activity

Bion later called the Work Group (W) (Bion, 1952). This activity was associated with the performance of a task and as such it is related to reality, its methods were rational. Every group meets for a purpose and, according to the capacity and skill of the individuals, they co-operate together. Unfortunately, Bion and Rickman were often in conflict with both the medical and the military hierarchy that brought an end to the first Northfield experiment. After only six weeks they were dismissed from their posts in spite of an improvement in the men's behaviour and morale. Bion may have been therapeutic for the men and the ward but he was anti-therapeutic for the military staff group at the hospital. He failed to maintain relationships with authorities, often ignoring protocol and neglecting to gain social sanction for his actions. This mistake orchestrated their downfall and others took up the baton in the work of the Second Northfield Experiment, presented in chapter eight.

In the field of the study of groups, Bion identified characteristics in the individual that he could not understand, except in the context of the individual as a herd animal. Like Freud, Bion noticed that group phenomena followed definite patterns, and that groups fluctuated between cooperative working attitudes and resistant attitudes. Resistant attitudes block work group activities that are undermined by powerful and chaotic emotional drives. These emotional drives are given consistency if they emerge from basic assumptions that are common to the whole group. Group organisation provides stability and permanence to a work group, but if the group is unorganised it is more easily submerged by basic assumptions. Individual distinctiveness has no part in the life of a group that acts on basic assumptions where the individual contributes implicitly and anonymously to the group mentality. The purpose of a basic assumptions group is to preserve the group in one of three forms: pairing, fight/flight and dependency (Bion, 1952; Bion, 1980). Bion later explained basic assumptions in terms of psychotic mechanisms based on his clinical work with schizophrenia:

> Just as the psycho-analysis of the psychotic must be regarded as differing from the psycho-analysis of the neurotic so, and for similar reasons, the interpretation of basic assumption group phenomena must be regarded as differing from the interpretation of W.(ork) Group phenomena. (Bion, 1952, p. 246)

Bion equated group mentality with a psychotic mentality, a mentality that becomes mindless. Here Bion was trying to conceptualise some radical inconsistency in the members of a group where the individual functions in two separate ways at the same time. On the one hand he or she can function mentally as an individual in a coherent way incorporating and expressing meanings, but as a group member dismantle meaning in the creation of a mindless group mentality where linking collapses (Hinshelwood, 2001). Group phenomena follow definite patterns; if a therapist is able to recognise these patterns they will be able to help group members become aware of their anxieties and resistances, thus enabling the work of the group to progress.

The aim of Bion's Tavistock method was that a group, as a collective entity, comes together to study intra-group tensions and covert processes that operate in groups (Banet & Hayden, 1977). Participants are provided with experience-based group opportunities to study their own behaviour as it happens. There are no recommendations on how to proceed or to stipulate what anyone will learn from the experience. The non-directive role of the group consultant is usually the subject of much concern among group members, which is deliberate, in the interest of getting members to pursue the group task. Participants typically explore issues of authority, responsibility, boundaries, projections, organisational structure, and large group phenomena. Bion was apparently suspicious of institutions and the folly of people in large groups (Winship, 2005). Few movements in the sphere of mental health interventions have equalled the paradigm shift from individual therapy to group therapy following the Second World War, where models of group therapy came to be applied across many different social groupings. Bion is generally regarded as the father of socioanalysis, which has its roots in the first Northfield Experiment. Socioanalysis is the activity of consultancy and action research synthesises methodologies and theories that are derived from psychoanalysis, group relations, social systems thinking, organisational behaviour, and social dreaming.

The cartel as a work group

Lacan's (1990b) idea of the cartel as a work group was derived from Bion and Rickman's (1943) analytic work on group function that Lacan (2000) saw as a potential site for the emergence of the subject. Lacan was also influenced by the efforts of students in the Humanities Department of the Sorbonne University who were in opposition to the way teachers delivered lectures. The students promoted small groups and formed a union as a means of working on a more egalitarian basis for teaching. The notion of training in small groups instead of lectures was based on anti-authoritarianism. Lacan used the cartel as a device to redirect the transference for each subject beyond the institutional ideals of a subject-supposed-to-know. The analysand supposes that the analyst knows something about the unconscious and views the analyst as the agent of the unconscious, thus the analysand refuses responsibility for his or her own unconscious productions. As a consequence, the subject-supposed-to-know has the function of establishing certainty at the expense of truth. The cartel is directed towards a transference to work; this is a reference to the ongoing reworking of psychoanalytic discourse through a particular transference that each psychoanalyst holds to psychoanalysis. This runs against the transference of a group that tends to adhere to an ideal, as proposed by Freud. The effect of a traditional organisational structure in analytic training schools was thought by Lacan (1980) to cause the trainee to become glued by an imaginary identification to the particular organisation or piece of knowledge. Often members do not recognise the transference to an ideal that is fostered in an organisation. It is an infantile dependency to those in authority that gives the comfort of professional respectability. This identification with an ideal fosters not only the subject's passive dependency but it also leads them to conform to the organisational mould that alienates their own truth. It was for this reason that Lacan proposed the cartel, as a social body with no head; an acephalic entity separated from the individual and their desire.

Lacan introduced two innovations in an attempt to preserve subjective freedom within the social body of the organisation that nevertheless requires regulations. "Cartels" and "The Pass" became the guarantors of subjective freedom within the institutional bond that mark the subject's journey of formation as a psychoanalyst (Lacan, 1990b). Cartels are the organisational process that can bind the fragmented organisational body together. The cartel aims to undercut the effect of the group's potential to dominate an organisation because the cartel is not defined by its permanence or by its hierarchical construction. What is required for the execution of a cartel is a small group composed of four individuals with the position of "plus-one" as the fifth member. The plus-one selects the members of the cartel and generates group discussion, although the outcome of the cartel is accorded to the efforts of each individual member. The creation of a cartel gives each member the opportunity to choose a theme of work that is in line with a common group theme and this becomes the umbrella title for the cartel. The cartel allows individual thinking that is open to all kinds of research in isolation that can then encounter work in common with others in a small group. Each person works in his or her own name with a genuine transference to the work.

After a period of approximately two years the cartel concludes and a scansion or division is introduced as an event of the cartel where its work finishes (Evans, 1997). Having a time limit prevents the gluing effects that Lacan opposed and it also avoids the inertia noticeable in unproductive work groups that go on and on. Psychoanalytic groups fall prey to the same kind of forces that Freud identified in all human groups where individuals identify with each other as members of the same organisation and install a leader in the place of an ego ideal. This means that something radically different has to occur to disturb and question this symptom coming into operation inside psychoanalytic organisations. So, the formation and dissolution of cartels is an attempt to tackle the problem of rank and hierarchy in an organisation. As small workgroups, cartels do not have a leader, per se; the plus-one is the functional leader of a minimal group; a modest or poor leader (Miller, 1994). The plus-one has a temporary purpose as a binding function and acts in the role of conductor for the group, as a witness who invigorates and elaborates on the effects of the group's work. The cartel is a knot that is made and unmade because of its permutations that reverberate throughout the psychoanalytic community, both local and international.

Lacan came close to developing a theory of group psychology in his 1945 paper on "Logical time and the assertion of anticipated certainty" (Lacan, 2004a). Here Lacan described a hypothetical situation in the form of an experiment where a prison warden offers three prisoners the opportunity of freedom if they can prove themselves through a test. The warden has five discs, three white and two black, which are placed on the backs of each individual prisoner out of sight of the others. They have either a black or white disk on their backs, they do not know which it is and they are instructed not to communicate with each other. The first task of the prisoners is to deduce the colour of their own disk. The warden then judges them on the logical reasoning of their decision. However, what they did not know was that the warden had placed only white disks on each prisoner's back. They had to come to a reasoned judgement about who they were, how they had been symbolically designated, and they had to provide an answer to the warden in order to be released. In the end, the prisoners simultaneously came to a solution that they were all white. Each prisoner noticed that both of his companions were white and that if he had been black the others would have reacted immediately. They did not do this, instead they hesitated and each inferred that they were not black. "One must know that one is a white when the others have hesitated twice in leaving" (Lacan, 2004a, p. 172). They observed the hesitation and movements of each of the others as they each tried to come to a logical decision and this created a necessary tension within the group in their relation to each other. Collectivity in the group is based on reciprocal relations where "[...] the truth for all depends upon the rigor of each [...]" (Lacan, 2004a, p. 173). Lacan's account of "the instant of the glance", "the time for comprehending" and "the moment of concluding" can be seen as attempts to grasp the inter-subjective relations in the group that are necessary for the subject to appear and where each individual has to deal with their existence in the group.

Organisations and group dynamics

The use of psychoanalysis as a tool of cultural enquiry and criticism of groups and institutions was first pioneered at London's Tavistock Institute before the Second World War. There is a rich, historical body of work that originated at the Tavistock whose traditions evolved into a psychodynamic theory of organisations. Group Relations is a method of study, training and development that was pioneered at the Tavistock Institute by Ken Rice, Eric Miller, Pierre Turquet, Isobel Menzies-Lyth, Gordon Lawrence, and others (Maltz & Witt, 2011). The field of group relations and systems psychodynamics applies its methods to working with groups, organisations, and communities. The focus is to engage the social sciences in addressing social problems of our times and, in particular, the relatedness of the individual to the group and the environment. Drawing on General Systems theory (von Bertalanffy, 1950) and field theory (Lewin, 1952) the socio-psychological tradition utilises psychoanalytic theory based on the works of Melanie Klein and the British Object Relations School, to link the psychological and social fields. This also includes key developments from Bion's theories of psychotic thinking and the use of social structures as a defence against anxiety with contributions from Jaques, Menzies-Lyth and others.

Armstrong (1996) supposed that what may contribute to an understanding of organisations is located in psychoanalytic clinical practice because without experience of that practice no amount of theory is likely to prove very useful. Amado (1995) also considers psychoanalysis the best theory for understanding the unconscious process of a human being because not only is it a theory and a practice but it is also a method of investigation that can be applied to a wider social context. Psychoanalysis applied to an understanding of organisations is therefore inevitable because institutions are built, experienced, and managed by human beings. Organisational psychoanalysis is one approach that claims to provide insights into the irrational character of institutional life, for example, how unconscious processes reveal the way people engage in self-defeating activities. Organisational psychoanalysis aims to expose and bring to the surface the conflicts, defences, and regressive tendencies prevalent in individual and collective behaviour, within the context of a contained relationship, so that solutions can emerge through discussion and discourse (Lawrence, 1995a).

Institutions have a natural tendency to become poor models of identification because the inherent organisational pathology is located in the pathology of the individuals who come to be identified with that organisation. Institutional dynamics refers to the process of relating the various component parts of an institution to the unconscious and the unacknowledged factors at play in individuals that interfere with the functioning of the institution (Obholzer, 1986). Hinshelwood (1988) examined the psychodynamic aspects of institutional pathology and the typical form of decline into institutional demoralisation that can become permanent due to a reverberation between individual personalities and detrimental institutional phenomena. When professional differences are hidden and loyalties are divided the stage is set for a debilitating form of conflict within the institution that is revealed in the form of personal distress and disputes between staff members. A spiralling decline in confidence in the institution is the result of factors, such as hidden personal conflicts, a growing culture of self-denigration within the institution, the absence of a generally recognised person in a position of authority to embody the institution and compensatory behaviour that is rigid and self-defeating in its circularity. Hinshelwood continues. The usual indicators of low morale mark this point. The influences that distort the institution's main task, undermine authority and confuse boundaries, are largely driven by the way anxiety is institutionally managed.

The social defence system and anxiety

The analytic arrangement between analyst and patient is based on the work of the transference where the unconscious is interpreted and its meaning put into words. Hinshelwood (1994, p. 288) argues that the transference relationship between patient and analyst is "[...] a culture created in the smallest institution of two". If the transference is applied to an institution we come to a dead end at the point at which an interpretation might be made. This is because in the hospital there is no psychoanalytic space available, nor is there the authorisation to present an interpretive understanding. Psychoanalytic insights are concerned with the structuring of the individual rather than the structuring of an organisation or institution (Jaques, 1995; Kirsner, 2004). According to this reasoning, psychoanalysis cannot view the institution in the same way it views a subject.

Another paradigm is that of the social defence system as observed in the psychoanalytic model of anxiety and defence. These social defences may be evident in the organisation's structure, in its roles and procedures, in its culture and in the gap between what the organisation says it does and what it actually does (Bain, 1998). An individual keeps anxiety at bay by using defensive manoeuvres but, in the case of an organisation, anxiety is avoided and defences are supported by the formation of collective sets of attitudes. Any change to the structure of an institution has the potential to arouse extreme anxiety in those who work there through the deployment of various defence mechanisms to counteract anxiety:

> Primitive defence mechanisms of projection, introjection, splitting, idealization and identification are reinforced and channelled through the way the institution operates in terms of organizing the decision-making process, task performance, role definition, hierarchical arrangements, staff training, distribution of responsibility, and so on. (Chiesa, 1993, p. 243)

Defensive attitudes are culturally drawn together into collective assumptions and practices that are not entirely rational. An important contribution from psychoanalysis is to acknowledge that most anxiety is unconscious and that its personal and institutional management remains similarly remote from conscious knowledge and control (Hinshelwood, 1994).

Theorists such as Isobel Menzies-Lyth and Elliot Jaques studied defensive processes in institutions over fifty years ago in the context of the psychoanalytic theory of organisations. Reputed in this field, Elliott Jaques made the observation that one of the main unifying elements that bind individuals to institutionalised human associations is the defence against psychotic anxiety. He claimed that it was badly organised social systems that produced psychotic anxieties leading to disturbance and acting out in work-based relationships. Institutions are used its members to reinforce mechanisms of defence against anxiety. Jaques (2003) described an organisation as an interconnected system of roles and positions with overt or covert mutual responsibilities and authorities. He thought that the main source of stress for staff in an organisation was in the failure to clarify their particular roles and specify the requirements of those roles. A lack of role definition could lead to a mismatch in the person's capacity to fulfil their role, creating problems in how accountability is interpreted by individuals, turning the organisation into "an unpleasant *paranoiagenic* zoo" (Jaques, 1995, p. 344). Jaques believed that dysfunctional organisations occur because we humans have a poor foundation for understanding how they function and have not learned how to construct adequate organisations. He sought to develop an organisational model where the system, the job function and lines of accountability were analysed without any reference to specific individuals.

Isobel Menzies-Lyth, a British object relations psychoanalyst and social scientist, developed the earlier link made by Jaques between individual psychotic anxieties and institutions, when she discovered that these anxieties could be unconsciously woven together in such a way that they constituted a social system of defence against anxiety. Institutional methods of defending against the anxiety, pain, and confusion that surround the performance of the primary task can be seen in the structure of the institution itself; the working practices and ultimately the staff relationships unconsciously defend against anxiety. An integral part of this defensive institutional process is that the defence is presented as an optimum way of performing the task (Menzies-Lyth, 1959). Her reasoning was based on her 1959 study where she observed nurses at the King's College Hospital in London who dealt with illness, death, and dying on a daily basis. Menzies-Lyth explained the unmanageable unconscious defences that were erected by nurses against the fear of death and destruction:

> The objective situation confronting the nurse bears a striking resemblance to the phantasy situation that exists in every individual in the deepest and most primitive levels of the mind. The intensity and complexity of the nurse's anxieties are to be attributed primarily to the peculiar capacity of the objective features of her work situation to stimulate afresh those early situations and their accompanying emotions. (Menzies-Lyth, 1959, p. 46)

The nurses, who had entered the field ostensibly out of compassion for human suffering and a strong desire to alleviate it, began to behave in thoughtless and routinised ways towards their patients as though they were less than human; they treated interactions with patients like they were relating to things or objects. People protect themselves from feeling overwhelmed by distancing and switching off; people who work in institutions, caring for the disabled or disadvantaged, are prone to suffering from burn-out. This leads them to being insensitive, careless and, in extreme cases, indifferent and even brutal to those in their care. These phenomena operate in all institutions in the form of defensive positions identified by Menzies-Lyth as: depersonalisation and categorisation, the denial of an individual's significance, the detachment and denial of feelings, and the avoidance of change (Menzies-Lyth, 1959, p. 51). Depersonalisation can be recognised in the use of identical uniforms, a rigid hierarchy of roles and responsibilities at different levels of seniority, orders that are followed without discretion or common sense, and staff who are expected to do stupid tasks or follow meaningless routines. The nurses became their roles and their skills and so they experienced themselves less as individuals.

A psychoanalytic understanding is very useful in orienting the observer to the nature of an institution and to the dynamic psychosocial processes that go on in institutions. Institutional defences manifest themselves in how the organisation structures its tasks, its principles, and its relationship with the outside world. Defences that are developed to deal with anxiety and inherent difficulties in collaborating with others to accomplish common tasks, appear in the structure of an institution and permeate its way of functioning (Menzies Lyth, 1990).

It is also an inevitable consequence of working in an institution that an individual will be drawn into performing one or other unconscious institutional tasks. Introducing serious change to an institution requires the restructuring of the social defence system and this implies the freeing up of underlying anxieties until such a time as new defences or better adaptations are developed. Central to this change occurring is a confrontation with the nature of an institution's leadership, especially during times of transition; and how well anxiety is managed and tolerated at senior levels of management.

Social defence theory helps us understand why it is so difficult to effect change in organisations, institutions, and communities, and explains how institutions are able to remain cohesive over time (Long, 2006). Without social defences those in the organisation would be exposed to overwhelming anxieties or other unbearable emotions. The presence of social defences allows people to work in these situations and problems arise when the defence system works against performing the task.

Leadership and authority

Hinshelwood (2000) drew on the therapeutic community ethos as a model for introducing new ways of thinking about the social relations in mental health institutions. Two of the key features of the therapeutic community ethos are the nature of the movement's ideology and the quality of leadership that expresses this ideology, enabling the group to come together (Manning, 1991). A leader's main role is to uphold the integrity of the community in the way he or she preserves the meaning and structure of the community (Norton & Bloom, 2004). A fundamental element of leadership for a group is the provision of an idealised object in order to sustain the fantasy of hope and immortality (Correale, 2006). Thus, a crucial task of leadership is the maintenance and expression of its beliefs because the organisation of the movement is the embodiment of those beliefs. This is typically portrayed in terms of the charisma of the leader and the commitment of the members (Manning, 1991). The leader effectively heads a new social movement and his or her followers and disciples are converts to a new cause. Charisma, and the inspiration it creates, is an important quality that engineers popular compliance in the relationship between leader and followers; the leaders authority is not questioned because the followers have faith that their special qualities set them apart from ordinary people (Weber, 1947). Maxwell Jones has been described as the "archetypal charismatic innovator"

(Manning, 1991, p. 90) who adopted the concept of the therapeutic community movement in a burst of enthusiasm, drawing a positive moral commitment to the community from his followers as discussed in chapter eight.

Thomas Main (1989) recognised that as a community of interdependent systems, from the human individual to the hospital as a whole, the institutions own health needed care and monitoring. He was aware of the need for clarity in the structure and in individual roles at each level of the hierarchy so as to minimise anxiety and conflict. He believed that the traditional culture operating in any organisation was decisively influenced and informed by the conduct of its leaders and how they related to one another. Institutional sickness can often be traced to the disappearance of a particularly important leader, usually the founder or a father figure, and this is why charismatic authority is notoriously unstable (Weber, 1947). An example of this occurred when Tom Main retired from Cassel Hospital in 1978; he had been their director for the previous three decades and his departure led to Cassel's stagnation and lack of direction, until they eventually generated a new arrangement (Hartnup, 1994). The loss of a leader is often followed by a phase of fragmentation that can only be resolved by the entrance of a saviour in the guise of a new leader or a new ideal. Charismatic leadership focuses on the character of the leader at the expense of the group but it is in fact the system dynamics that give rise to such a form of leadership. Challenges that need to be better understood are that for the leader to effectively lead he or she must be "allowed" to lead effectively by those being led and that the organisation is "allowed" to effectively follow, while authorising their leader to lead (Maltz & Witt, 2011, p. 2).

Natural hierarchies assert themselves wherever human beings organise themselves to work on a task (Jaques, 1995). Organisations are justified as having to be hierarchical because of the belief that it is necessary for obedience. Those at the top of hierarchies tend to carry the anxiety of others in an institution or have it projected onto them. Loss of control results in chaos, so part of the role of those at the top of an institution's hierarchy is to ensure that there is compliance and obedience. Institutions that have a rigid, authoritarian organisation have an associated culture that defends against anxiety that is frequently associated with a narcissistic leader. As external demands and fiscal pressures stress leaders they tend to become more autocratic and surrender democratic decision-making for punitive and controlling measures. Such reactions are borne by the workers who react by displacing their frustration on those lower down in the pecking order. This culture reinforces the belief that thinking has to be accurate and certain with no room for error; it becomes dangerous to have thoughts that are different from the majority. In actual totalitarian states, narcissistic leadership is called the "cult of personality" (Lawrence, 1995a). Joseph Stalin would be an example of this.

Obholzer (1996) argues that the stirring up of envy in the leader can cause serious problems for an organisation, where envy is acted out and directed at particular staff members in the form of blocking, bureaucratic obstruction, responses that do not facilitate creative ideas, and stealing acknowledgments. The leader's capacity to recognise and contain such feelings and actions, as well as the ability to facilitate and foster creativity, is an important quality. "The leader's capacity to bear the institutional 'transference' appropriate to the role, without being carried away by it, is from a psychoanalytic perspective an equally important capacity" (Obholzer, 1996, p. 54). This has to do with the leaders awareness of the projections that have to be carried on behalf of the membership, and to be aware of the risks to the leader, and thus to the institution, of such processes. Strategies in communication and leadership help to move an institution towards a more flexible position where hidden conflicts and disruptive splitting are exposed, while encouraging accurate reality testing as to the aims and effectiveness of the institution. Those in leadership positions are obliged to take a global perspective; to listen and regularly appraise what is happening in the institution so as to recognise defence mechanisms, different levels of conflict and group dynamics that tend to paralyse processes of confrontation, circulation and exchange (Vigorelli, 1998).

The proverb "a fish rots from the head down" means that when an organisation fails, it is the leadership that is the root cause. The success of an organisation in a complex changing environment relies on how senior managers and leaders to interpret the inner and external realities of the institution. A sense of community enhances the functioning of individuals in an institution where members matter to the leader, to one another and to the group as a whole. They have a shared belief that their needs will be met through their commitment to being together. A sense of community is derived from being a member of a group that provides boundaries, emotional safety, a sense of belonging and identification, personal investment, and a common symbol system; secondly that members can influence the group; thirdly that the group provides integration and fulfilment of needs; and finally that the individual experiences a shared emotional connection (McMillan & Chavis, 1986). A leader inspires team members to enhance their personal resources to reach their potential and in the words of Martin Luther King (March 31st 1968):

> Ultimately a genuine leader is not a searcher of consensus but a moulder of consensus. On some positions cowardice asks the question, is it safe? Expediency asks the question, is it politic? Vanity asks the question, is it popular? But conscience asks the question, is it right? And there comes a time when one must take a position that is neither safe, nor politic, nor popular but he must take it because conscience tells him it is right.

The dominant culture of psychiatric institutions

Anxiety experienced in a psychiatric institution is different from that of any other institution because the business of psychiatry is madness, potential violence, and a fear of personal fragmentation that is connected to the loss of reality in psychosis (Hinshelwood, 1987). The dominant culture, supported by the anxieties of both patients and staff, can be hypervigilant and hypersensitive to the dangers of any emotional responsiveness between people and has the potential to lead to a serious disruption of the mind. Within this culture, there is the belief that any spark could ignite a fire. As a result, there is a deliberate and profound deadening of lively interactions (Hinshelwood, 1994). Fear of madness and violence, including suicide, gives rise to a deep suspicion of anything that may be seen as stimulating or enlivening; the defensiveness against this relies on techniques for deadening all contact and by numbing stimuli, particularly of the emotional kind. "The problem of pathological dependency is universal in psychiatric hospitals" (Hartnup, 1994, p. 4). This was especially evident on the long-stay wards of the old mental hospitals where all efforts directed at change were resisted in spite of decades of attempts to improve the quality of life for patients by providing more stimulating environments.

In her research of in a British mental hospital Bott-Spillius (1990) found that any type of therapeutic innovation that was introduced to the wards of the hospital was unsuccessful. Ward staff would embrace a new therapeutic innovation with enthusiasm but ultimately there was no obvious efficacy.

Bott-Spillius observed a culture of "not knowing" in the institution where staff actively strove to preserve the prevailing status quo and avoided the introduction of any change measures. Maintaining the customary features of practice served as a defence against anxiety inherent in the work of the staff in the institution. "So long as people in the external society have feelings of horror and dread of madness, mental hospitals will be pressed into accommodating madness in a way that will relieve society of responsibility and allow its members to regard themselves as sane" (Bott-Spillius, 1990, p. 609). The first step in the change process is the acceptance of madness, or the dread of it, as social and personal facts. This is a better position, for both the patient and society, from which to make madness more bearable rather than curable or beyond understanding.

For staff who work intensively with disturbed and psychotic patients the intolerance of doubt or not knowing is intensified: what arises is an almost delusional demand for certainty and absolute knowledge. Psychotic patients, especially those who are paranoid, are internally dominated by very archaic superegos (Rosenfeld, 1988a). This is described as a mafia like structure of the Other which imprisons the patient with its omnipotent, persecuting demands. It knows no doubt, it opposes thought, and the patient feels tyrannised into allegiance to this internal structure. Such a process occurs not only on an individual level but can become part of the structure of a ward, service or institution. When the omnipotence of the patient is met with the omnipotence of the mental health service, the service will act accordingly as though it was able to provide magical solutions or use mechanisms of denial to avoid facing damage, limitations or conflict. If omnipotent institutionalised systems take over, the institution itself can become indistinguishable from the patient's internal world. The development of rigid social defences against anxiety encourages the very conditions for psychosis to emerge because there is no space in which it can be tolerated and worked through. The capacity for thinking is removed and the institution ceases to be able to contain and tolerate thinking. Tolerance of doubt and not knowing are preconditions for the effective management of very disturbed patients (Bell, 1997). The work in psychiatric services is a struggle to preserve thought; it is this balance which is needed and which is so difficult to achieve. There needs to be tolerance of when it fails because the work never proceeds in straight lines; it is more like a constant zigzagging or tacking back and forth.

As the environment in an institution is experienced as becoming more uncertain, the management of the institution becomes more anxious, putting pressure on managers to bring organisations into being that offer certainty. In this way they are supported by the majority of other staff in bringing into existence authoritarian organisations that generate "totalitarian states-of-mind" in the participants of the institution (Lawrence, 1995, p. 32). Such an organisational culture diminishes the capacity for thought, so staff, at all levels, become less able to relate to the external environment that is perceived as being in a state of flux. They become entrapped in the inner, political environment of the institution, in a life of action and reaction, preoccupied with personal survival. This frame of mind does not allow them to anticipate in any way and so crises repeat themselves until they reach such a magnitude that the enterprise fails.

Idealisation

Ideologies are formal systems of belief that are held with great resolve and emotional investment; they have self-containing features that are opposed to being challenged from an objective rational point of view (Rapoport, 1960). Ideologies influence an individual's perception and interpretation of the world around them in terms of the rules of their ideology and the special importance of their own particular orientation. Idealisation and denigration are commonly used defences in institutions where aspects of the environment are welded into a kind of unity by filling the gaps in knowledge with projections that supply the belief system on which action is based. The presence of psychoanalysed subjects makes no difference to the efficiency with which an organisation is managed nor do psychoanalytic insights necessarily lead to organisational knowledge or wisdom (Jaques, 1995). Main (1989) warned that idealising the psychoanalytic method, with a lack of regard for the importance of the environment leads to many wasted efforts, painful failures, fruitless arguments, and the discouragement of many budding therapists. The idealisation of psychoanalysis in an institutional setting ultimately undermines the effectiveness of both. "Certainly, the ideals of the institution must be questioned by the presence of psychoanalysts, but in no case should psychoanalysis take their place" (Stevens, 2002b, p. 3). Frequently, the structure of an institution promotes a universal value that is binding for all, whereas the analytic ethic places the value on what is particular in each singular case. This assumes the presence of psychoanalysts or analysands who are at least civilised and enlightened in their orientation towards psychoanalysis.

Lacan was questioning the operation of this ideal during the time he was censured and expelled by the International Psychoanalytical Association (IPA) in 1964 and later when he dissolved his School in 1980 (Lacan, 1977, 1980). Some of the consequences for an institution that is glued to an ideal are the exclusion of external influences, the labelling of atypical behaviours as deviant and an elite that takes care of everything. That which is not approved by this select few, is subsequently excluded or forbidden. The action of the International Psychoanalytical Association introduced something essential for Lacan in the function of large groups or organisations in his thinking about psychoanalytic praxis and the training of analysts. This process led, that same year, to the Founding Act where Lacan (1990b) referred to the objective of the work in psychoanalysis as inseparable from the provision of an analytic formation.

An example of idealisation at the institutional level occurred at Nonette, a psychoanalytic facility orientated to the work of Lacan in the Clermont-Ferrand area of France. In 1988 the legal and financial authorities gave their official approval for the psychoanalytic treatment of psychoses according to Lacan's teachings to proceed at Nonette. The treatment of psychotic and autistic children, adolescents, and young adults was based on the work of François Tosquelles who originally introduced institutional psychotherapy to Nonette during the 1970s (Cottes, 2002). The staff group there organised themselves around a comfortable psychoanalytic philosophy that placed priority on speaking with each other and in discussing everything in staff groups. The imperative "It must be spoken" resulted in nobody speaking about anything except the team and its tensions, crises, feelings, and the reinforcement that the jouissance of this generates (Cottes, 2002, p. 8). The staff were dominated by the idealisation of speech and this was later referred to as the era of the "reign of speech" where speaking was the ultimate and misdirected goal:

> Speak-up meetings were organized throughout the day, the week, for everyone (children's meetings: in-patient, in the classroom; staff meetings called institutional meetings. And the whole of this collective) caregivers and cared-for, everyone was submitted to and

> structured by the imperative; "It must be spoken". This according to an ideal that could be formulated in this way: "Each cared for everyone (givers and receivers of care), all the time". The effects were, at first, very positive, but came to an impasse, a major crisis toward the end of the 70s. (Cottes, 2002, p. 7)

As the number of patients admitted to Nonette grew, the limitations of the reign of speech became obvious and was demonstrated in an impasse in the work with the patients (Cottes, 2002). However, the influence of Lacan's teachings in psychoanalysis was starting to take on more importance at the institutional level, so the focus was redirected away from the preoccupation of the staff group and back towards the treatment of patients. This shift in awareness of the staff occurred when their priority shifted towards the study, discussion, and research of psychoanalysis applied to the treatment of psychosis in the institution. The work was formalised by the creation of another group, The Clinic Relation that facilitates psychoanalytic research around the limits of the speaking treatment for psychosis by learning about the status of language in psychosis:

> [...] the transference to the work of psychoanalysis, or rather the double interest of an engagement in the contribution to knowledge, is necessary to support this encounter. It is a paradoxical support that doesn't aim at suturing the division, but at keeping the gap clear. Psychoanalysis allows this division which is at stake in the encounter with the psychotic. (Cottes, 2002, p. 8–9)

At Nonette the influence of the ethics of psychoanalysis became important at the institutional level where idealisation of the group dynamics was interrupted so that the work of the treatment could proceed.

Internal models and the analytic attitude

According to analysts of the Italian Psychoanalytical Society, an analytic attitude involves the capacity to divide the mind into parts that coexist simultaneously, as both participatory and reflexive.

> The internalization of models of the primitive functioning of the mind provides the analyst-therapist with an interpretive framework

> for relational phenomena connected with his patient's life, which can be used not only in the setting as it is traditionally understood, but also in different operative contexts. In this way the accent is shifted from psychoanalysis as a technique to the analytic attitude, understood as the capacity to subdivide one's own mind into two coexisting parts—one participatory and empathic, the other cognitive and reflexive—forming, as Bion might say, a sort of binocular vision. (Scortecci, et al., 1993, p. 197)

An integrative approach produces adaptability, flexibility and a range of choice for the internal scaffolding of the analyst, to interpret what might be going on for the patient and how to deal with it at the level of the individual, the team and the organisation. The hope is that the analyst will be able to introject the model and integrate it into a kind of internal object, minus the ritualistic and idealised institutional aspects. Thus an interpretive framework shifts the accent from psychoanalysis as a technique to an analytic attitude of mind.

A culture of enquiry is an analytic attitude that is central to the process of thinking about the dynamics of an institution with the aim of sustaining a therapeutic culture (Main, 1989). The underpinning of a culture of enquiry is the practice of psychoanalysis applied to an institutional structure with the aim of preserving the uniqueness of each individual and thwarting the temptation to idealise psychoanalysis or the institution (Hinshelwood & Skogstad, 1997). "It both requires and sanctions instruments of enquiry into personal and interpersonal and intersystem problems, and the study of impulses, defences, and relations as these are expressed and arranged socially" (Main, 1989, p. 141). In the early days of the Cassel Hospital everyone, including the staff and patients, idealised it to the place of a special hospital and this was reinforced by people calling it "The Castle", which reflected a sense of superiority and invited the envy of outsiders (Hartnup, 1994). Cassel's director, Tom Main (1989), recognised this as a problem; it was not possible to establish a psychotherapeutic culture in an institution with a dominant culture such as this. Main set out to find a solution at the level of the institution that led to establishing a culture of enquiry that involved all aspects of the hospital. Therapeutic communities have to continually regenerate themselves in order to maintain an ethos of enquiry and awareness so that the dangers of normalisation, routinisation, and institutionalisation can be circumvented. The whole staff effort needs to focus on understanding and tolerating the pressure from mutual projections and the tendency to turn creative thought into ritualised practice. Thinking about the unconscious dynamics between patients and staff and of the whole institution requires an active effort and is fundamental to the culture of inquiry. As the level of complexity within any situation intensifies so does the need for collaborative, calm, diverse, and intelligent problem solving and this can only be accomplished in an atmosphere that values mutual respect and open communication (Norton & Bloom, 2004).

Holding the institution in mind and being aware of how it functions means understanding the dynamics that flow between patients and those who work towards their care in the institution. This means being mindful of the institutional dynamics within which the work proceeds and ensuring that in the process of individual treatment the larger group is not forgotten or undermined. Winship (2005, p. 242) explains psychoanalytic thinking in an institutional context as follows:

> [...] it is actually a function of psychoanalytical thinking to be inside or "underside" the organisation in order to subvert the dominant culture where necessary. To be inside and irrelevant is as meaningless as being outside and isolated. To fail to adopt a critical or dialectical position in relation to the dominant culture [...] may be rather more inclined to pathological conformism than good diplomacy. In this sense there is no misunderstanding when colleagues perceive the radical nature of psychoanalytic thinking; we might say that the organisation ought to be suspicious. Psychoanalysis has built its most impressive and influential work on radical hypotheses that across time and the drifts of paradigms, have stood to become pillars of new convention. The clinical challenge is one of de-constructing the faulty premises of self and organisation [...] offering the dialectical space for the necessary process of objectivity in evaluation and self-reflection [...].

A timbre of psychoanalytic subversion challenges the potential stagnation of the cultural order of an organisation but to succeed in applying psychoanalysis in an institution it must be constantly questioned on all levels so as to "[...] erase the institution from inside" (Grasser, 2003, p. 89). This implies the ability to acknowledge and face what will always be a symptom there in the determinants of the super ego that tends to dominate in institutions.

Austen Riggs Centre

CHAPTER FIVE

Psychoanalysis and institutional models

This chapter and the next present several institutions selected for their historical roots, their contribution to the psychoanalytic field and for the unique ways they have adapted themselves to meeting the needs of a targeted population i.e., those patients diagnosed with serious psychiatric disability. Firstly, the intention is to highlight some fundamental principles that guide the application of psychoanalysis in psychiatric institutions in the form of institutional models. An institutional model provides a structure for understanding an institution's characteristics and a basis for examining and explaining it through the use of psychoanalytic theory and practice. A model is a construct that organises information and so allows a better understanding of the nature of a complex phenomenon by virtue of its analogous structure. For example, the British therapeutic community movement is significant as a model that emerged as an alternative treatment for mental illness, providing a link between psychoanalysis and the institution through an emphasis on group and community processes. Thus, this model forged a bridge between inpatient psychiatry and community mental health during deinstitutionalisation.

Secondly, these models provide a framework for thinking about three well-known American pioneering psychiatric hospitals oriented according to psychoanalytic theory in this chapter and chapter six. The Menninger Clinic created a psychoanalytic milieu program, Austen Riggs Center applied a therapeutic community model, and Chestnut Lodge Sanitarium placed priority on an individual treatment approach. All these facilities admitted patients with a diagnosis of psychosis and/or borderline personality disorder for treatment, although Chestnut Lodge probably had the highest caseload of patients with chronic psychotic disorders, such as schizophrenia. These institutions functioned as psychiatric hospitals for over eighty years each and were influenced by psychoanalysis for at least sixty of those years.

Theoretical models of institutional practice

Characteristics of institutional functioning were studied for over twenty-five years in the protracted research of the Serious Pathologies (*Patologie Gravi*) Study Committee of the Italian Psychoanalytical Society (SPI) (Scortecci, et al., 1993). The Study Committee comprised a group of Italian psychoanalysts who all worked as psychiatrists in psychiatric institutions. In 1978 the Italian parliament passed "The Mental Treatment Act", also known as "Law No 180", where a mentally ill person's civil and political rights were guaranteed by the constitution and through legislation declared that no new psychiatric cases could be admitted to long-stay psychiatric hospitals (Colucci, Norcio, & Sindici, 2000). Spurred on by the government's mandate regarding deinstitutionalisation the Serious Pathologies Study Committee focused on the theoretical and practical side of the psychoanalytic treatment of psychosis in the search for a suitable institutional model. These psychoanalysts wanted to broaden the analytic function in institutions through the integration of a number of theories based on psychoanalysis. In Italian psychiatry several schools of thought have been identified: the Basaglia School from Franco Basaglia who championed the anti-institutional movement in the 1960s; the Milanese School with a mix of influences from S. H. Foulkes, Eliot Jaques, and the Kleinian tradition; and finally the Roman School that is identified with Wilfred Bion and group phenomena in institutions (Correale & Di Leone, 2001).

The Study Committee synthesised these psychiatric schools and the outcome was the institutional field model; a multifaceted psychoanalytically derived model. It provides an example of how models merge, overlap, and diverge, how some aspects are gleaned from additional models resulting in a final version that works. The contributions of a number of approaches were brought together in the creation of a framework for the individual in relation to institutional life. There is the work of Wilfred Bion, Donald Winnicott, and Didier Anzieu discussed elsewhere in this book. Claudio Neri used the theories of Anzieu and Bion in his work on group analysis where he elaborated the idea that illusions tie groups together. According to Neri (1993), groups perform binding functions and the group itself acts as a container for powerful, explosive feelings that are channelled into action.

Kurt Lewin's (1952) field theory of mutual interdependence strongly influenced the institutional field model. Lewin's general message was that human systems could only be understood and changed if the members of the system were involved in the inquiry process itself. Thus all members of an organisation ought to be involved in the change process. José Bleger (1967) refers to the psychoanalytic frame in his work with psychotic patients. Bleger's definition of an institution is a relationship that lasts for years where a set of norms and attitudes is maintained. He proposes that the psychoanalytic situation comprises the process and the frame. The institution is the frame that holds the constants within which institutional processes occur. Eliot Jaques (1955) researched social institutions that he believed unconsciously defended themselves against psychotic anxiety. Bleger used the work of Jaques as well, as object relations theory to propose that this is the depositing of the psychotic part of the personality into the institution, that is, "the undifferentiated and non-dissolved portion of the primitive symbiotic links" (Bleger, 1967, p. 513). From the integration of these theories the institutional field model is formed and its important functions are derived (Correale & Di Leone, 2001). Unified these functions are said to provide a global outlook for the investigation of life in institutions based on careful, controlled teamwork so that a therapeutic effect can be established in the group work of the institution. The teamwork can be regarded as having two fundamental purposes:

The first purpose is that of holding, in Winnicott's sense this is an environment that provides affective limits and containment:

> This "unity of intents", this "being with" the patient, is what ultimately "holds", what more than anything else can facilitate cohesion. In this way it is possible to provide the patient with the necessary support apparatus which allows him to rely on new forces that help him to (re)acquire the sense of continuity of being,

> interrupted or prevented from taking solid shape by environmental "impingements". (Scortecci, et al., 1993, p. 201)

This allows patients to be held in such a way that they are protected from further fragmentation, thus facilitating gradual integration. The holding function can be developed by the team in a range of ways from the capacity to tolerate projection, splitting, and acting out, the acceptance of fusional needs and the willingness to allow oneself to be used as an inanimate object at times, for the individuation of the patient. The attitude of the team has the equivalent of a structuring function.

The second purpose regards the therapeutic function of institutional staff in facilitating the creation of a significant personal relationship that evolves and opens up a space for the patient to "gain access to metaphorical thought and regain possession of the world of symbols" (Scortecci, et al., 1993, p. 201). This can only happen if the team is able to maintain the holding function and withstand the pressure of "symbiotic and fusional demands" of the environment. Establishing a central, meaningful relationship with the therapist integrates and organises a patient's split-off parts that can become indistinctly and confusedly transferred to the institution and its members. The team offers itself as a receptive field to the various aspects of the patient's mental life and are more distinctly recognisable to the patient if the central relationship is in place.

Institutional models

Vigorelli (1998, pp. 33–40) identified four particular institutional models that reference psychoanalysis:

The first is the bifocal model that is a modification of the classic institutional setting that emphasises the dual therapeutic relationship between patient and therapist. In this model the institution serves as a container for intensive psychotherapy in a protected environment where patients are housed for a long time. The classic example of the bifocal model is Chestnut Lodge in the United States (see chapter six) where patients receive individual psychoanalytic therapy five days a week no matter how disturbed they are and where the average length of stay is two years. Patients' progress to a step down program geared towards rehabilitation before moving into the community to a supervised living facility. They frequently continue their therapy as outpatients residing and possibly working in the nearby town.

The second is the integrated group model that is based on interventions that involve a number of professionals who coordinate the dynamic process of working together with an open attitude in response to a patient's distinctive needs. It has links to the case management system but is informed by psychoanalysis. A team of professionals ensures that the psychotic transference is spread beyond a single therapist, shouldering complex issues, to it being dealt with by the team collectively. The model is successful when team members have constant interaction about the patient and operate on different levels of integration to provide the scaffolding a patient needs. The slow progress of the work in psychosis is dependent on the protective system that the team provides in how it holds and supports over time. This model was introduced by Giovanni Zapparoli using an approach that included different treatment methods and was widely adopted in both public and private institutions in Italy during the 1970s (Zapparoli & Gislon, 1999a). In elaborating this model, Zapparoli drew from a range of clinical experience and an assortment of theoretical formulations: Rosenfeld and Racamier; clinicians from Chestnut Lodge, including Feinsilver, Ping-Nie Pao, and Searles; ego psychology proponents Margaret Mahler and Edith Jacobson, as well as Giovacchini.

A third institutional model is the therapeutic community model that emerged as an alternative treatment for mental illness providing a link between psychoanalysis and the social group of a psychiatric institution. The therapeutic community movement promoted an emphasis on group and community processes where the individual is respected as unique and self-determining. During deinstitutionalisation this model formed a bridge between inpatient psychiatry and community mental health. Chapter eight is dedicated to the therapeutic community model.

The fourth model is the community network model. It incorporates the previous three models within a series of coordinated structures offering therapeutic interventions that service the same geographical area where patient lives. This system draws on resources from the patient, their family, their environment, and the social structure of their community mediated in a dynamic weave with the therapeutic team. Patients can progresses through their stages of illness and treatment in the context of a lively interaction with the therapist, the group and the institution with a permeability in the boundaries and where information is circulated from the inside to the outside environment. What emerges is an inter-system map with numerous operating centres that, although autonomous, have regular exchanges. Therapeutic continuity is provided through the connection between the therapeutic couple, the small integrated group working with the patient, the residential and daytime community structures and the network team.

Sector psychiatry

The community network perspective has its roots in the systemic approach of the Tavistock Institute of Human Relations and the Grubb Institute in London, which includes the theories of Bion, Jaques, Miller, Rice, and Turquet. With psychiatric treatment beginning to reflect an open hospital and community approach following the upheaval produced by the Second World War, a mental health private organisation, *l'Association Sante Mentale* (Mental Health Association) was created in France by a group of psychoanalysts from the Psychoanalytic Institute of Paris. These psychoanalysts were Philippe Paumelle, Paul-Claude Racamier, Serge Lebovici, René Diatkine, and René Angelergues (Gittelman, Dubuis, & Gillet, 1973). This endeavour led to several collectively authored books *La Psychanalyse D'Aujourd'hui* (*Psycho-Analysis Today*) in 1968 and *Le Psychanalyste sans divan* (*The psychoanalyst without a couch*) in 1970. At the same time in post Second World War France there was a climate of antipsychiatry gathering at Saint Alban hospital in Lozere that also produced a new psychiatry that heralded institutional psychotherapy.

This pioneering mental health group promoted a new multidisciplinary approach to psychiatry in which psychoanalysis played a major role. Philippe Paumelle proposed an alternate model for institutional treatment in public psychiatry and in 1957 lobbied for the principles of sectorisation to be put into practice in Paris. Credit for sectorisation has also been attributed to psychoanalysts François Tosquelles and Henry Ey. The basic principle of sector psychiatry was that a psychiatric team would be responsible for patients with mental health problems within a defined catchment area; the continuity of professional relationships and appropriate attention would be ensured to all patients regardless of diagnosis, prognosis or socioeconomic factors. Although the framework was based predominantly on the medical model, Paumelle worked to reform psychiatry by integrating it with psychoanalysis. He saw that the role of therapeutic teams was crucial and encouraged collegiate structures and a psychoanalytic praxis that was equal to the problems posed by psychiatry. The essence of Paumelle's principles was the absolute priority of therapy over assistance for the patient including their family and caregivers. The community network model adopted a comprehensive internal and external, individual and group oriented perspective. It highlighted the essential requirement of dynamic dialectical exchanges between the individual patient, the group and the institution with the permeability of boundaries where information is circulated from the inside to the outside environment.

Paumelle's idea developed into a contract with the social security system to provide community and hospital treatment in the thirteenth arrondissement of Paris, a low socioeconomic neighbourhood that housed a very heterogeneous population of North African families and foreign workers with the highest rate of mental illness (Gittelman, et al., 1973). The sector's psychiatric team consisted of a psychoanalytically trained psychiatrist, social worker, and nurse. The project presented a strategy based on community centred psychiatric interventions, including outpatient treatment, group therapy, and home hospitalisation. The target of the intervention was frequently the family of the designated patient who were treated in situ in their own sociocultural network or community by the team as a small therapeutic group. Intensive individual psychotherapy became available for those who needed it, as well as group therapy, psychodrama, family therapy, and relaxation therapies. The interventions of members of the team, be it the prescription of medication, budgetary assistance or a psychotherapy session, were all deemed to be of equal therapeutic significance. To deal with the team's anxiety concerning the work with psychotic patients, the supervision and training strategy focused on internal models that helped them develop ways to metabolise or digest the raw anxiety. This was so that important information, otherwise unavailable, could be extracted and utilised in the team's work with patients and families in crisis (Woodbury & Woodbury, 1969, p. 622).

In 1961 the French government and civilian agencies formalised the pilot project in sector psychiatry in the thirteenth arrondissement and it was not long before all of Paris was divided into twenty arrondissements each corresponding to a sector. A sector, in turn, was usually further divided into smaller units, each with its own mental health team. The thirteenth arrondissement, for example, had six teams each responsible for a mini-sector. When a patient required hospitalisation every effort was made to have him or her treated and followed up by the same therapist. Thus, the patient did not have to adjust to new people because treatment was ongoing with little interruption and with greater effectiveness. For the patient the advantages of the continuity provided by a mobile team were practical as well as psychological. The success of the thirteenth arrondissement pilot project led to the entire country becoming sectorised for mental health purposes (Woodbury & Woodbury, 1969). *L'Association de Santé Mentale du 13e arrondissement* (ASM13) in Paris was an experiment in sector-based psychiatry that played a unique and seminal role within the reforms to French psychiatry after the Second World War. It was a test case for a new way of practicing psychiatry and a new type of institutional patient care that reflected a psychoanalytic approach to the treatment of psychoses. It was also intended to serve as a global critique of society and its relationship to the mentally ill. The psychoanalytic elaboration of care, the development of new socio-health approaches, and the work on collective stigma towards the mentally ill were all tightly enmeshed aims of the experiment.

Institutional psychoanalysis in the United States

In the inter-war years on the other side of the world in the United States, psychoanalysis had changed from an interest group of partially trained psychoanalysts into a profession with its own training institutes and a strong national association where a new remodelled psychoanalysis was being established. From the 1930s psychoanalysts from Europe migrated to North America so that by the 1940s a significant majority of the world's analysts lived there. The nature of the psychoanalytic training of the early analysts in America was based on their propensity to adapt and develop their own approaches, including modifying the analytic method in its application to the treatment of psychosis. Ferenczi thought the Americans had a tendency to be satisfied with a superficial acquaintance with psychoanalysis, avoiding the basic tenants, such as submitting to a personal analysis as a fundamental part of analytic training. Freud too was sceptical about the way the Americans were adapting psychoanalysis.

The Menninger brothers went to Europe in 1934 to follow through on their interest in creating a psychoanalytic hospital. Karl Menninger met with Freud and asked him about the use of psychoanalytic principles in the administration of a hospital and the programming of the patient's routine, to which Freud replied that he had never tried it and did not feel very optimistic about it. At the same time William Menninger conferred with Ernst Simmel on the same question and he received quite a different answer, thus establishing a connection that was to continue for some years with Simmel's sanatorium at Schloss Tegel serving as a model for the Menninger Clinic (Menninger, 1982; Simmel, 1937). As a result of this connection and the unfolding events in Europe pre-Second World War, the Menninger Clinic started to recruit émigré analysts who were fleeing the Nazis.

The Menninger clinic

The Menninger clinic opened in 1925 as a private psychiatric hospital in a farmhouse. It was established by the Menninger family in Topeka, Kansas and consisted of a clinic, a sanitarium and a school of psychiatry. C. F. Menninger and his two psychiatrist sons, William and Karl, were interested in what psychoanalysis could offer the mentally ill with the possibility of translating it to the treatment of larger groups of people in the sanitarium or hospital. In the 1930s, a small group of dedicated clinicians began to develop methods of applying psychoanalytic ideas to hospital treatment. They codified the treatment program to include specific approaches to treating a range of severely ill patients, particularly those suffering from depression and schizophrenia, by applying Freud's ideas based mainly on libido theory and early ego psychology (Schlesinger, 2007). The hospital milieu was designed to encourage patients to develop healthy living patterns and to correct their personality distortions that contemporary psychoanalysis evidently held responsible for their illness.

One special feature of the Menninger program in its quest for continuity of care was that as patients improved they had the option of moving into housing that had different levels of supervision and support. The Menninger Foundation also maintained a network of family care homes, provided by local Topeka residents, for patients who were continuing their treatment as outpatients but were not yet ready for independent living. A social worker supervised these homes and held monthly meetings with the families. Eventually many of the patients moved into places of their own locally and continued in psychotherapy in a similar arrangement to Chestnut Lodge and Austen Riggs. Unlike Simmel's approach where individual psychoanalysis was installed at the heart of institutional treatment, individual treatment was not part of the Menninger program but was conducted separately on campus on a one by one referral basis. Once patients were admitted they might spend two or three years sheltering within the institution's walls, "[…] building an identity, a network of friends, a way of living apart from the world outside" (Goode, 2003, p. 1).

The psychoanalytic milieu

The type of institutional milieu at the Menninger Clinic was derived from traditional psychiatric practices combined with a unique adaptation of Ernst Simmel's psychoanalytic approach at Schloss Tegel, mingled with a large dose of military common sense: "A psychoanalytic hospital was to be both a hospital and a school in which patients would 'learn to live'"(Menninger, 1982, p. 9). The milieu at Menninger was conceptually different from that of a therapeutic community milieu. Menninger devised a milieu composed of organised activities and patterned staff attitudes prescribed for each patient, even if they were in individual therapy outside the milieu. Treatment was conceived as a relearning or corrective experience through specific regimens of occupational and recreational therapy that comprised a roster of carefully chosen activities and a set of attitudes with which patients were to be addressed. Activities and tasks were designed to compensate for the patient's presumed deficiencies in sublimating drives, by effectively defending against them, or by allowing socially acceptable channels for drive expression.

At Menninger the hospital was seen as a screen where old patterns of behaviour were projected and studied, and deviant behaviour interpreted. The institution fostered a repetition of the drama and conflict of past relationships in the form of a regressive transference neurosis; the manner in which this was manifest was then open for interpretation by the analyst. Karl Menninger (1962) stressed the importance of structure in the therapeutic setting. Here the patient's daily program was divided between work, play, study, and creative activity, including certain rules and regulations based on personal freedom. *The Guide to the Order Sheet* (Menninger, 1982) was a set of therapeutic interventions central to milieu therapy at Menninger Clinic that operated as a communication link between the physician and the hospital staff to ensure uniformity of approach towards the patient. According to the guide, the doctor's written orders were instructions addressed to all staff members who had contact with patients about particular management devices and general attitudes they were to adopt with each individual patient. The inclusion of the whole team, including physicians, nurses, aides, therapists, housekeepers, and grounds-men, in treatment decisions was innovative at the time because the treatment was based on an understanding of the patient's needs and a treatment that was carried out in a humane way akin to moral treatment.

Therapeutic prescriptions were made for each individual patient on an order sheet where a list of management devices was formulated on the basis of psychodynamic principles. This list was intended to correct the patient's disturbances aimed in particular at the aggressive and the erotic drives. Prescriptions for each patient focused on their individual assets, liabilities and vulnerabilities, and were directed to where the patient's conflict appeared most pronounced. For instance, the way to correct the aggressive drive was to relieve conscious and unconscious guilt through the direct expression of hostility. In addition, attitude therapy guided hospital staff to behave in a uniform manner and with a consistent approach towards the patient. William Menninger believed that patients reacted more to feelings and manners than to words, so the atmosphere created by an attitude was seen as particularly important, especially for those patients diagnosed with psychosis. The main general attitudes on the order sheet were: active friendliness, indulgence, passive friendliness, watchfulness, matter-of-factness, and kind firmness. Based on *The Guide to the Order Sheet*, an example of a treatment prescription would be the following:

> […] for a patient suffering from a severe psychotic depression, one might prescribe that the nursing staff assume a kind but firm, rather matter-of-fact attitude towards him, holding him to punctuality in rising in the morning and seeing him through a demanding schedule of activities during the day. He would be assigned daily some hours of work on menial, non-gratifying tasks such as participation in house cleaning; if vigorous and in good physical health, he would spend at least an hour in the gymnasium punching a bag or doing strenuous exercises; and he might be put to work on a group project in occupational therapy requiring precision and cooperation with others. Expressions of delusional guilt feelings and irrational pleas for mercy would be ignored; instead, all workers would assume a task-masterish attitude towards the patient in the hope that through the prescribed combination of symbolic penitential activities and harmless externalized motor discharge of self-directed aggression the patient would regain a workable equilibrium. Later on an expressive-supportive psychotherapy course might be prescribed. (Menninger, 1982, p. 7)

The Menninger Clinic leaned towards a pedagogical approach both in the training of staff and in the treatment of patients. Without the constant training and education of staff to ensure they remained faithful to the guide, with a focus on consistency in its application, this kind of program would not have succeeded. By the 1980s, the order sheet was viewed as an anachronism.

At its peak, Menninger had two hundred and eighty or more patients in intensive treatment, seventy of them in psychoanalysis. In 1945, sixty-two per cent of patients were treated in psychotherapy (modified psychoanalysis) or formal psychoanalysis. By 1965 this had dropped to twenty-three per cent with only one patient in formal psychoanalysis (Hills, 1968). In 1945 the majority of patients admitted were indiscriminately referred for individual psychoanalysis without assessment for appropriateness and suitability, and certainly, no distinction was made regarding structural difference. The change between 1945 and 1965 reflected a lessening in therapeutic optimism where the only patients referred for individual psychotherapy were those considered to have a favourable prognosis. At the same time as the scope of psychoanalysis was narrowing at Menninger, there was more than a one third increase in the number of patients receiving psychotropic medication and the introduction of the newer modality of group therapy. Consequently, over the ensuing twenty years patients diagnosed with psychosis were considered unanalysable and were not referred for psychoanalysis because of the presumed high failure rate. Almost fifty per cent of the patients admitted in 1945 had a diagnosis of psychosis and twenty years later it was at forty per cent. It is a mystery as to why a modified and less rigid form of analysis that was of longer duration was not attempted with this group of patients when the environment was clearly experimental and evolving. Repeatedly, the avoidance of presumed failure was responsible for giving up hope or not persisting with longer treatments because the outcomes might appear negative.

The psychoanalysts at Menninger were housed in the North office building that provided over twenty small consulting rooms where patients, both inpatient and outpatient, came for their individual therapy sessions. Adjoining this was the building that accommodated the Topeka Psychoanalytic Institute and the Topeka Psychoanalytic Society offices. The intellectual atmosphere, and indirectly the therapeutic programs, was further strengthened by the constant influx of prominent scientists, clinicians and scholars from diverse fields who came to visit the Menninger Clinic. Up until the 1970s the Menninger Foundation represented the core of ego psychology in America and trained eight per cent of all their psychiatrists (Kernberg, 1997).

Psychotherapy research project

The Menninger Clinic embarked on a Psychotherapy Research Project in 1954 that lasted nearly thirty years. The overall aim of the research was a naturalistic study of psychotherapeutic treatment in that institution. Using the case histories of forty-two patients in treatment for significant mental disorders, including psychosis and personality disorder, the investigators sought to uncover the roots of how psychoanalysis and psychotherapy actually worked, what changes could predictably occur over the course of treatment, how those changes were brought about and how they evolved over time. The project's case histories and therapeutic insights aimed to provide hard evidence of the efficacy of psychoanalytically informed therapies in varying situations. As a director of research at Menninger and the project's principal investigator, Robert Wallerstein (2000) recorded the study's findings in collaboration with at least thirty-seven other Menninger professionals over the life of the endeavour that resulted in the publication of *42 Lives in Treatment: A Study of Psychoanalysis and Psychotherapy*. The patient sample was drawn from the Menninger hospital population who were in intensive inpatient treatment between 1952 and 1954. Patients who were acutely psychotic, who had organic brain disorders or whose treatment was expected to be of short duration were excluded.

In the project, patients were divided into two groups: half of the selected patients were in psychoanalysis and the other half were in "other modes of expressive and supportive psychoanalytic psychotherapy" (Wallerstein, 1989, p. 195). Variables were conceptualised according to clinical judgment and the patient's intra-psychic functioning, and then defined in terms of psychoanalytic theory and certain idiosyncratic terms employed only at Menninger. Data analysis followed a case-by-case clinical examination, a complex prediction of treatment efficacy and a semi-quantitative comparison of patient variables. Treatment approaches ranged from the most analytic-expressive type of analysis, through to the most supportive type of psychotherapy. Wallerstein (2000) claims that in the research sample there was an adverse loading of much sicker (possibly psychotic) patients who were placed in psychoanalysis and some were in treatment with inexperienced analysts under supervision. This was by way of explaining why six patients dropped out of psychoanalysis and were converted to a more supportive psychotherapy. The rigid application of classical psychoanalysis by inexperienced psychoanalysts to the treatment of a difficult, sometimes hospitalised, patient population was a problem in the initial conceptualisation of the project. Another issue to be considered is the uniqueness of the transference relation between patient and analyst that does not conform to research protocols and does not seem to have been taken into account.

Overall about sixty per cent of patients, in either psychoanalysis or psychotherapy, showed moderate to very good clinical improvement. Of the forty-two cases in treatment (six were referred for analysis and five for psychotherapy) eleven were judged to be failed cases showing significant issues with alcoholism, drug addiction, and paranoid-borderline traits. These patients either terminated prematurely or developed transference psychosis, and six died while in treatment. The findings for both psychoanalysis and psychotherapy tended to converge rather than to diverge in outcome. The results showed no significant difference between psychoanalysis and psychotherapy as to which approach demonstrated better findings, except that all forms of therapy included a substantial amount of supportive work in the treatment of this cohort of patients. Across the whole spectrum of the project the treatments that carried more supportive elements accounted for more of the changes achieved. Irrespective of the therapeutic approach the group of sicker patients gained better overall results with a more supportive therapy.

A significant discovery from the research was the appropriateness of predicting which patients were suitable for particular modes of therapy. The authors had great difficulty in identifying the difference between classical psychoanalysis that used the interpretive uncovering of intrapsychic meanings directed towards analysing defences and supportive or ego building psychotherapy (Wallerstein, 1989). The supposed classical form of analysis was ultimately not used in the study because modifications to the method were constantly required to adapt to interruptions to the treatment, for example, a patient's need for periodic re-hospitalisations. In addition, the termination of treatment required a prolonged weaning process for many patients and that meant extra sessions and telephone contact between sessions that was thought to be outside the confines of the classical method. Any patient accepted into psychoanalytic treatment requires deviations from the norm and this is inevitable especially with outpatient and hospitalised patients.

The modified analysis practiced at Menninger demanded flexibility in its application and new parameters were created for its use with more unpredictable patients. The downgrading of psychoanalysis to psychotherapy when it was modified was a common mind-set for psychoanalysts of this era. Preconceived ideas about the nature and definition of psychoanalysis and psychotherapy were challenged by the research, as were predictions regarding outcomes of treatment:

> [...] that the therapeutic modalities of psychoanalysis, expressive psychotherapy, and supportive psychotherapy hardly exist in ideal or pure form in the real world of actual practice; that real treatments in actual practice are intermingled blends of expressive-interpretive and supportive-stabilizing elements; that almost all treatments (including even pure psychoanalysis) carry many more supportive components than they are usually credited with; that the overall outcomes achieved by more analytic and more supportive treatments converge more than our usual expectations for those differing modalities would portend; and that the kinds of changes achieved in the two ends of this spectrum are less different in nature and in permanence than is usually expected. (Wallerstein, 1989, p. 205)

The overall project findings were not predicted and the researchers concluded that the psychotherapeutic approach must be matched to the appropriate patient and employed by a trained psychoanalyst with skill and understanding. They were beginning to see that each patient was unique regardless of the diagnostic criteria and so required a singular approach to the treatment with the flexibility to respond appropriately to whatever contingency may arise.

In recent times, the Menninger Clinic like other psychoanalytic hospitals has come under the influence of the managed care movement and has had to evolve with the times, although its length of stay remains longer than most hospitals. In parallel with the Austen Riggs Center, it has developed a reputation as a facility for treatment resistant patients with complicated diagnostic problems. The intensive psychoanalytic approach that was once the clinic's specialty became marginalised in recent times as advances in neuroscience inspired the introduction of new pharmacological treatments and brief psychotherapies. The psychoanalytically oriented programs are now based on empirical research with a focus exclusively on process and outcomes. During the 1990s the Menninger's budget was increasingly constrained so they tried diversifying and had to seriously downsize several years later. Nevertheless, financial difficulties intensified and in 2005 the Menninger Clinic was moved to Houston, Texas and amalgamated with the Baylor College of Medicine and the Methodist Hospital at the Texas Medical Center. As a consequence the Topeka Institute of Psychoanalysis no longer exists.

The Austen Riggs Center

The Austen Riggs Center is a private, not-for-profit, open psychiatric hospital in Stockbridge, Massachusetts that offers a continuum of treatment programs within a core clinical framework that includes inpatient, residential, and day treatment, as well as aftercare. Their ethos values the dignity of the individual, the importance of human relationships and the centrality of a sense of community. The mainstay of the treatment at Austen Riggs is individual psychoanalytic psychotherapy modified to meet the needs of an unstable ego within the context of a therapeutic community (Geller, 2006). An intensive psychotherapeutic treatment program encompasses, milieu and group therapy, family therapy, individual therapy, and an activities program (Shapiro & Plakun, 2008). Psychopharmacologic intervention plays a significant part in the treatment program and an internist provides on-site medical consultation, diagnosis, and treatment. The length of stay in the treatment program is averaged at around six months in which time the patient's care is followed up by the same individual therapist with four times weekly sessions and by the same clinical treatment team throughout their entire stay.

Patients are admitted for an initial four to six week assessment period where a comprehensive interdisciplinary evaluation is carried out from multiple perspectives: psychological testing, psychodynamic and social opinion regarding psychotherapy and group interactions, psychopharmacologic opinion, a full medical and psychiatric examination, a nursing assessment, a social work assessment and a family evaluation that takes into account the influence of previous generations (The Austen Riggs Center, 2005). The culmination of this evaluation phase is at a two-hour individual case conference. Time is devoted to discussion of what has been learned during the initial period of work with the patient, and the entire clinical staff is invited to review the full range of clinical material. Furthermore, the patient is invited to attend the case conference to help frame the discussion and ask questions. After this evaluation, a recommendation is made for further treatment and the patient meets with his or her therapist and treatment team to design a treatment plan. This rigorous assessment is a unique feature of Austen Riggs Center.

In the therapeutic milieu patients take authority for their own treatment in how they address the tensions of living in an open community setting where each patient is involved in creating a mutually respectful society. This is achieved by: examining behaviours and understanding them as a way of communication; maintaining responsibility for insightful self-management; and using patients' perspectives to recognise concerns that arise at the level of the organisation as a whole. The nursing focus, as in other therapeutic communities, is on the development of reliable interpersonal relationships in a safe community environment in order to enhance the patients' potential for facing and modifying problematic behaviours. The activities program includes an interpretation-free zone called the studio where patients paint, work in clay, and do other crafts providing them with opportunities to become students in a variety of creative enterprises that are taught by professional artists and craftspeople (Luhrmann, 2000). The teacher-student relationship encourages curiosity and focuses on developing strengths and assets. Austen Riggs assists the patient to move towards a healthier sense of self-responsibility including the ability to maintain internal controls.

The Inn hospital program is located in the hospital building and has a capacity of forty beds. A patient's admission has three distinct phases each with a particular treatment focus: initially there is an intensive evaluation and treatment phase, then an intensive milieu phase for patients requiring an inpatient level of care, and finally the transition phase that prepares patients for discharge or the move to a residential or partial hospital program. The Inn residential program operates as both an inpatient and residential facility providing for patients who still require a structured treatment setting. The Elms residential program is located in a cottage on the grounds and provides a structured group living situation that emphasises the mastering of independent living skills. The Lavan residential program is housed in a building in the town of Stockbridge; it offers an independent living environment in a group setting with an emphasis on self-management.

The Stockbridge Institute for the Psychoneuroses, renamed The Austen Riggs Foundation in 1919, was founded in 1907 by Austen Fox Riggs who developed a system of treatment based on talk therapy combined with a structured routine of daily activities that emphasised a balance between work, rest, play, and exercise. Austen Riggs was succeeded in 1947 by Robert Knight, who came from the Menninger Clinic and led the Austen Riggs Center to becoming recognised as a centre for American ego psychology (The Austen Riggs Center, 2005). Knight moulded the Center around his philosophy that the borderline schizophrenic patient needed more organised support between treatment hours than living at home could provide. He believed that the answer lay in the therapeutic setting, such as an open sanatorium, where patients are able to stay in charge of themselves. Under Knight's directorship a therapeutic community environment was developed at Austen Riggs Center. This followed the pioneer work that came from Tom Main at Cassel Hospital and Maxwell Jones at Henderson Hospital in England, see chapter eight.

Erik Erikson was recruited in the 1950s and spent ten years working and teaching at Austin Riggs. His application of psychoanalysis was also founded on ego psychology aimed at helping the patient's ego become stronger and heal itself by mediating between the demands of unconscious internal pressure and the pressures of the external world (Edward Shapiro & Fromm, 2000). The goal of therapy was the patient's progress through the various stages of the life cycle, and the degree to which their psychological development or pathological outcomes could be identified. In the consulting room, the therapist was expected to practice self-observational vigilance but it is unclear if this involved submitting to a personal analysis. With Otto Will's arrival as director of Riggs came his wealth of experience in the individual daily psychotherapy of psychotic patients at Chestnut Lodge. Will carried on the work that Knight and others had established in underscoring the need for an open setting, intensive psychotherapy, and a milieu that functioned synergistically with the individual psychotherapy (Geller, 2006). Will identified financial reasons for the scarcity of psychoanalytic facilities because very few patients were able to afford such a long treatment and government funding was often directed in favour of biological research with its promise of more rapid and dramatic results. Added to this was the expense of running such a facility, with suitable staff who required intensive, prolonged training. Borderline or psychotic patients treated in private centres were often treatment failures elsewhere; they did not respond quickly to treatment, making the kind of work unappealing to a lot of clinicians. At this time, Austin Riggs was in danger of becoming an anachronism like so many other similar facilities.

Current successful strategies

When Edward Shapiro came from McLean Hospital as medical director to Austin Riggs in 1991 he decided to reorganise the way things were done (Geller, 2006). In the context of a health care landscape that was rapidly changing Austin Riggs had to adapt. In order to survive they had to address their limited resources with a series of budget cuts. Thus, they decided to offer a wider array of treatment options with corresponding financial flexibility. During 2002, the number of patients funded by insurance alone was almost twice as high as the percentage the year before which was interpreted as an indication that insurers might be recognising the cost benefit of longer term treatments for persons with treatment refractory disorders (Ellen, 2003). Austin Riggs began to move towards specialising in a niche market for treatment resistant patients (Plakun, 2011). Of those patients admitted during 2004 eighty-seven per cent had treatment refractory mood disorders with a secondary diagnostic overlay of forty per cent substance use disorders, twenty one per cent had eating disorders, fourteen per cent Post Traumatic Stress Disorder and ten per cent had a psychotic disorder (Geller, 2006). Although Austin Riggs does not provide primary treatment for substance abuse or dependence, nearly half of the patients continue to have significant substance difficulties. Signs of success were a median length of patient treatment at eight months, an increase in capacity to seventy-five beds and the facility operating at full occupancy with a four year waiting list (Plakun, 2006).

In addition, Austin Riggs developed a management structure that brought together the financial staff and clinicians to address a framework for the patient's treatment. A Resource Review Committee was formed in 1991 that comprised the Chief Financial Officer, the Utilization Review Coordinator, the Clinical Director and the Director of Admissions (Shapiro, 1997). In the past the crucial clinical and financial discussions about treatment were made without the patient being involved or properly informed, leaving the patient as a passive recipient of treatment rather than an active agent in it. At Austin Riggs the patient and their family are now brought into the conversation about finances and treatment arrangements between the hospital and the external third party payee or health fund. Finances are candidly discussed at admission and beyond to help the patient figure out how to make the most of the resources available to them. Patients who have come from emotionally deprived backgrounds tend to transfer their insecurity onto money issues. The process, although challenging for the patient, exposes them to the truth of their situation; it authorises them to speak and act as the critical agent of change with an added analytic dimension. In 2003, the most intensive level of inpatient hospital care at Riggs costs US$870 per day, while the least intensive aftercare costs were US$105 per day (Ellen, 2003). The patient is invited to take responsibility for choosing less expensive treatment options within the system and to negotiate the terms themselves in order to find a balance between treatment needs and resource limitations. This produces a working link between financial and clinical thinking as the patient's therapist helps them mediate the pressures and sustain a realistic perspective while the therapeutic processing work continues.

The psychotherapy dyad

The therapeutic couple of therapist and patient are embedded in the larger context of the Austen Riggs therapeutic community. Individual psychotherapy is informed by a blend of psychoanalytic principles based on Eriksonian ego psychology with influences from Lacanian and object relations theory (Muller, 1999). It is in the approach to the therapy where the mix of theoretical influences is most apparent; a third element is said to keep the psychotherapy dyad grounded in reality. This is the "analytic intersubjective third" that is a guiding frame that structures the roles and relationships of the therapeutic dyad in the treatment, enabling therapist and patient to transform symptoms that arise in the transference and counter transference into usable signs.

The analytic situation is composed of three subjects: the analyst, the patient, and the analytic third which is continually being generated by the unconscious interplay between analyst and patient but remains separate from their individual experiences and is perceived differently by them both. Meissner's (2006) research on the analytic Third led to the conclusion that the third is the way the analyst maintains autonomy within the matrix of the analytic process and is synonymous with the maintenance of an authentically neutral stance, synonymous with the therapeutic alliance. Muller elaborates on the alliance between therapist and patient calling it an ethical pact that operates as a representative of the analytic Third that authorises speaking subjects to carry out their tasks in the treatment. The analytic Third is a structure of signification that grounds the position of the dyad in "[...] an evolving contextualised relationship, serving as the basis for any interpretive speech act" (Muller, 2007, p. 226).

Frequently, the therapeutic dyad moves towards a regression to the early mother-infant relation and this dynamic is articulated in the transference as an impasse in the therapy that puts the analytic third at risk. For example, if the "analyst's desire" is not in place the patient will not be able to articulate his or her own desire with the possibility of a power struggle developing in the transference that could cause the dyad to cease to function. The analyst's desire is a Lacanian concept that is fundamental to psychoanalytic treatment as it aims for the analysand's own unique truth to emerge in the analytic treatment. If the therapeutic frame of the analytic third is at risk it needs to be taken to supervision or to a consultant. The consultant grounds the situation in its larger context intervening as the representative of the analytic third that can be seen as the place of a Name-of-the-Father (Muller, 1999). The consultant's position is to hold the dyad and stabilise the relationship by opening a signifying dimension that grounds the positions of patient and therapist, interrupting the impasse and thus making it possible for them to keep on going. Each member of the dyad is recognised without taking sides as the consultant addresses what is occurring between the patient and therapist, mediating a relation with each other through the other. The chief intervention is to reinstall the framework of the third that contextualises the dyad and amplifies its symbolic dimension.

A psychodynamic hospital such as Austen Riggs provides the space for the patient to discover the words to symbolise their interpersonal experiences through the responses of others and the interpretive work of the therapy (Fromm, 2006). Behaviour signifies an intention to communicate meaning and the therapeutic community works at interpreting behaviour and giving voice to its significance. In a community where life is examined there is no space for private behaviour, all behaviour is potentially interpretable, but this does not rule out private thought and speech.

The experience of examined living

Patients and staff work collaboratively at Austen Riggs in large and small therapeutic groups to facilitate the work of examined living. The work of an open therapeutic community relies on the way patients assume authority and in how they take on the challenges and responsibilities of citizenship (Charles, 2008). This notion of subjectivity is also central to the approach to the treatment at GIFRIC in Canada, discussed in chapter seven. Patients elect their leadership for an eight-week period and that leadership works with staff leadership in administering the hospital. Patients run the community through a system of self-governance: they plan meetings and group activities, they reach out to other members who are isolated, alienated or alienating and they help orient new members, as well as, recognising and celebrating milestones, such as someone's discharge. This mobilises an individual patient to assume a citizen's role where full membership of the community implies assuming responsibility and following the rules and laws of that community. As the hospital is an open facility, there are no locked doors nor is there the capacity for restraining patients. The model expects everyone, no matter how disturbed, to work collaboratively in the running of the milieu and the whole centre. Disturbed patients are not admitted until they are able to take responsibility for managing themselves with assistance.

The group is a powerful tool for learning and this provides a wealth of opportunities for projection, the reworking of old problems from the family of origin and for encountering new problems. The community is also a social system where "[...] resistance, irrationality, and pressure to silence threatening ideas all emerge" (Parish & Elmendorf, 2007, p. 379). To counter these destructive elements the milieu fosters the idea of examined living that is similar to a culture of enquiry that was established at Cassel Hospital in England. All members of the therapeutic community, including the staff, are encouraged to collaborate in being open with each other and to the organisation as a whole in an effort to understand the meaning of previously obscured re-enactments. The openness of staff to self-examination is an important element in community life because it shows that human and institutional dynamics apply to all.

Within the open setting of the therapeutic community a subsystem of staff and patient representatives has been established called the Task Group that creates a space for review and reflection on the meaning of disruptive behaviour or issues that are of concern to others. As described earlier, the analytic third embodies the community as a social and ideological context for treatment, and the Task Group is its most concentrated representative. The group mediates, listens, and holds in mind impartial standards that govern action in the community. "In practice, this kind of group works in a range of ways, offering observations and perspectives about how members view or feel affected by the person and the problem presented" (Parish & Elmendorf, 2007, p. 382). They try to understand what is going on, including the role of the community as a whole, in the problem and then offer ways to help repair relationships between members. The community is the context in which treatment happens and it supports the broader therapeutic aim of translating symptoms into language.

Tanya Luhrmann (2000) was an anthropologist who spent time observing the work at the Austen Riggs Center and she described the complex culture around several paradoxes. The first paradox was that emotions were an important focus in most clinical discussions yet there was an implicit message that feelings were not to be displayed, except in a calm formal way. The second paradox was that psychotherapy was confidential and took place in private, yet the environment of examined living demanded that everything be open for discussion. The third was the existence of a solid hospital hierarchy that was consistently flattened in the service of an egalitarian democracy, and finally, there was much discussion about limits and boundaries yet the hospital was open; it had no concrete constraints, no doors, and no security:

> Thus, to live in the culture successfully as a doctor (or another staff person) meant that you had to talk about your own emotions in public and in depth, but not express them; you had to keep secrets but know when to share them; you had to behave democratically but with a deep respect for hierarchy; you had to substitute talk about responsible living with your patient for (instead of) taking responsibility for that patient's life by keeping her under lock and key. (Luhrmann, 2000, p. 14)

Research at Riggs

Research on the patient population at Austen Riggs was first introduced by Robert Knight in the 1950s and then Otto Will during the 1970s. Since 1992 the Erik H. Erikson Institute for Education and Research has been conducting an ongoing, naturalistic, longitudinal follow-along study of treatment outcome in patients at Riggs. The follow-along study examines change in patients' diagnoses and symptoms during and after treatment at the Center. In addition, the study measures psychodynamic constructs, such as defence mechanisms and intrapsychic conflicts. Variables such as treatment duration and outcome as a function of diagnosis are studied to see if there is any demonstrable benefit from longer term treatment that continues after symptoms have subsided up until there is measurable character change. Recent research on treatment resistance derived from the Follow-Along Study identified 226 patients admitted between 1992 and 2001 and reported that:

> [...] individuals with self-destructive phenomena can recover with time and treatment, despite the presence of treatment-refractory disorders. Although 85% of those studied showed improving courses, strikingly sustained recovery was obtained in the majority, ranging from 50.6% of those with suicidal ideation to 77.2% of those making suicide attempts immediately before admission. (Perry, et al., 2009, p. 33)

Psychodynamic therapy with these patients suggests that the outcome of such work depends in part on the therapist's success in three tasks:

> 1) careful negotiation of, and ongoing attention to, the establishment and maintenance of the working alliance; 2) recognition that the use of the vicissitudes of the therapeutic alliance may be the central initial therapeutic action in work with suicidal patients; and 3) "taking" the transference as it is offered, rather than "refusing" it, with careful attention to the way our countertransference-based inclination to refuse transferences may lead to enactments that can, unwittingly, give patients reasons to choose suicide over continuing the arduous therapeutic work. (Plakun, 2001, p. 275)

Another study (Owen, 2011) examined therapeutic alliance in the psychotherapeutic relationship as a predictor in patient outcomes. Results revealed several techniques that were meaningfully related to patient improvement. These were: the linking of current feelings or perceptions to the past, focusing attention on similarities in patients' relationships that repeat over and over again and identifying recurrent patterns in patient actions, feelings, and experiences.

In North America, psychiatric institutions that grew up with psychoanalysis as an experimental approach tended to enhance it as a model for the treatment of patients and for the organisation of the institution. In this way, they learned and evolved their models. The Menninger clinic adapted Freud's theories to the whole institution, creating a milieu that was organised by operationalising psychoanalytic concepts for institutional treatment. Today the rationale for these artificial devices could be seen as manipulative and eccentric interpretations of Freudian doctrine, but this did work as an approach to milieu treatment that all staff believed in and thoughtfully applied with respect for the individuality of the patient. A significant contribution was the Menninger Clinic's longitudinal research project on the nature and efficacy of psychoanalysis in the treatment of more disturbed patients. This effort remains the most extensive and detailed examination and follow up of psychotherapy and psychoanalysis that has ever been done. Findings showed that the more supportive the therapy, the better the overall results for the patient irrespective of the approach being psychoanalytic or psychotherapeutic. The rigid application of classical psychoanalysis did not show great efficacy in an environment such as the Menninger Clinic and a broader, more supportive and more inclusive therapeutic approach was recommended.

In their institutional approach, the Austen Riggs Center amalgamated a number of theoretical orientations drawn from an Eriksonian version of ego psychology with influences from Lacanian and object relations theories in their therapeutic community model. Over many decades each of the directors of Austen Riggs have brought with them their unique experience of alternate models of psychoanalytically informed hospitals that were honed for a particular patient population. The innovative use of the concept of the analytic third opens up an understanding of the therapeutic experience, allowing the process to be examined and appropriate interventions made. The Center also made creative changes in order to embrace the demands of a patient population that were difficult to treat and remain viable. In this setting the negotiated management of limitations becomes the framework for psychoanalytic interpretation.

The institutional models discussed in this chapter are informed by psychoanalysis and bring together a number of conceptual approaches to provide a framework for understanding an institution and a structure for clinical practice from which a unique perspective can be drawn. Institutional models are also internal objects of the analyst's mind that have been transformed by the characteristics of his or her own mental apparatus in the institutional context. Each institution contains a portion of the individual's personality in the sense that at least one part of the individual's identity shapes itself by belonging to a group, institution, ideology or party.

Chestnut Lodge Insane Asylum.

CHAPTER SIX

Hospital based individual treatment

This chapter focuses predominantly on Chestnut Lodge and the factors that contributed to the practice of psychoanalytically oriented psychotherapy for each individual inpatient. The hospital based approach at Chestnut Lodge has been described as a bifocal model that emphasises the dual relationship between analyst and patient, with technical alterations to the psychoanalytic classical method for the treatment of psychosis, in a highly protected institutional environment. Although diagnostic classification was less rigorous than it is today it seems fairly certain that the majority of patients admitted to Chestnut Lodge would satisfy the criteria for schizophrenia. Chestnut Lodge provided a stable container for a prolonged inpatient stay that initiated, maintained, and sustained the therapeutic process. The therapist and the administrator took up leading roles with the whole team effort supporting the assumption that all patients needed intensive therapy with a view to structurally changing their personalities.

Few mental hospital superintendents in the United States were willing to experiment with the use of psychoanalytic treatment methods for very disturbed inpatients, however, William Alanson White was one who played a major role in the introduction of psychoanalysis to the United States, advancing its role as a theory and treatment method.

He was superintendent of the Government Hospital for the Insane, later called St. Elizabeth's Hospital in Washington in the 1930s. White was very open to new ideas and new forms of treatment and was keen to accept psychoanalytic concepts once they were fully justified. He planned an extensive system for the practice of the psychoanalytic method, although modified through experience to be used to understand and treat psychotic patients at St. Elizabeth's Hospital. The plan was to train staff to be able to approach any personal problem the patient might have and be able to treat them without prejudice. Edward Kempf, Lucile Dooley, and Harry Stack Sullivan all worked at St. Elizabeth's applying psychoanalytic principles to the treatment of psychotic patients.

Harry Stack Sullivan

In 1922 Harry Stack Sullivan was a thirty year old physician who only had experience in surgery and internal medicine when he accepted a position at St. Elizabeth's Hospital in Washington and came under the influence of William Alanson White and Edward Kempf. White believed that Sullivan had promise and assisted him in securing employment at Sheppard and Enoch Pratt Hospital in Towson, Maryland. His claimed success in the treatment of young male patients with schizophrenia using milieu therapy became noteworthy in the history of American psychiatry. Sullivan (1931a) claimed marked improvement in forty-eight out of seventy-eight cases of schizophrenia that he treated but these numbers were mainly for statistical purposes and ought not be considered an indication that he conducted cures, especially in the light of diagnostic variability (Wake, 2006, p. 325). Sullivan studied and applied psychoanalytic theory in the interviews he conducted with psychotic patients for research purposes but he did not see patients in individual analytic treatment whilst at Sheppard and Enoch Pratt (Schulz, 1987). Instead his focus was on the milieu of the ward.

Central to Sullivan's therapy of psychosis was an emphasis on clear communication so that patients could grasp and then put their experience into speech. According to Sullivan, the persons with whom the patient had personal contact were of great importance in determining the course and outcome of the illness (Sullivan, 1931b). He theorised that it was the psychotic person's interactions with others that precipitated anxiety, and accordingly it would be the relationship with the significant other of the clinician or attendant where the goal of recognition, understanding, and exploration should occur. The practice at Sheppard and Enoch Pratt was to use the diagnostic criteria proposed by Kraepelin and Bleuler to which Sullivan added Freud's psychoanalytic principles. Sullivan's patients frequently received such diagnoses as "psychopathic personality with incipient schizophrenia" or "psychopathic personality with recurring psychotic episodes" or even "psychoneurosis in a psychopathic personality" (Wake, 2006, p. 347).

Sullivan observed that the psychotic patient used language more as a means of defence than as a method of communication and encouraged them to reconstruct their experiences so that they could gain insight into their situation. He revolutionised the field by introducing the concept of "participant observation" (Krim, 1994). Sullivan (1954) saw the clinician's perception of the patient in the role of the participant observer as screened through their own past experiences contributing to their interactions with patients. In cultivating self-observation clinicians could become authentic observers and so be more aware of their own anxiety responses to the patient. The position of participant observer was one who responds to the patient's communication with an inquiry or comment, to which the patient counters with further thoughts or feelings and so a greater idea of the patient's experience is achieved. Sullivan observed himself closely to explore the impact that the patient had on him and, in this way, linked his thinking to that of Sandor Ferenczi with reference to the countertransference. Sullivan created opportunities for positive interactions where patients could speak to someone in particular who would not produce anxiety but provide the type of communication that would enhance their capacity to formulate and clarify their own issues. He observed that providing an experience of reciprocal trust, which he felt many patients had missed during critical periods of development, was beneficial in validating their personal worth so that they became a "person among persons" (Sullivan, 1931b, p. 532). When the patient was more settled, Sullivan recommended reconstructing the actual chronology of the psychosis with the patient using free-association to fill in failures of memory.

In order to record and analyse the speech and interactions of patients in his research, Sullivan installed crude listening devices on his desk, in the ceilings and in the bathroom of the inpatient unit while a secretary, stationed on the floor below, documented all that transpired (Chatelaine, 2001; Schulz, 1987). Generally, Sullivan preferred to observe patients from a distance and had the aides talk to patients and then report back to him.

Sullivan engaged in very little talking with individual patients outside of staff conferences and structured clinical interviews. Clinical files show that Sullivan was only engaged in the intensive treatment or special interviews of patients from around 1929 after the establishment of his own ward at Sheppard and Enoch Pratt where "discussions of homosexuality occurred almost exclusively in the course of special interviews" (Wake, 2006, p. 328). Sullivan thought that talking about homosexuality was therapeutic for the patient; he believed that social stigmatisation of homosexuality was the major cause of schizophrenia as the result of sociocultural inhibitions that led to a patient's failure in interpersonal relations.

Milieu therapy

For the most part, Sullivan's (1931a) ideas embodied the influence of social sciences in psychiatry based on his intense scrutiny of psychotic inpatients over an eight year period. The only tools he found to be of any use in the treatment of schizophrenia "[...] are the *psychoanalytic* procedures and the *socio-psychiatric* program which the writer has evolved from them" (Sullivan, 1931b, p. 529). Sullivan's milieu therapy was not significantly influenced by psychoanalysis, at least in his early days at Sheppard and Enoch Pratt when it was basically an experiment to which the theory was progressively and retroactively applied. Sullivan felt that any good therapy with a patient could be ruined by only a brief contact with an unsuitable person, whether that was staff or family; psychiatric staff were, in general, considered unsuitable people, especially the nurses. Therefore, immediately upon admission patients on Sullivan's ward were placed in the all-male ward milieu in the company of specially chosen attendants and were kept segregated from the destructive influences of those Sullivan regarded as inappropriate. Visits with people were strictly monitored and many visitors, including relatives, were restricted.

Sullivan thought that attendants who were successful in getting along with psychotic patients were potentially schizoid themselves, so he staffed the hospital unit with shy, introverted, homosexual male attendants. The attendants were specifically chosen and trained by Sullivan, who was said to be homosexual himself. Sullivan's patients were, for the most part, also young male homosexuals with schizophrenia that he personally selected from the general hospital population to be intensively treated on his ward, the Special Receiving Service, in 1929 (Wake, 2006). Sullivan would watch interactions between patients and staff very closely and if he noticed an alienated patient sitting over in the corner by himself Sullivan would approach an attendant and coach him in ways that he could make tentative advances towards the patient (Chateline, 2001). Physical contact between aides and patients was permitted to enable patients to express themselves without being rejected. From 1929, when Sullivan became director of his own ward, physical contact was upgraded to affectionate contact that brought censure from the Hospital's Board of Trustees (Wake, 2006). Sullivan was encouraged to leave Sheppard and Enoch Pratt the following year when his experiment was just reaching its peak.

In the early 1930s, Sullivan started training as a psychoanalyst and received 300 hours of personal analysis from Clara Thompson, who had been analysed by Ferenczi at Sullivan's urging (Hornstein, 2000; Thompson, 1957). By then Sullivan was increasingly dissatisfied with psychoanalysis as a method of treating psychosis and, in his independent way, developed his own theory regarding personality development. Sullivan's interpersonal view of human development was similar to that of the object relation's theorists where the infant is seen as motivated primarily by the need for object relatedness rather than drive satisfaction. Like Winnicott, Sullivan believed that there was no psychology of the infant independent of the psychology of the infant-mother dyad. Although Sullivan published, supervised and lectured about his approach, especially the seminars he gave to the staff at Chestnut Lodge, he had great trouble transmitting his theory and practice to others. He could at times be irritable, sarcastic, aloof, and highly judgmental of students, staff, and colleagues; his speech was at times illogical and discouraged any verbal exchange (Hornstein, 2000). Sullivan's observations and conclusions about psychotic patients were insightful, offering guidelines for institutional treatment. Conversely, Sullivan tended to flout the law in the way he carried out his research, beyond what would be considered ethical even by the standards of the 1920s, and this complicates the legitimacy of his work. In spite of this he still has a loyal following today and is considered the father of interpersonal psychotherapy, which arose out of his research in the institutional treatment of psychotic patients, see chapter two.

Chestnut Lodge Sanatorium

Chestnut Lodge Sanatorium was a small private psychiatric hospital located in Rockville, Maryland in the United States. Dr Ernest Bullard founded The Lodge, opening it as an adult inpatient psychiatric facility in 1910. Ernest's son, Dexter, joined him in 1925 as assistant physician and the sole staff member until 1931 when he became medical director and continued in that role for the next thirty-eight years. Following the family line, Dexter Bullard's son, Dexter junior (known as "Rusty" Bullard) took over directorship until 1995, when Wayne Fenton stepped in as its last director. Unfortunately, like the Menninger Clinic, Chestnut Lodge struggled with increasing overheads before finally closing its doors insolvent in 2001. It was Dexter Bullard senior's vision to specialise in the psychoanalytic treatment of psychotic patients when he invited Frieda Fromm-Reichmann to join him at The Lodge following her immigration from Europe prior to the Second World War in 1935 (Bullard, 1952). Harry Stack Sullivan and Frieda Fromm-Reichmann were distinguished figures known for their work with severely psychotic patients, many of whom were diagnosed with schizophrenia. Fromm-Reichmann was an intrepid pioneer who was willing to work with psychotic patients in long-term psychoanalysis, and had the ability to engage and tolerate disturbed behaviour. She was influenced by Sullivan who was often invited to Chestnut Lodge to give sessional lectures during the late 1930s and early 1940s; it was during this time that he began to operationalise his theory and practice of interpersonal psychotherapy.

The Lodge campus ultimately stretched over a hundred acres with a number of buildings on the grounds that housed residences, inpatient units, consulting offices, a dining room, a high school for adolescents, and various recreational and occupational therapy facilities. In the period between 1940 and 1975 demographics showed that the average length of stay at Chestnut Lodge was approximately two years, and the vast majority of patients were of a higher than average intelligence coming from affluent families who could afford to support the costs of admission there (Schultz, 1963). Patients were initially admitted to locked inpatient units or cottages; after a thorough assessment they were established in four to five times a week mandatory intensive psychoanalytically based psychotherapy. Patients who were too disturbed to leave the ward for sessions in the psychotherapist's consulting room were seen in situ, even if they were in restraints. The therapy work took place within a structure that prevented patients from hurting themselves or others; disturbed patients were housed in locked wards and restraints were uses in addition to continuous baths or wet sheet packs (Fromm-Reichmann, 1947). Patients progressed to a step down program geared towards rehabilitation before moving on to a supervised living facility. When the patient was able to leave the hospital, he or she usually continued therapy as an outpatient, living and possibly working in the nearby town of Rockville much the same as patients at Menninger Clinic and Austen Riggs.

Dexter Bullard described psychoanalytic psychiatry as "an interpretive psychiatry based on the fundamental contributions of Freud and his followers" (Bullard, 1939, pp. 526–527). He applied psychoanalytic thinking to a wide range of institutional contexts, such as issues associated with nursing care on the ward, treatments such as hydrotherapy, the choice of recreational or occupational activities, in addition to dealing with administrative problems. He believed that so called chronic psychotic patients did change in analytic psychotherapy and there was evidence that some did recover (Stanton & Schwartz, 1954). An experienced medical staff member supervised every psychiatric therapist's work with a patient. Each patient's progress was reviewed by medical staff and charge nurses at twice weekly case conferences, weekly staff meetings dealt with administrative issues and new admissions, the physician met with the nurses and therapy staff weekly to discuss patients and the entire therapeutic staff of the hospital met monthly. Fromm-Reichmann maintained that nurses and allied staff also receive some supervision with regard to transference and countertransference responses. Bullard recommended that nurses were analysed at fees they could afford and he often subsidised some of their analyses himself. "All of the supervising nurses, some of the practical nurses and the recreational and occupational therapists have been or are being psychoanalyzed" (Fromm-Reichmann, 1947, p. 338). Bullard acknowledged the difficulties encountered in an environment where analysed people, those undergoing analysis and the unanalysed had to work together because every person's actions were seen as having unconscious meaning and routine events took on symbolic significance (Bullard, 1954). In an effort to deal with this, Bullard instituted weekly staff meetings to interpret and deal with conflict as it arose.

Frieda Fromm-Reichmann

Frieda Fromm-Reichmann considered herself a psychoanalyst in her practice of intensive psychodynamic psychotherapy in psychiatry and that her orientation was based on the training she received at the

Berlin Psychoanalytic Institute, her analysis with Hans Sachs and her supervision by Sandor Ferenczi (Hornstein, 2000; Silver, 2000). Her work in European sanatoria is discussed in chapter three. Differing in opinion from Freud, Fromm-Reichmann felt that psychotic patients were capable of transference relationships that were extraordinarily intense and that countertransference difficulties were of a specific quality and difficulty. Reminiscent of Ferenczi's view, she believed that no patient was so hopeless as to be beyond help. Her early work was based on the observation that psychotic patients were extremely sensitive and tended to withdraw. For that reason, she encouraged the therapist to avoid thinking, saying or even feeling anything that might trigger the patient's fear of closeness (Fromm-Reichmann, 1947). Fromm-Reichmann did not put patients on the couch and was more flexible with session lengths saying that an interview ought to be determined by the patient's clinical needs rather than a compulsive adherence to the clock. She did not recommended free association with psychotic and borderline patients because it carried the possible danger of inducing and increasing disintegrated thinking (Fromm-Reichmann, 1950). She also cautioned away from too much content interpretation of schizophrenic productions in favour of understanding the genetics and dynamics of what was being communicated. Interpretation should be left up to the patient because a great deal of psychotic communication was not immediately understandable.

Fromm-Reichmann claimed that the repetition of experiences from infancy in the transference were crucial to the analytic treatment of psychotics. Fromm-Reichmann thought that the therapist's role was to make up for inadequate mothering through constant warmth and encouragement towards the building of a harmonious relationship. Fromm-Reichmann (1947) first used the term "schizophrenogenic mother" and wrote about the loving aspects of the maternal principle that instils security in a child, in addition to the dangerous influence of the domineering mother. It was thought inappropriate for a therapist to offer closeness, friendship and love to a patient because it would leave the patient torn between an intense longing for and an equally intense fear of a symbiotic merging with another. Her approach to the therapeutic task was to identify the distortions within the transference relationship and communicate to the patient verbally and non-verbally that the therapist was not the person the patient thought she was (Fromm-Reichmann, 1947). The next step in the treatment was to try to determine what in the patient's early life may have been the basis for the distorted perceptions.

The therapeutic relationship was seen as a collaborative effort to discover the inherited and dynamic roots of a patient's anxieties, blind spots, defences, and other symptoms. Fromm-Reichmann described delusions and hallucinations as symptoms that occur "[...] due to the bursting through into awareness of an unbearable surplus of repressed or dissociated thoughts and feelings [...]" (Fromm-Reichmann, 1950, p. 178). In twenty years of experience treating mainly severely disturbed psychotic patients, Fromm-Reichmann claimed that "the majority emerged sooner or later under intensive dynamic psychotherapy" (Fromm-Reichmann, 1954, p. 411). After this, they would continue in treatment four to six times a week for a number of years in a quieter state of illness and ultimately recover their insight. The recovery of insight was considered the benchmark of a cure. When a relapse occurred Fromm-Reichmann ascertained it was due to either a failure in the therapist's skill in evaluating the patient's capacity to endure psychotherapy or unrecognised problems in the transference, and other relapses were due to events beyond their control. These relapses could be handled successfully if the therapist did not become "too frightened, too discouraged, or too narcissistically hurt by their occurrence" (Fromm-Reichmann, 1954, p. 411).

The social system of the mental hospital

Detailed studies of staff and inpatients within the social system of a psychiatric hospital were relatively rare prior to Second World War. The Stanton and Schwartz socio-psychiatric study of fifteen disturbed women in a psychiatric ward at Chestnut Lodge in the early 1950s is of particular interest because it reports on observations of the relationship between staff and patients in an institution organised according to psychoanalytic principles. At the time, Chestnut Lodge employed 165 staff to care for sixty patients. Alfred Stanton, a psychoanalyst and psychiatrist employed at Chestnut Lodge, and Morris Schwartz, a psychoanalysed sociologist, collaborated for over three years on the study of how patients participate in an institution in the context of their psychiatric illness and treatment (Stanton & Schwartz, 1954). Aided by a grant from the National Institute of Mental Health and added support from the Washington School of Psychiatry, Stanton and Schwartz's study described the particular social circumstances of staff-to-staff and staff-to-patient interactions, and identified the significance and the consequent impact on the patient's development and stability.

In the case of the institution, social experience is determined by people who are themselves arranged according to a formal pattern of organisation based on the purpose of the institution, the institution's practical necessities and the requirements of each individual in the institution. A mental hospital, like all institutions, functions in a highly organised way to fulfil the needs of the human beings who inhabit it. The prescribed activities of staff and patients are not only on the institution's terms but their own informal terms and are reflected in the symptoms or emotional responses of individuals; an example of this would be staff morale. The interdependence of the formal and informal structures in the Chestnut Lodge study is highlighted by incidents where the formal structure of the hospital was inadequate, such as insufficient staffing or overcrowding of patients on a ward. The informal tacit solution to the problem was for staff to sabotage the structure, in the form of taking shortcuts that may compromise a patient's treatment. This would produce a response in the psychiatrist, who had to deal with the problem in order to find a solution (Stanton & Schwartz, 1954). The formal organisation is by its nature incomplete, ambiguous, contradictory, and impossible to achieve. It is because of this that the informal organisation comes into play to bridge the gap in an attempt to influence or change the formal structure itself.

At Chestnut Lodge, there was a hidden collusion amongst staff where the existence of prestige was openly denied but was covertly promoted. The institution's hierarchy of status placed psychoanalysts, typically psychiatrists and senior administrative staff, at the top of the pecking order. The patient was under the authority of psychiatrists; the practice of therapy was the exclusive domain of psychoanalysts and the administrator had the decision making power in the hospital. Trained nurses, aids, and allied health staff received supervision and most of the staff had been or were receiving analysis from the resident psychoanalysts (Fromm-Reichmann, 1947). Nonetheless, they could only aspire to some on-the-job training under the guidance of expert doctors and would never become psychoanalysts themselves. The American Psychoanalytic Association's 1938 rule prohibited membership to lay psychoanalysts, making it particularly difficult for potential analysts and those analysts who migrated from Europe before, during and after the Second

World War (Kirsner, 1998). Freud did not like the American trend of turning psychoanalysis into "a mere house-maid of psychiatry" (Ernest Jones, 1957, p. 323). Medical authority was assumed; with it came a benign but patronising certainty about the way things ought to be done that was steeped in a history of hegemony.

Hospital culture and staff attitudes

The Stanton and Schwartz study was primarily directed at the staff with the aim of breaking down stereotypes that were entrenched in the hospital's culture by identifying the reflexive nature between certain symptomatic behaviours and dysfunctional social attitudes (Stanton & Schwartz, 1954). Much of what occurred in the hospital that influenced the therapy of patients went on outside the conscious awareness of the particular personnel involved. Thus institutional dynamics that were at play in the lack of improvement in the chronic symptoms of some patients in prolonged therapy were possibly an expression of unconscious negative attitudes on the part of the hospital staff (Bullard, 1954). The pattern of these involvements represented only a part of the larger pattern of difficulty within the staff group at Chestnut Lodge. A distorted stereotype perpetrated by senior staff was the belief that the hospital was a perfect haven for patients. This idealised belief went unquestioned and led to rationalisations for decisions based on an allegiance to this stereotype that blinded them to other realities. The constitution of an ideal has a universalising value for all those who work in an institution. Similarly, many procedures at Chestnut Lodge were performed for the function of fulfilling certain needs of the hospital but were couched in terms that made them seem to be for the benefit of the patient. The hospital's central priority was devoted to the provision of psychotherapy to the majority of patients throughout their admission and beyond. This was a very expensive exercise that threatened the hospital's economic viability on a number of occasions. One hour in every patient's day was given much higher priority than any other hour in the day of the hospital's life; this inconsistency was perpetuated with the special individual therapy being homogenously applied to all patients for their own good regardless of individual choice or relevance.

The idealisation of the individual therapy over the other needs of the institution meant that a great deal was sacrificed for that sole purpose, such as overcrowded wards and insufficient staffing. This imbalance produced conflict that was naturally played out in the patient's treatment and reflected in the high turnover of ward staff. Nevertheless, many patients were said to be actively involved and participated equally in their therapy, which was not simply a product of compliance (Stanton & Schwartz, 1954). Idealisation is a problem associated with institutional practice and is of particular concern in the choice of how psychoanalysis is applied. Stanton and Schwartz's examination of the clinical and administrative procedures at Chestnut Lodge marked a significant stage in the development of the hospital as it brought into focus the existence of stereotypes that had grown up around the way the hospital functioned and how uncritically things were accepted. They found that when existing practices were scrutinised, the frequently unrecognised forces that influence patient and staff behaviour were exposed. As differences of opinion between staff were investigated it became clear that administrative, therapeutic, and nursing procedures reflected their own personal needs rather than those of the patient. As a consequence, the roles of administrative psychiatrist was separated from that of the psychoanalyst to clarify role definition for each patient and separate the ward based decision making from the psychoanalytic process.

The place of nurses in the social system

The charge nurse carried out the crucial role of co-ordinator of the ward: she was the intermediary between ward staff, the psychiatric administrator and the psychoanalyst, as well as, liaison between the ward and the rest of the hospital. Staff nurses and aids spent a lot of time with patients; their role was primarily a supportive one, enhancing patients' self-confidence and promoting a feeling of achievement tailored to the level of the individual's psychopathology and stage of treatment. They talked, listened, and read to them; they discussed issues around their treatment and they took care of the patient's physical condition and environment (Stanton & Schwartz, 1954). Nurses frequently came to the Lodge with little experience and training, and the aids were laymen on the lowest salary. Graduate education in psychiatric nursing was provided in a one-year course and aids received on the job instruction. Furthermore, nurses and aids were required to understand basic psychoanalytic principles so they could interpret subtle dynamics in patients and in the ward environment.

The problem at Chestnut Lodge was that the morale of nurses and aides was low, as evidenced by the rapid turnover of staff and poor retention rates, with a fifty per cent chance of nurses leaving "under a cloud" (Stanton & Schwartz, 1954, p. 107). Over the two year period of Stanton and Schwartz's research twenty-two nurses left the hospital; the most common reason for leaving was dissatisfaction with the hospital, usually in the context of irreconcilable differences with another staff member. A major criticism made by staff and patients alike was that there were not enough nurses and the wards were overcrowded. If a patient was disturbed, the policy was to spend time with them talking and listening until they settled down. However, nurses were often so busy they did not have enough time to do what they ought to be doing. As a consequence nurses became anxious and used other methods to control disturbed patients including seclusion, sedation with occasional use of barbiturates for prolonged sleep therapy and restraint with cold wet sheet packs, together with continuous baths, massage and back rubs (Stanton & Schwartz, 1954). The wet sheet pack was a procedure given for the sedative effect it had on patients who suffered from symptoms such as sleeplessness, restlessness, anxiety states, mania, the catatonic excitement of schizophrenia. It consisted primarily in enveloping the patient compactly in wet sheets and dry blankets for around two hours under supervision by a nurse (Kennedy, Helms, & Dykstra, 1936).

Isabel Menzies-Lyth's (1959) research on nurses in England sought to understand nurses' dissatisfaction and why they resigned from their jobs in such high numbers. She found that hospital based nurses unconsciously defended against anxiety that was endemic and was embedded in the routines of the nursing service, in particular by the senior nurses. Nurses often went into the field out of compassion for human suffering with a strong desire to alleviate it. However, the stress of dealing with staff shortages and an increased workload nurses tended to behave in thoughtless and routinised ways towards patients. The consequence of this is unbearable conflict that is followed by a switching off or withdrawal of sensitivity; to protect themselves from feeling overwhelmed the nurses treat patients as though they are not quite human. To be insensitive, off-hand and, in extreme cases, uncaring, and even brutal is associated with burnout. The jobs of nurses and aids were the lowest in prestige among the clinical staff at Chestnut Lodges, affording them little job satisfaction with no chance of progress in their careers, as opposed to the psychiatrist psychoanalyst who had a strong career path.

Due to the high staff turnover, nurses were commonly promoted to charge nurse after only several months on a ward, and in a few months they were promoted further to nursing supervisor. This meant that a small core of experienced nurses who could assume clinical responsibility were usually promoted away from patients to administrative roles. Direct patient care was therefore in the hands of neophytes with little clinical experience. Typically as nurses gained experience, they were moved away from patient contact, and as psychoanalysts gained experience they moved towards more patient contact, but only for one of the twenty-four hours in a patient's day.

The special patient

An illustration of the unacknowledged chronic and intense conflict that occurred between staff was when a nurse took special interest in a patient, defensively justifying the patient's need for special attention (Stanton & Schwartz, 1954). This would inevitably lead to the patient's condition improving when the nurse was on duty and getting worse when she was away. Initially, the special relationship was reinforced and colluded with by the rest of the staff but then slowly they would start to distance themselves. It was generally found in the cases studied, that the patient served as a bridge over which two incompatible attitudes were being fought out. The struggle was maintained and accentuated by the patient who selected and distorted the material that was gathered from respective staff members and fed back to the other one, and by the staff themselves in their inability to face the problem directly. Ultimately angry outbursts from the patient to the nurse would occur or the nurse would increasingly experience hostile feelings towards the patient. The nursing supervisor would identify the problem as "a delicate issue" and discuss the matter with the administrative psychiatrist who would typically generalise it as an "erotic transference and countertransference situation" (Stanton & Schwartz, 1970, p. 325). The problem was managed either by transferring the nurse to another ward or by asking her to work in her personal therapy on the reasons for her over-involvement. In circumstances when the splitting was brought out into the open, discussed, and addressed properly, the disagreement was resolved, which incidentally, led to an improvement in the patient's mental state. The willingness to consider the other person's point of view can lead to collaborative work on behalf of the patient that results in marked improvement in the splitting process.

Nevertheless, the fact that this scenario occurred regularly indicates a pattern; continued observation in the course of the study revealed a story behind the scenes, crucial to the development of the issue (Stanton & Schwartz, 1970). There was always a second senior nurse who globally undermined the first nurse behind her back while spearheading the same concerns the first nurse had about the patient. The reason for their disagreement about the patient was never discussed when these two nurses were together forming a triangulation and this would lead to a polarisation in roles towards the patient and inconsistencies in the patient's management. Quietly the other nurses would watch and take sides, usually against the first nurse who would find herself isolated and scapegoated. Progressively she would start to show signs of strain as she became more preoccupied with the patient; her sleep would become disturbed resulting in irritability to a point where her anger might produce an outburst directed towards the patient. Subsequently, she would be either transferred to another ward or left with no recourse but to resign, ostensibly for unethical conduct. In an attempt to deal with this repeated scenario, the senior psychiatrist met more frequently with ward staff and identified issues for discussion, but this only dealt with the superficial problem at hand not the fundamental issue that amplified the controversy and maintained the split. The solution senior staff arrived at was to rotate nurses from ward to ward on a regular basis so that they would not became attached to a patient anymore. In this way, a policy of rotation and replaceability of nurses was introduced to deal with the problem of nurses' over-attachment with patients, but this arrangement meant that the charge nurse and the administrator were the only permanent staff on the ward during a patient's stay. The staff conflict was viewed and treated administratively rather than properly understanding the meaning of what was happening psychoanalytically. With no real attempt at an answer, the conflict and splitting was doomed to be repeated over the ensuing years and decades.

Hildegard Peplau confronted something of this entrenched conflict in her dealings with Chestnut Lodge, although it must be said that she was a passionate and determined woman who could rub people up the wrong way. Her initial impression was garnered over the winter of 1941–1942 during field placement at Chestnut Lodge as part of her degree in interpersonal psychology at Vermont's Bennington College

(Callaway, 2002). She attended evening seminars and discussions at Bethesda Golf & Country Club with Harry Stack Sullivan and others where she listened and absorbed everything. Peplau recalled that her time at Chestnut Lodge was very rich; she received weekly supervision from Dexter Bullard and attended Fromm-Reichmann's lectures, even lunching with her on Wednesdays where they talked about clinical issues. She completed her degree and went on to do her master's degree in psychiatric nursing. Peplau's lifelong work was dedicated largely to extending Sullivan's interpersonal theory for use in nursing practice. Her book, *Interpersonal Relations in Nursing*, was completed in 1948 but its publication took four more years because it was ground-breaking for a nurse to contribute this scholarly work without a co-authoring male physician (Peplau, 1952).

By 1949 Peplau was a nurse educator at Columbia Teachers College when she obtained a grant for a postgraduate nurse program in psychiatric hospitals. She optimistically approached Dexter Bullard with an idea for postgraduate nursing students to do field placements at Chestnut Lodge. Although she had Bullard on side she neglected to consider the director of nursing, Emmy Lanning, who did not understand or approve the objectives of the course. Here we find a fundamental bias; Lanning thought that although nurses could be therapeutic they should not offer a patient anything approaching psychotherapy (Callaway, 2002). Consequently, the two women clashed because Peplau believed that psychiatric nursing would fit very well into Chestnut Lodges therapy program. With tensions mounting, students were caught in the crossfire between the expectations of the Teacher's College and the practices of Chestnut Lodge. Peplau acknowledged failure and withdrew the program. One of the chief ambitions of Peplau's career was for graduate-degree nurses to practice psychotherapy and contribute to research but she met with a great deal of resistance along the way before this was achieved.

Follow up studies

The psychoanalytic culture at Chestnut Lodge placed high value on all forms of information about patients' and all facets of the patient were seen as potentially useful. Great efforts were made to record and transcribe clinical conference discussions, and observations about the patient were recorded, reviewed and documented on an annual basis by the entire medical staff in a case conference. From the early 1940s all these reports on the patient's treatment were transcribed by a court reporter for the hospital records (McGlashan & Carpenter, 2007). This huge database has proven useful over the years for outcome studies associated with the Chestnut Lodge Research Institute. A follow-up report of 302 patients admitted to Chestnut Lodge over the decade 1948 to 1958 showed that patients diagnosed with schizophrenia comprised sixty-three per cent of the patient population and were all currently hospitalised, while the psychoneurotic group of patients comprised nineteen per cent of the total population and were largely located in the functioning group at follow up (Schultz, 1963). This proved that the psychotic group of patients were more difficult to treat, their overall treatment took much longer and their prognosis was less secure. Another long-term follow-up project and outcome study of 454 patients admitted to Chestnut Lodge between 1950 and 1975 was conducted during the 1980s (McGlashan, 1984, 1986). The results were consistent with other outcome studies (DeSisto, Harding, McCormick, Ashikaga, & Brooks, 1995; Harding, 2003; Harding, et al., 1987) that indicated one third of patients diagnosed with chronic, treatment resistant schizophrenia improved significantly, a third were described as recovered and the remaining third were unchanged.

McGlashan believed that patients at Chestnut Lodge spent years in psychoanalysis to no avail before they received antipsychotic drugs and were then able to reclaim something of a normal life (McGlashan & Nayfack, 1988). However, McGlashan's use of a worst-case scenario to make a general point about the failure of analysis to bring about change in patients is skewed. McGlashan altered the focus of his research towards Kraepelinian psychiatric diagnostic criteria rather than its original aim as an outcome study associated with psychodynamic psychiatry based on the philosophy of the treatment of psychosis at Chestnut Lodge (Bechgaard, 2003). Methodologically the research did not fulfil the demands for a study of process and outcome of psychotherapy; instead the results were only able to illuminate different kinds of illness course in relation to variable groups of diagnostic and predictive factors. In the end, we are none the wiser from McGlashan about how the psychotherapy with psychosis worked at Chestnut Lodge.

One thing seems certain and that is that each therapist applied the psychoanalytic approach to the treatment in his or her own unique way. Frieda Fromm-Reichmann claimed that the sole use of psychotherapy informed by psychoanalysis could cure schizophrenia (Fromm-Reichmann, 1954). She said that most patients emerged from their psychosis whilst in therapy and that if they continued in their treatment for several more years it would lead to the eventual recovery of insight. Almost four decades after Fromm-Reichmann's death McGlashan wanted to prove her wrong and contradicted her supremely optimistic view of a psychoanalytic cure for psychosis recommending a more flexible form of psychotherapy. Wayne Fenton, the Lodge's last director, confirmed this conclusion. He thought that supportive psychotherapy was more appropriate for the treatment of psychotic patients where a pragmatic approach helped the patient to interpret and adapt to reality. Primarily a system of care was advocated for chronic schizophrenia based on a community-oriented multidisciplinary team, the foundation of which included pharmacological and psychosocial approaches.

The conflict over medication

The introduction of antipsychotic medications in the 1950s started a revolution in psychiatry worldwide. Chestnut Lodge had to decide how it would deal with this new force after having devoted so much time and energy to the intensive psychotherapy of schizophrenia. There followed many years of intense and bitter debate about this issue amongst the staff. The usual practice was that almost all patients were taken off medication when they were admitted so that they could start intensive psychotherapy. Then, depending on the progress of the therapy, a patient's medication regimen may be reinstituted. The opinion was that antipsychotic medication interfered with the therapeutic process causing a sealing-over to occur which negatively impacted on the therapeutic process (Levine, 1990). There was also a number of staff who felt equally as intensely that to deny a patient some relief from their distress in the form of a pharmacological intervention was unethical. The issue was debated in staff meetings and case conferences for years that polarised the staff into two camps. This was reminiscent of earlier conflicts and divisions.

The Osheroff case had a decisive effect on the question of the use of medication at Chestnut Lodge in the 1980s. Dr Rafael Osheroff had been treated with antidepressants and psychotherapy for long standing problems with anxiety and depression by different psychiatrists for several years with little effect (Klerman, 1990). He was apparently poorly compliant and his mental state had deteriorated in the context of protracted marital problems and interpersonal conflicts with colleagues. In 1979 Osheroff admitted himself to Chestnut Lodge where intensive psychoanalytic psychotherapy was prescribed in keeping with the hospital's treatment guidelines. He developed an intense negative transference towards the therapist assigned to him and, by association, the hospital that led to an ongoing standoff. Finally, a senior consultant intervened suggesting a transfer to another hospital. Osheroff later claimed that his therapist had persisted with psychotherapy for seven months withholding medication that he said caused unnecessary suffering. So Osheroff initiated a lawsuit against Chestnut Lodge for negligence in not administering drug treatment on the basis that there were no Randomised Controlled Trials to attest to the efficacy of the psychoanalytically oriented treatment practiced there. The case was settled out of court but served as a salutary lesson that the tide was turning. The Osheroff case presented a confrontation between two forms of knowledge in psychiatry, evidence based medicine and clinical experience, where one form of knowledge dominates, excludes and invalidates another form of knowledge as the sole support for a treatment's efficacy (Robertson, 2005). Many patients, including disturbed psychotic patients, derive benefit from psychotherapy even when the patient is considered to be a treatment failure in the eyes of biological psychiatry. The intolerance of pluralism is the attempted annihilation of one form of knowledge by another and reduces a complex human experience to a simple matter of brain chemistry.

Together the effects of the Osheroff case and the results of McGlashan's long-term follow-up study played major roles in promoting change at Chestnut Lodge. Inevitably, medication was used more and more regularly so that by the late 1980s eighty per cent of patients at Chestnut Lodge were prescribed some form of psychotropic medication (Chiesa, 1988). By this time the hospital population comprised approximately ninety adult inpatients and thirty adolescent inpatients, and around fifty day patients (Levine, 1990). The staff to patient ratio was radically different in the 1980s in comparison to the 1950s with a total of around thirty-five clinicians; most were psychiatrists and nurses, there were also several psychologists, social workers and occupational therapists on staff. The treatment model was still based on the therapist and administrator split with each patient under the care of two doctors, the psychotherapist and the administrator who took responsibility for the patient's day to day care on the ward. The patient's diagnostic picture was relatively similar to that of thirty years earlier, with approximately sixty per cent of patients having a diagnosis of schizophrenia or schizoaffective disorder, twenty per cent with borderline and other personality disorder and twenty per cent with a mixture of affective disorder and character pathology (Judd, et al., 2002).

The practice of psychotherapy

During the 1940s a group of psychoanalysts interested in the intensive study and treatment of schizophrenia assembled at Chestnut Lodge and pioneered the intensive psychodynamic psychotherapy of Frieda Fromm-Reichmann and the interpersonal psychotherapy of Harry Stack Sullivan. From this a tradition persisted for the next sixty years. Marco Chiesa from Cassel Hospital in England visited the Lodge in the late 1980s. He observed the psychotherapy being practiced there through the eyes of his Object Relations background. Disturbed and chronically psychotic patients were not generally seen at Cassel because these patients were part of their exclusion criteria. Chiesa identified a theoretical orientation at Chestnut Lodge that ranged from Ego Psychology to the Interpersonal Theory influenced by Sullivan and Fromm-Reichmann. Important contributions had also been made by psychoanalysts such as Ping-Nie Pao, Otto Will, and Harold Searles to name a few.

Chiesa thought that certain theoretical approaches, such as making use of countertransference feelings and the way the so-called real relationship between the therapist and the patient was dealt with, were controversial and unlike the work of most British psychoanalysts (Chiesa, 1988). During an analytic session some therapists at Chestnut Lodge shared their thoughts, feelings, and fantasies with their patient, and at times enacted the patient's projections in a way that Chiesa found inappropriate. He stated the reason for this was that in the symbiotic stage of the therapy the therapist and patient can become fused in a mutually dependent situation where systematised delusions may be accepted and colluded with. Harold Searles worked at Chestnut Lodge from 1949–1964 and advanced the concept of therapeutic symbiosis based on countertransference identification that for him constituted a major force in the psychoanalysis of psychoses (Searles, 1963). Therapeutic symbiosis was said to allow the patient to eventually respond by identifying with the supposed healthy model of the analyst, reminiscent of the analyst's healthy ego in ego psychology. Chiesa saw the elimination of difference between patient and therapist as a breach that was evidenced by examples of therapists responding to a patient's request for a more personal relationship so that they became engaged in social interactions. Chiesa supposed that this would increase the patient's existing ego weakness, but he also acknowledged how taxing it is for therapists to work with a high degree of disturbance and fragmentation: "[...] this modification of technique may stem from the intense and often unbearable countertransference feelings of despair, hopelessness and failure evoked in the therapist during the course of therapy" (Chiesa, 1988, p. 324). Theoretical differences can be confronting and need to be struggled with.

In working with psychotic patients, Ann-Louise Silver identified the principles of insight-oriented psychotherapy based on an Interpersonalist approach that guided her work at Chestnut Lodge for the twenty-five years she was a psychiatrist there. From her perspective, the approach to each new patient is based on the assumption that every human strives towards positive effectiveness and mutuality (Silver, 2001a). Therapists must respect the profound dilemma experienced by psychotic patients and not provide facile reassurance or pretend that they understand the extent of patients' experiences. The therapist's endurance will be tested and patients will confront the therapist to provoke a defensive response, but with greater self-awareness in the form of one's own analysis and supervision this can be borne. Silver highlights the necessity for flexibility, humour, and creativity when working with psychotic patients even if it means getting outside and walking with the patient. Unlike the treatment with neurotic patients, the psychotic patient needs help to organise the topics under discussion and this requires the therapist to engage dynamically in the dialogue rather than waiting to make an interpretation. Silver insists on an honest and ethical stance that is mandatory in the therapist's conduct towards the patient (Silver, 2001b). She claims that her treatment results were far more gratifying in the era prior to the use of psychotropic medications at Chestnut Lodge and is convinced about the efficacy of psychotherapy as a significant treatment of psychotic illness.

Silver's conclusions are echoed by Harold Searles who, after leaving Chestnut Lodge, saw psychotic patients four or five times per week in private practice, where he focused on a modified psychoanalytic treatment:

> After some five years of my work at Chestnut Lodge, developments in the therapy of various of my patients brought home to me the realization that even the most deep and chronic symptoms of schizophrenia are to be looked upon not simply as the tragic human debris left behind by the awesome glacial holocaust which this illness surely is, but that these very symptoms can be found to have—or, perhaps more accurately, in the course of therapy can come to reveal—an aspect which is both rich in meaning and alive, one now sees, with unquenched and unquenchable energy. (Searles, 1963, p. 249)

Searles's psychoanalytic background included ego psychology, object relations theory, and interpersonal psychotherapy. He applied a combination of these theories to the treatment of psychotic and severe personality disorder both in private practice and in the institutional context at Chestnut Lodge. He integrated a sophisticated and original conceptualisation of the pathology of internalised object relations with a theory of technique based on transference and countertransference analysis.

Chestnut Lodge was a tertiary care psychiatric hospital that treated patients with psychosis in long-term intensive psychotherapy, regardless of their prognosis or severity of their illness, when the only alternative for them was the back ward of a mental asylum. The work with psychotic, and at times very disturbed patients, frequently stirs up conflicted feelings for those who work closely with them, especially when the intrinsic demand is that these anxieties be contained or hidden. It is the nature of the communication between staff and the level of understanding about complex institutional dynamics that allows an effective integrating outcome to occur for the patient. Equally the state of organisation or disorganisation of an institution will have a reciprocal impact on the internal state of its members who will in turn reflect this back, having a mutual effect on each other in an ongoing way. The phenomenon identified at Chestnut Lodge where unacknowledged chronic and intense disagreement between staff inevitably led to splitting and conflict that was passed on to the patient. The idealisation of psychoanalysis and the institution inevitably produced a trend where its dominance was toppled by opposing forces, demonstrated by the competitive battles regarding the introduction of the routine use of pharmacotherapy. Institutions that use psychoanalysis to guide the treatment of psychosis reveal a number of similar characteristics, regardless of their theoretical orientation.

All three facilities, Menninger Clinic, Austen Riggs Center, and Chestnut Lodge discussed in chapters five and six functioned according to institutional models derived from psychoanalysis that were applied in very different ways: the Menninger Clinic developed a psychoanalytic milieu, Austen Riggs became a therapeutic community and Chestnut Lodge placed emphasis on the dual therapeutic relationship between analyst and patient. These institutions frequently shared staff and evaluated their performance with respect to the standards that the other set. The staff at Chestnut Lodge were divided on patient issues with those for the institution's administration on one side and those who sided with the patient on the other. The spurious controversy between economic and administrative objectives that focused solely on the therapeutic purpose of individualised treatment, rather than the collective issues of the whole institution, echoed the age-old push-and-pull of the individual versus the group. In contrast to other hospitals oriented to psychoanalysis, Chestnut Lodge did not advocate a therapeutic milieu model, which could have provided a more constructive and supportive perspective to contain the internal conflict and how it was understood and managed.

Hampstead War Nursery.

CHAPTER SEVEN

Institutions oriented to Freud and Lacan

This chapter addresses the psychoanalytic treatment of the psychoses from a Lacanian perspective and presents institutions that have employed the theories of Freud and Lacan as a foundation for their work. Applied psychoanalysis is the extension of the work of psychoanalysis to a group, an institution, or an organisation. It refers to the concepts and principles of psychoanalysis that are used to orient psychoanalytic practice in its institutional context; in the medical domain and associated therapeutics this includes the research of psychoanalytic concepts in the clinic and a critique of the results of the analytic experience. Applied psychoanalysis establishes a psychoanalytic viewpoint within the psychiatric field. Issues associated with group and institutional transference were central to the founding documents of Lacan's various schools and pronouncements on the training of analysts. Experience and knowledge of the theory of psychosis and its application in the treatment are fundamental to understanding the aims of the analytic work in a psychiatric institution. Psychoanalytically oriented inpatient treatment settings have developed in a number of pioneering centres around the world over the past century covering the treatment of adults, adolescents, and children. The theoretical foundations that sustained treatment practices in these centres are in stark contrast to the institutionalising and antithetical culture present in traditional psychiatric settings.

Concepts that help orient institutional treatment

Lacan's discussions about psychosis are among the most original aspects of his work; his most detailed discussion of psychosis appears in his seminar, *The Psychoses* (Lacan, 2002a). As discussed in chapter two, what gives psychosis its structure is the foreclosure of the Name-of-the-Father in the place of the Other and it is this failure of the paternal metaphor that gives psychosis its essential condition (Lacan, 2004b). Foreclosure of the Name-of-the-Father translates into a modification of the nature of language and its effect on signification that is received by the psychotic subject as an absolute enigma. In psychosis, the conditions of the subject's relation to the Other are completely different from that of neurosis because the symptom in psychosis is the symptom of the Other. The Other in Lacanian psychoanalysis is complicated and Lacan (1991) referred to at least two "others": the (big) Other *O* (A for French *Autre*) in the symbolic is an effect of speech, distinguished from the (small) other *o* (*a* italicised French *autre*) that is a projection of the ego. The psychotic subject relates to a bizarre and irregular Other whose interest in him or her is mysterious, obscure and, most of all, malevolent and perverse. The Other manipulates: it talks, it reads thoughts, it commands actions. The place of the Other of language is imposed as hostile by the fact of its enigmatic nature. "Schreber himself pointed out that something in him was at a certain moment profoundly disturbed. A fissure appeared in the order of his relations with the Other, which he mysteriously calls soul murder" (Lacan, 2002a, p. 208). Schreber's "soul murder" delusion was manifest as a central phenomenon linked to his conception of the transformation of the world that he believed was at the root of something enigmatic.

Lacan referred to the development of an unshakable certainty in psychosis that constitutes the elementary phenomena that develop into delusional beliefs. The production of a symptom in psychosis is an attempt to symbolise the unspeakable real and to manage jouissance that pushes the subject towards the Other to seek the signifiers that might name this real that invades. Jouissance is experienced as a confrontation with an overwhelming terror that is carried by the jouissance of the Other. Fundamentally, jouissance is linked to an excess that in psychosis leaves the subject in the position of an object for the Other's devouring and deadly enjoyment. It is at the core of this encounter between the subject and the Other's jouissance that an intervention is required because it is the Other that has to be treated in psychosis. In the style of presence that orients the institutional response, it is best to be on the same side as the subject facing this Other; to be an Other who would simply witness and support the subject as guarantee of order and a limit in the face of the intrusive, unbridled Other that harasses him (Zenoni, 2002, p. 6).

For the psychotic subject the encounter with the analyst, the "subject-supposed-to-know", is a triggering factor: "As soon as the subject who is supposed to know exists somewhere [...] there is transference" (Lacan, 1977, p. 232). The analyst is often thought to know the secret meaning of the subject's words and the significations of speech of which even the speaker is unaware. "This is why the Other of knowledge can be encountered sometimes in the guise of an erotomanic transference or an aggressive confrontation" (Zenoni, 2002, p. 6). The analytic work in an institution provides a place that allows the subject to say something about the Other that he or she has to try to interpret and treat. "His passage in [the] institution will then be a proper crossing to sit in this place from which he can treat his Other, lighten himself of its burden" (Vlassembrouck, 2002, p. 6).

Lacan's main question where psychoanalytic organisations were concerned was that of how to form a group that is not based on a belief in the big Other and the primacy of the master's discourse. The master's discourse is one of Lacan's four discourses or types of social bond from which the other discourses, the university, the hysteric, and the psychoanalyst, are derived (Lacan, 2007). In society the relationship between the master and the individual stems from the unquestioned power of the master that is exercised by virtue of the authority of the master's position. In the master's discourse, the master can be either an individual or an institution. The master's discourse is inherent in the foundations of an institution, "and it isn't enough to refer to psychoanalysis and analytic theory to subvert this" (Rouillon, 2002, p. 2). In order to work in an institution, one has to deal with the ramifications of the master's discourse. The appeal that a subject addresses to an institution is a demand from the master's discourse based on the identification to an ideal, and in this way the subject does not pose his or her own questions. An institution that is informed by psychoanalysis presents itself as an incomplete master, castrated of knowledge, a not-all master. Thus by not responding it becomes possible to introduce a gap and provoke a question, which affords the opportunity of making the symptom emerge. Thus it is possible to arrange a boundary in the master's discourse so that the subject can be represented by his or her own question in the place of the Other. This practice aims at a clinic of the particular with reference to the ethics of psychoanalysis. In an analysis the psychoanalyst represents an unknown desire for the analysand but in the institution this occurs by introducing the function of the unknown desire in the place of the normalising ideal of the institution so that the institution becomes particular for each subject.

Institutions lean on the Name-of-the-Father as a regulator of jouissance. An institution that works with psychosis has a choice: it can adhere to a blind idealisation that promotes jouissance of the superego or it can apply an ethic regarding how jouissance is received. Hence, an institution has the opportunity of operating as a place of asylum, as a guarantee of order and as a limit in the face of an intrusive, uncontrolled Other. The theories of psychoanalysis are fundamental to understanding approaches to the patient's treatment in institutions. Institutions that operate psychoanalytically to support the work with psychosis do so in a specific way by allowing a space for the person without any other agenda. The development of a negative transference is a common occurrence in psychiatric institutions and this frequently leads to patients discharging themselves either unchanged or relapsed (Freud, 1912b). Each clinician has to be responsible for how they face the specificity of the transference, especially in the work with psychosis, for example, to strongly recommend or impose something on to a psychotic patient risks a persecutory encounter. This stems from the knowledge that the transference in psychosis is problematic. To work with subjects who are psychotic there has to be no pre-programed response to their discourse and the subject needs to be given the opportunity to communicate what is of fundamental importance to him or her. This offers them the possibility of constructing what they need in order to reconnect with the world. For the subject an institution's treatment objective, educative projects, and rehabilitative agenda are translated via the superego as an injunction or as advice that puts them in front of the Other's will and tends to compromise the subject's ability to unfold and deal with their issues. Psychoanalytic treatment in a Lacanian sense requires the removal of any pedagogical, adaptive or normalising therapeutic motives and interventions that impose a directive onto the subject to improve, adjust or progress (Zenoni, 2002). Instead the psychotic subject requires a simple set of rules as a guide and a range of possibilities placed before them so that they can select or make use of them, as or if they choose, when they choose.

Language and the body image

The concept of the body image has a long tradition in psychoanalysis in the theory and treatment of the psychoses. Lacan's (2004a) theory of the mirror stage marks a turning point in a child's mental development and typifies an essential libidinal relationship with the body image. Lacan said that a psychotic process develops because the subject had been alienated in a pathological form of mirror stage. Subsequently, when certain vital limitations are freed up, an aggressive drive is liberated triggering a dramatic delusional process. The mirror stage occurs in infancy between the ages of six to eighteen months when the child discovers its own reflection in a mirror; it is an identification that transforms the child as he or she assumes an image, ideal ego or *imago*. The mirror stage marks the primordial recognition of one's self as "I" at a point before the entry into language and the symbolic order (Lacan, 2004a). Françoise Dolto evolved a theory that focused on the concepts of the "unconscious body image" and "symbol-generating castrations" (Binet, 1999). The body image is the unconscious symbolic incarnation of the desiring being, before it is able to say "I". It is a representation without words reflecting the first relational experiences to the mother that develop from physical and psychical needs. Symbol-generating castrations mean the necessary separations from beloved partial objects and the renunciation of the symbiotic participation in the mother's body linked with archaic fantasies of omnipotence; a necessary pre-condition for symbolisation. The child becomes a social being by means of these castrations; able to verbalise and to have an unconscious body image that corresponds to its physical maturity. Psychosis is connected with a mutilated body image that originates in failed castrations.

Jacques Lacan recommended that the psychoanalyst think carefully before undertaking the treatment of psychosis; he advised that caution be exercised in this area because of the potential pitfalls. Of central concern are the technical and theoretical problems encountered in the application of psychoanalytic treatment to the psychoses. See chapter two for further explanations about Lacanian theory on psychosis.

Institutional psychotherapy

French psychiatry was ideologically destabilised by the ideas of Foucault, Tosquelles, Dauмézon, and Lacan in the post Second World War climate of anti-psychiatry and by those who gathered at Saint-Alban-sur-Limagnole, a French psychiatric hospital in Lozere where they produced a new psychiatry that heralded institutional psychotherapy (Reggio & Novello, 2007). The principles of institutional psychotherapy came from the acknowledgment that asylums have pathological effects and the recognition that each human being is unique. François Tosquelles was a hospital psychiatrist, psychoanalyst and founder of the institutional psychotherapy movement. In 1940, after the defeat of the Spanish republicans, he was forced to leave his native Spain, and Tosquelles found work at the Saint-Alban Hospital, bringing with him a passion for change borne through his war time experiences. His Catalan antifascist militancy meshed with the French Resistance that had already been established at Saint-Alban. His collaboration with Lucien Bonnafé, André Chaurand, Jacques Schotte, and many others in the Resistance led to Saint-Alban becoming the crucible of an experiment based on the discoveries of psychoanalysis directed towards the institutional treatment of psychosis (Reggio, 2004). The TGPSI or *Groupe de travail de psychothérapie institutionelle* was a work group for institutional psychotherapy founded at St Alban in 1960 and continued by Felix Guattari at La Borde Clinic (Guattari & Genosko, 1996).

Tosquelles felt strongly about a global concept of the human being. In his psychoanalytic practice he treated children and adults, individuals and groups, using the techniques of classical psychoanalysis and psychodrama (Reggio & Novello, 2007). Tosquelles was a leading reformer and theorist of sociotherapy, with its emphasis on communal life in the institution and simply listening to the patient. Whether in the psychoanalytic study of delusional manifestations and other elements in the behaviour of psychotic patients or in reflection to the transference, for both the patient and the therapist, Tosquelles was known for his capacity to make complex psychoanalytic problems accessible and clear. He established links between the world of psychiatry and the discoveries of psychoanalysis, phenomenology, and anthropology. Tosquelles introduced institutional psychotherapy during the 1970s when he was clinical director at Nonette, an institution for psychotic and autistic children, adolescents, and young adults in the Clermont-Ferrand area of France, referred to in chapter four. Nonette was under the direction of the *Comite Central d'Entreprise* (CCAS) which was essentially the board of directors of Electricity and Gas of France (EDF-GDF) (Cottes, 2002). For two decades Nonette had been a traditional educational facility for the children of EDF-GDF employees who had learning difficulties or were diagnosed as retarded, later found to be psychotic and autistic. Over the first ten years, Tosquelles brought other psychoanalysts to work there, many of whom were oriented towards the work of Jacques Lacan. During 1987–1988, CCAS increased their commitment to Nonette and doubled the funding for the psychoanalytic treatment of psychoses according to Lacanian theory and practice because their outcomes proved their effectiveness. From that time on to this day Lacanian psychoanalysis has been practiced at Nonette.

La Borde Clinic

La Borde Clinic (*la Clínica de La Borde* also known as *La clinique de Cour-Cheverny*) is located in a château near the town of Cour-Cheverny in the Loire Valley of France. It was a private psychiatric clinic until 1953 when Jean Oury developed it into what he thought an asylum ought to be; a place of refuge, shelter and sanctuary (Reggio & Novello, 2007). At La Borde, Oury and Felix Guattari, together with Michaud and Jenny Aubry and others, furthered the institutional psychotherapy movement that had been initiated by Tosquelles at St Alban. Oury opened up what he called, "a non-deductive ontology […] to create a space of syntax" (Reggio, 2004, p. 7). Still in operation today, La Borde is an innovative psychiatric clinic with a capacity for over one hundred inpatients and fifteen day patients. It is an open hospital that specialises in the treatment of psychotic patients; there are no locked doors and the patients actively participate in the running of the facility (Guattari & Genosko, 1996). In 1973 La Borde was threatened with closure ostensibly due to their excessive overheads and prolonged lengths of stay, and yet, they have managed to adapt and keep going.

La Borde was born from a lineage of psychiatric practice that used psychoanalysis influenced by Lacan, to explore the relationship between patients and psychotherapists (Mozère, 2002). According to the principles of institutional psychotherapy, the common assumption of responsibility is said to have therapeutic effects, although it does not necessarily draw from the therapeutic community model. The clinic took the lead in the development of a new practice of psychiatry in which care, research and formation were integrated in a collective step. Following Tosquelles, Oury perceived patients in a holistic way regarding them as fellow human beings rather than as sick people, thus he redefined the role of the doctor-patient relationship. Oury supposed that it was simultaneously necessary to look after the institution and to look after each patient. This could be achieved by returning initiative and responsibility to patients by developing situations where they could work and express their creativity.

Félix Guattari joined the clinic at La Borde in 1955 as a militant interested in notions of desire (Massumi, 1992). Guattari was one of France's leading innovators in the field of psychiatry and psychoanalysis, and his activities as a member of the anti-psychiatry school focused primarily on the reform of institutional practice. Guattari became Oury's principal collaborator, revolutionising their model of institutional psychotherapy and producing a large body of theoretical work that is described in a book co-written with the philosopher Gilles Deleuze in 1972 called *Anti-Oedipus*. Guattari's unconventional theories of "schizoanalysis" are unfolded as a process meant to replace Freudian interpretation with a more pragmatic, experimental, and collective approach rooted in reality. Guattari adopted a model of schizophrenia as an extreme mental state induced by the capitalist system as a way of maintaining normality (Deleuze & Guattari, 2004). In line with the ideas of R. D. Laing, schizophrenia was viewed as an inventive positive experience that expands the limits of life through the pragmatic proliferation of concepts. Guattari wanted better care for patients outside of the imprisoning system of psychiatric hospitals and clinics and his post-Marxist version of capitalism provided a new definition of mental illness, and of the micro-political means for its subversion. He sought to push the movement in a more political direction toward what he later described as a "political analysis of desire" (Guattari & Genosko, 1996). The injection of a Lacanian psychoanalytical discourse into a custodial institution led to a collectivisation of analytic concepts. For example, transference came to be seen as institutional, fantasies were seen to be collective and desire was a problem of groups and for groups. Guattari remained at La Borde for forty years carrying out research and establishing it as a training place for philosophy, psychology, and ethnology students, as well as, psychiatric nurses and social workers.

The group at La Borde argued that most of the time social status and roles made people's conception of themselves rigid and inflexible, leading to stereotype and hierarchical behaviours. The aim, therefore, was to abolish the doctor-patient hierarchy in favour of an interactive group dynamic that would bring the experiences of everyone to full expression in such a way as to produce a collective critique of the power relations in society as a whole (Massumi, 1992). The staff rotated in taking turns in doing the cooking, in dispensing drugs and giving injections, in doing the housework, the laundry and the gardening, in looking after the library, in editing a local paper or in supervising the production of theatre or musical events. Everyone (doctors, nurses, patients, the locally recruited lay staff, friends, visitors, and students) took part in the clinic's activities, whether they were considered as work, hobbies, or leisure. All were considered to be part of the therapeutic task to the extent; Jean Oury was said to have remarked that even the doorknob had to be therapeutic (Mozère, 2002). Everyday arrangements, meetings, groups and discussion workshops, special events such as the theatre, a festival or a shopping trip; everything from the hospital bus to the telephone switchboard were in the charge of patients and staff together, including the printing of the local paper.

An unwritten law at La Borde was that the institution must take care of its staff who were not regarded as any more or less normal than the patients. Therefore, as far as possible in organisational terms, the question of desire holds importance. This means that working on a hobby or a passion, for example, was regarded as a strong incentive for that person to invest in his or her work. Changing roles and tasks led to innovations and experiments that offered everyone the opportunity to change, to create new ways of living and to enable them to get free of inappropriate, alienating or fixed behaviours. This approach liberated, what Deleuze and Guattari called "molecular and molar power" where the individual was not hindered by fixed categories or stereotyped attachments (Massumi, 1992). From this came the notion that the self may be an irrelevant category and that one is more a multiple being who is unfinished and can change according to encounters and circumstances.

Among the many distinctive aspects of La Borde is the annual summer tradition in which the boarders and staff work together to perform a play, choosing from a range of classical works. *La moindre des choses* (in English "Every Little Thing") is a film by Nicolas Philibert where he records the daily life of the clinic, including the dispensing of psychotropic medications, while they are rehearsing for the annual play in 1996. The film shows all activities being organised by staff and patients together. Another film *La Borde ou le droit à la folie* (in English "La Borde or the right to insanity") by Igor Barrère (1977) takes into account the creative and productive dimension of madness, and redraws it removing the repressive dimensions of traditional psychiatry and psychoanalytic conformism. As would be expected, the film calls into question the hierarchies and the divisions of the labour making the institution the central therapeutic device.

Institutional approach at Le Courtil

Le Courtil (in English "the courtyard") presents an alternative psychoanalytically influenced approach to the institutional treatment of patients with psychiatric disorders. It is a 150 bed psychiatric hospital founded in 1982 and located at Lille-Roubaix-Tourcoing in Belgium, on the border with France. Its mandate is the treatment of psychotic and severely disturbed children, adolescents, and young adults; this includes schooling and day centre treatment as well. The work at Courtil is influenced by the shared relationships with other institutions that are part of the International Network of Institutions in the Freudian Field that was created in 1993; they are Antenne 110 (located in Brussels and directed by Antonio Di Caccia), Mish'olim in Tel Aviv and Nonette at Clermont-Ferrand in France. For over twenty years the work at Le Courtil has been strictly based on psychoanalytic principles with reference to Freud and Lacan so that the whole institution works towards the treatment of the patient by integrating the analytic work. The treatment is a variation of the classical analytic treatment as individual analysis only takes place off-site. In not offering individual psychoanalysis Courtil avoids the pitfalls associated with conducting prescriptive forms of psychoanalysis and maintains flexibility in what the institution can offer.

A new resident admitted to Courtil is informed of two basic rules: one is that violence is forbidden and the other is that he or she is under an obligation to meet once a week with a "referent" with the aim of establishing a space for the talking work, although this is not the exclusive domain for talking. The function of the referent is to represent a desire that the subject works at elaborating, for example through the reconstruction of his or her history and developing an understanding of the cause of their symptoms. However, the treatment at Courtil is primarily arranged through the work of "intervenants"; someone who comes between the subject and the Other, helping them to manage the jouissance that invades the subject. Most of the intervenants are not psychoanalysts but civilised analysands, meaning that each one is at work in their analysis and enlightened in their orientation to the analytic doctrine. There are unanalysed staff who also work at Courtil and they are expected to participate in the clinical seminars and to respect the logic of the psychoanalytic doctrine that underpins the work. In the institutional approach to the treatment of psychosis, the positions of intervenant and referent represent a shift from the usual way of working where psychoanalysis can become marginalised or idealised in an institution, and so becomes unworkable and ineffective (Stevens, 2002a; Stevens, 2002b).

Le Courtil is a working community supported by regular seminars, case presentations, and workshops. Importance is placed on the training of the team and the transmission of psychoanalysis, the formalising of the study of clinical cases, the work of the management of the institution and the organisation of the patient's treatment. Clinical cases are studied and elaborated according to Lacanian psychoanalytic theory within the treating teams, during meetings and seminars. The clinical elements that are brought out during the workshops, as well as in the subject's daily life experiences, all help to identify what is at stake for each person, case by case. An intervention cannot be defined unless the minimal elements necessary to orient each case are recognised and placed at the team's disposal. This allows the team to work out what decisions need to be made, such as, the making or refining of a diagnosis, the offer of a more specific perspective on the work with a subject, and as a guide for interventions. It is important not to understand too quickly what a subject means when they speak:

> It is only at the price of letting go of the idea of knowing what is going to happen that one can leave the child the possibility of elaborating the speech that is proper to him/her. Moreover, it is only from such a position that the work can open onto the surprise and the invention. (Besserer, 2002, p. 8)

The role of intervenants

The purpose of the workshops at Le Courtil is to make a space that provides an opportunity for the subject's speech to emerge. The treatment of psychosis aims to provide a framework for the patient either by a push to construction in speech or by such structures as the daily program of workshops. It is through the intermediary of speech that the subject can construct something of their own history that organises his or her symptoms. The production of objects is secondary to the signification with which the subject accompanies its production, whether it is a work of art or the creation of something. Workshops are limited to one hour's duration and take place at regular times in the morning and in the afternoon on the same day of the week thus creating a predictable routine. The workshop is led by the same intervenant and involves the same individual patients each time. In the workshops the intervenant occupies the role of witness, a place of reception or as an address for the patient, similar to the position of "secretaries to the insane" described by Lacan in his seminar on *The Psychoses* (Lacan, 2002a, p. 206). This position means actually being physically present and designates the place of one attending and watching an event but, more importantly, the presence implies the fact of being in the place from which one speaks, of being involved and of taking part (Besserer, 2002). Being occupied with something such as a crossword puzzle, the intervenant is also attending to everything that is going on but avoiding the element of invasion caused by the gaze:

> [...] this mode of presence plays on a certain absence—the absence of a gaze, but also the absence of "omnipresence" (if you will, and

> in default of finding a more correct term) since I am occupied by other things than directly by what the children do. It is interesting to note that the moment that one is no longer waiting, the child begins to ask. I am frequently solicited, in this way, by one or another child, who asks me to read what he has written or to help him draw a picture. This mode of presence is supported by speech. Not a speech which comes up with a solution to the question [...] but rather speech constituted as a relaunching. It is one way to signify to a child that there is something there to be gotten at, but this style of intervention is obviously not generalizable. (Besserer, 2002, p. 7)

At Le Courtil it is the responsibility of the team in the clinical seminars to research how the dialectic of the work can facilitate an awareness of the position of the persecutory Other. They have learned how to locate the persecutory Other quickly and hopefully are able to avoid falling into that position. At the core of this encounter between the subject and the Other's jouissance the intervenants act to address the Other in the form of a response that situates the subject's signifiers (Poblome, 2002). It is a question of allowing the subject to begin to discern what has happened to him or her so that some distance might be made from the horror, and to potentially provide a small space where speech can be elaborated. The work in the treatment of psychosis has to do with facilitating a compromise between the real of jouissance and the order of the world and its ideals (Zenoni, 2002).

The Name-of-the-Father as regulator of jouissance

Hoornaert suggests that Le Courtil operates like as an intermediary prosthesis or a suppletion that takes the Name-of-the-Father as one of its working references. "Courtil works with a reference to the Name-of-the-Father which is inevitable but insufficient" (Hoornaert, 2002, p. 1). This is because the underside of the paternal metaphor comes in the form of a constricting jouissance of the superego. Thus, an institution that works with psychosis has a choice: it can either deny the reality of this intrusion by adhering to a blind idealisation that promotes jouissance of the superego, or it can apply an ethic regarding how jouissance is received that takes into account the incomplete nature of the law. Institutions lean on the authority of the Name-of-the-Father as a regulator of jouissance but within it there is the imperative that paradoxically pushes it toward a forbidden jouissance. This is exactly where a major difficulty in the work with psychotic subjects is encountered because the absence of an ethic concerning the reception of jouissance pushes the psychotic subject for a response that comes from a position of mastery. This is based on the assumption of certainty that is often reproduced in various forms of therapy with psychotic patients, for example, where there is no structural theory to act as a compass for the work. The work with psychosis is a question of putting the events of the patient's life into order, like the secretary function referred to previously, so that at some point it might lead them to elaborate a delusional metaphor that could potentially constitute the first period of work in an analytic treatment. For the psychotic subject the broken links of the signifying chain must be re-established and delusional knowledge put into question, until the subject is able to perhaps construct a suppleance or a substitute for the Name-of-the-Father (Haarscher, 2001). Careful consideration is given to the practice of psychoanalysis at Le Courtil where the treatment of psychotic subjects is central to their cause. They aim to deposit analytic discourse at the very heart of the institution with the intention of disrupting the development of institutional ideals. This is achieved through the production of psychoanalysts who are concerned with establishing analytic concepts as the foundation of the institution and where the clinical elaboration of psychoanalysis is constitutive of the clinic.

The psychoanalytic treatment centre GIFRIC

GIFRIC (*Groupe Interdisciplinaire Freudien de Recherches et d'Interventions Cliniques et Culturelles*) was founded in 1982 in collaboration with the Robert-Giffard Psychiatric Hospital in Quebec, Canada. The Psychoanalytic Treatment Centre for Psychotics or 388, this refers to the street number of the centre, is a non-profit private centre for the psychoanalytic treatment of young adults with psychosis aged eighteen to thirty-five years (GIFRIC, 2009). The Centre integrates the position of psychoanalysis within that of biological psychiatry, that also includes neurobiology and psychopharmacology, into the treatment approach because it was considered necessary to unite the two perspectives for a broader clinical approach (Apollon, 1991). GIFRIC's approach combines an intensive program of socio-cultural and artistic activities, together with the psychiatric and psychoanalytic treatment. The first problem the psychotic subject encounters is his or her ability to make a demand for treatment; this means they have to independently request a treatment on their own behalf rather than under the direction of someone else, such as a parent, a doctor or the voices. Those who are referred by a psychiatrist or their family are turned away; in order to be accepted at the centre everyone must address a personal demand on the basis of their commitment. This is because a necessary precondition for treatment to proceed is the recognition of a subject beyond the delusional or hallucinatory phenomena (Apollon, 1991). Applicants do not necessarily make a demand for an analysis but they do need to make a demand for help on their own behalf. Importance is placed on the person being responsible for comprehending and managing the causes of their own difficulties.

From the beginning the subject is registered in a treatment program that comprises a timetable of activities set up to establish the minimal framework of a symbolic system. The treatment aims at the "social re-articulation" of the psychotic subject by giving them the means of actively participating in their lives (Cantin, 2009). It restores an experience of subjectivity where patients have a degree of control over their personal and social life so that they are able to derive some satisfaction from it. The individual psychoanalytic treatment is integrated as part of the total treatment program and is on a continuum from medium to long term and beyond the hospital environment. In the analysis the subject's demand encounters the analyst's desire, not as an answer but as an opening for the transference that inaugurates the process of the analysis (Apollon, et al., 2002). In the absence of the signifier Name-of-the-Father in psychosis, the analyst is the loci of address for the subject and this is where he or she makes a demand and enters language as a subject. This concerns the subject's assumption of responsibility for their own structure and so for the ethics of their desire. The key to the treatment is the transference between patient and analyst. Patients are expected to participate in a psychoanalytic treatment that is completely separate from the 338 therapy and activity programs, and their analyst has no involvement in the program either.

The team that organises the patient's care at GIFRIC consists of a psychiatrist, a social worker, an analyst, and an "intervener". Adopted from the intervenants position at Courtil, the intervener's role is to assist the patient in a crisis (Gibbs, 2007). Four rooms on the third floor of the house at 388 have been set aside twenty-four hours a day seven days a week for patients in crisis where an intervener is available to them. Patients are called *usager* (meaning in English "to make use of") because they are expected to make use of the space provided by the intervener who accompanies them through the psychotic experience. All interventions are governed by analytic perceptions drawn from weekly team meetings where the patient is considered as a subject in the context of his or her own history with his or her own theory about what has happened. Each patient admitted to 388 works towards identifying a unique project or personally meaningful activity that helps to rebuild their broken social link. There is no formal group therapy at 338 but the group process does have a containing function for delusions and encourages ways of rebuilding their social links. The protected space of the program facilitates each patient in locating their desire by using a variety of media that is placed at their disposal so that they can express their experience of psychosis in the context of their personal history.

Transference in the work with psychosis

Through the transference the spontaneous work of psychosis and delusional elaboration takes place, fostering a new social bond that develops between the psychotic subject and the analyst's desire (Apollon, 1991). The transference is an experimental social link where the psychotic subject can speak extensively with the analyst about his or her delusions. The patient's delusional certainty is not challenged and he or she is not confronted with any word or action that could promote persecution or generate erotomania; hence the psychotic subject is given the opportunity of encountering their psychosis in a new way, working on it with those who act as companions. The therapeutic effort sustains a new position for the patient regarding absence and it is to that position the patient directs his speech, filling in the void with new found knowledge (Apollon, et al., 2002). This logic is similar to that of Le Courtil where a space is left vacant so that the subject may use it for speech rather than having it imposed on him or her.

The psychoanalytic treatment of psychosis is based on the place where the analysand's demand encounters the analyst's desire. The analyst's desire is central to installing the transference and bringing the subject into the analytic process. The framework of the analytic treatment is anchored on the side of the Name-of-the-Father, the symbolic father (Bergeron, 2002). The intention of the treatment is to separate the subject from the imaginary relationship with the Other that persecutes them and dictates their every action. To do this the subject is invited to take personal responsibility in the process of their treatment by paying with a written account of a dream, presented to the analyst at each session. They are also asked to bring memories of events that have never been spoken of before. The dream represents the payment of a symbolic debt for the person's right to exist and to speak, and so to subjectivity and individuality. The dream produces signifiers that lead to memories from the psychotic subject's history and they open up gaps or loose threads in the delusional formation; thereby the delusion is put into question. The work of the dream limits the jouissance of the imaginary Other, allowing for symbolic castration and the emergence of the law of the father. The subject will only produce dreams if the analyst's desire is in place. Gradually the dream, in answering the analyst's desire, will provide the subject with meaning which produces an easing of the delusional certainty, thus introducing the subject to a new logic regarding meaning. From this point the subject works with a new production concerning knowledge that will insert itself in a new social bond where the subject's history can be articulated:

> The psychotic engaged in transference will encounter a boundary that limits the certainty of his delusion, so that the signifier, supported by the analyst's desire, will be able to discover its trace through the writing of the symptom, to connect the unbound drives to an object in fantasy. (Apollon, 1991, p. 125)

Potentially, for the first time, the psychotic subject in analysis is being listened to and being asked to say more rather than being restricted, watched and labelled. The analyst's desire to know opens up a means for the reshaping of the subject's position with regard to the Other's demand in psychosis.

Direction of the treatment

At GIFRIC there are logical steps in the direction of the treatment based on the theories of Freud and Lacan and derived from research outcomes at 388 (Apollon, 1991). A change in the subject's position can take between eighteen to thirty-six months of treatment to reach. The production of a subjective position involves a restoration of the identification of the subject to their speech and the reconstruction of some part of their history as a referential substitute for their delusional certainty. Through the renewal of the body image in time and space in the treatment the subject develops a point of reference. The Other's signifiers determine how jouissance is constitutive of the subject's body in the real which is a major struggle in the treatment because now there is something at stake for the subject that was not there before. A sign that the transference is installed occurs when a gap of uncertainty grows around the subject's delusional theory and only the presence of the analyst can compensate for the absence and the hole that the subject is left with. Through the transference there is the production of an object of fantasy that is a substitute for the absence of the signifier of the Name-of-the-Father. This is an object that signifies a modification of the effects of the Other's jouissance indicating the subject's change of position in the structure that will have to be constructed again and again at each emergence of psychosis. The generation of a social link is grounded in the signifiers of the psychotic subject's desire offering a way to build relations with others, which includes the exploration of the ethics of the social link where the subject confronts the lack in society.

GIFRIC utilises Lacanian thought as a discipline, an inquiry and as a way of understanding the stakes of the psychoanalytic process that are unique and viable for the clinic of psychosis (Hughes & Malone, 2002). They have been conducting research on family speech and kinship structures for almost twenty years. The study's main focus is on family discourse and structures that are unique to the family. A psychoanalytic and anthropological perspective determines a new analysis of family phenomena based on an ethical paradigm that regulates the relationships between family members. The family is the principal client, thus any intervention concerns the whole family unit, not just a particular individual (GIFRIC, 2009). The clinical objective is to make it possible for individual members of the family to coexist. An institution can be considered psychoanalytic when its clinical activities are conceived, implemented, managed, and evaluated according to psychoanalytic theory. The institutions presented in this chapter demonstrate that and how Lacanian theory is applied in the particular institution.

The Cassel Hospital.

CHAPTER EIGHT

The therapeutic community

The main aim of this chapter is to trace the therapeutic community movement by means of its psychoanalytic and social links within institutional psychiatry during a time of change in the mental health care system in Britain. The therapeutic community model is an essential contribution to modern institutional psychiatry with antecedents in pedagogy, psychoanalysis, and social medicine. It is oriented in the long-term dissatisfaction with the state of mental hospitals and the changing human relations that took place between the two World Wars that resulted in the development of new knowledge and the desire for more egalitarian social policies. Added to this was the incompatibility of the spirit of modern psychiatry with huge centralised institutions that took on the custodial and welfare responsibility for the mentally ill. After Second World War the therapeutic community approach was adopted by most psychiatric hospitals; starting, initially, with the open door policy where wards were unlocked and patients had free access to social and occupational amenities within the hospital. This less controlling approach was a return to moral treatment methods echoing the traditions of some of the mid-nineteenth century asylums that showed concern for human rights and respect for people with mental illness. It was a common-sense approach where the individual was usefully occupied in a calm, emotionally containing social and physical environment.

The ways psychoanalysis was applied in therapeutic communities were, initially, via the individual therapy that was practiced in conjunction with the work of the therapeutic community, as demonstrated at the Cassel hospital in England. Then psychoanalytic theory was used to understand the meaning of individual relationships within the community, with particular reference to transference and countertransference distortions that often characterise therapeutic relationships. Then finally, psychoanalysis was used to describe and understand the institution as a whole organisation that is made up of sections that interrelate. The emphasis on a multidisciplinary approach to community mental health during the second half of the twentieth century came from the growth of social psychiatry. Social psychiatry is a branch of psychiatry that focuses on the interpersonal and cultural context of mental health; this includes the psychosocial effects of mental illness and social approaches to prevention, treatment and rehabilitation of mental illness (Neve, 2004). This resulted in a strong psychoanalytic orientation and a social model of therapy that was grounded in the philosophy of health care, thus the traditional role of the doctor was superseded by the concept of the treatment community.

The therapeutic community movement reached its peak before the dominant paradigm of biological and evidence-based psychiatry, and it preceded the worldwide agenda of deinstitutionalisation. Although the volume of therapeutic community activity was relatively small outside the United Kingdom and Europe, it has had a recent resurgence in popularity, especially in forensic psychiatry and in the treatment of addictions. In this book the focus is predominantly on the democratic therapeutic community model that traditionally depended on two types of psychiatric problems: borderline personality disorder and psychosis, in particular patients with chronic schizophrenia. At the Cassel Hospital patients were commonly diagnosed with neurosis and personality disorder and at Henderson Hospital patients with diagnoses of psychosis and psychopathy were admitted for treatment.

The genesis of the therapeutic community

Historically, British psychoanalysis in psychiatry formed the matrix for the development of the therapeutic community model that, according to Malcolm Pines (1999a) was based on a number of overlapping elements. British psychodynamic psychotherapy at the Tavistock Clinic was influenced by both psychoanalysis and social factors at a time when psychoanalysts came into creative contact with psychiatry as barriers were finally ruptured with the wartime need for cooperative psychological management. Also, British psychiatry was emerging from its lethargy regarding mental illness as hospitals began to open their closed wards and admit voluntary patients. Tom Main and Maxwell Jones pioneered the development of the therapeutic community model during and following Second World War, each in his own way, and independent of the other, but with the same guiding principles. Tom Main was a psychiatrist psychoanalyst who came from a Tavistock background to Northfield Military Hospital and later became director at the Cassel Hospital in Surrey. Maxwell Jones was a psychiatrist from the Maudsley Hospital who went to Mill Hill Military Hospital and afterwards to Belmont Hospital also in Surrey. Both men relied on the resources and support of government departments of health and labour respectively (Manning, 1991). On the whole, what emerged from these two innovative experiences at Northfield/Cassel and Mill Hill/Belmont was very similar in terms of the concentration on the functioning of the hospital community. Out of Northfield came a philosophy for the therapeutic community and from Mill Hill came a method. The idea that the community itself might serve as an instrument of therapy developed at these hospital-based therapeutic communities and the idea was taken up in modified forms by other British psychiatric hospitals and went on to develop an international following (Jones, 2004).

The Northfield experiments

The application of psychoanalytic theory in institutions and organisations was presaged at the Military Neurosis Centre at Hollymoor Military Hospital in Northfield, Birmingham, England (Jones, 2004). It was here that group psychotherapy and the therapeutic community model were developed in the treatment of soldiers suffering, mostly from neurotic disorders, who had not responded to ordinary disciplinary measures in their army units. Military psychiatric services were faced with many psychologically traumatised soldiers who were expected to convalesce and return to the front line. Two treatment trials, known as the Northfield experiments, were conducted between 1942 and 1948 and they brought together a group of talented people: Wilfred Bion, John Rickman, Siegfried Heinrich Foulkes, Harold Bridger, and

Tom Main who all collaborated to develop group psychotherapy in the therapeutic community model (Campling, 2001; Pines, 1999a; Whiteley, 2004). These men were the primary shapers of psychotherapeutic theory and practice in the United Kingdom over the following decades and are still strongly influential today.

In the beginning, Wilfred Bion (1961) was appointed director of the Training Wing at Northfield at the end of 1942. He and his colleague John Rickman, who had been in analysis with both Freud and Klein, instituted a disciplined program of daily parades for the soldier-patients where a period of time was spent in group discussion; it was this innovation that characterised the first Northfield experiment. Group discussion provided the men with an opportunity "to step outside their framework and look upon its working with the detachment of spectators" (Bion, 1959, p. 16). Bion and Rickman were soon in conflict with both the medical and the military hierarchy, and after only six weeks were dismissed from their posts despite an improvement in the men's behaviour and morale. Bion failed to maintain relationships with the authorities often ignoring protocol and omitting to gain authorisation for his actions. This neglect orchestrated his downfall. Bion's clinical experiments and ideas about group dynamics, as they emerged from his brief involvement at Northfield along with his prior experiments with leaderless groups, set a new tone for psychoanalytic work. See chapter four.

A few weeks after Bion left, Foulkes arrived at Northfield and the whole purpose and philosophy of Northfield hospital underwent a major revision. The entire hospital became the social field and the behaviour of individuals within it were subject to the forces inherent within that social field (Harrison, 2000). Foulkes instituted ward-based group therapy sessions and focused on the unit as a single entity. He structured the wards like communities, encouraging mutual support and cooperation in living, with non-directive group discussions to examine and understand the process. The whole community was seen as both the patient and as the instrument of treatment with the aim of educating and training the community in the problems of neurotic defences and interpersonal relationships. Foulkes consulted with various departments in the hospital when problems were arising, in order to study the situation in a group setting and facilitate the emergence of a group resolution. He argued that if the psychotherapist resisted the temptation of being made a leader, his patients growing independence, spontaneity, and responsibility, together with personal insight into their social attitudes, would reward him or her. Foulkes initiated the bringing together of all the players involved in the common project that become an essential component of the therapeutic community concept.

With the arrival of Harold Bridger at Northfield a few months after Foulkes, the conception of "hospital-as-a-whole" became more obvious (Whiteley, 2004). Activities were introduced, both in the hospital and in external community projects, as a means of studying and increasing the patient's opportunities for group interaction. The hospital at Northfield grew into a self-governing community in which the patients were expected to take a responsible part. Ward meetings changed to involve patients in the administration of the hospital where representatives from each ward were elected and attended a weekly meeting of ward representatives. The ordinary army discipline and procedures continued to provide the framework for the new tasks and activities but links were also forged with the local community where employment opportunities were found in the local community and with neighbouring farms or the local agricultural college. The institution opens up and spreads out so that attention is directed to what is going on in the outside world and it acts as a counterbalance to what the group internalises. Tom Main was the last to come to Northfield, arriving towards the end of the war to take charge of a division of the hospital. He brought with him experience in the early treatment of battle exhaustion and of the resolution of a threatened mutiny on the Italian front. Main took up the concept of the hospital as a whole coining the term "therapeutic community" (Main, 1989). Main's contribution was to acknowledge the involvement of broader interrelated systems at work in the environment. Rather than coming into confrontation with the existing military order in the hospital, as Bion had done, he took into account the needs and expectations of the military system, the status quo of the conventional psychiatric treatment system and integrated them with a psychoanalytic way of working with the group (Whiteley, 2004). In 1947 Main was appointed director of the Cassel hospital where a tradition of psychoanalytic treatment existed and in this environment he established his therapeutic community model.

The Second World War served as a significant catalyst for change and innovation even though wartime psychotherapy was not very effective because the majority of servicemen were not returned to active duty, most being downgraded or discharged after treatment. In spite of this, group and milieu therapies were adopted within the British National Health Service (NHS) and in the private sector (Jones, 2004). The Northfield experiments are an example of the evolution of an institutional model borne from the need to treat a particular target group, and the assimilation of different perspectives honed to produce the therapeutic community model.

Democratic therapeutic community model

A therapeutic community usually refers to a small cohesive group of people in an environment where patients are called "residents" and have a significant involvement in decision making and the practical running of the institution (Campling, 2001). A resident's peer group brings strengths and creative energy into the therapeutic setting in establishing a strong therapeutic alliance. The day-to-day social experience of living and working together in a shared environment is seen as being of equal importance as formal therapy, and the structure is such that the two are closely integrated and inform each other. Democratic therapeutic communities are based on ideas of collective responsibility, citizenship, and empowerment (Kennard, 2004). They are deliberately structured with a flattened hierarchy and decision-making is delegated in such a way that encourages personal responsibility and avoids dependence on professionals:

> Democracy in health care treatment settings might be described as the introduction to therapeutic encounters of consensual decision making procedures, derived and adapted from political theory. Democracy, from this perspective might be viewed as algorithm of patient empowerment. The interest in genuine (rather than tokenistic) democracy in therapeutic settings rests most explicitly with the application of the principles of the Therapeutic Community (TC). (Winship, 1998, p. 3)

One of the principles of the therapeutic community is for the hospital, institution, or community service to examine and treat itself as a living and learning situation. A culture of enquiry is central to the process of thinking about the dynamics of the whole culture of an institution with the aim of sustaining a therapeutic culture. The capacity to sustain a culture of enquiry needs support and one of the most important ways of sustaining this is to be clear about the central focus of the work. Holding the institution in mind and being aware of how it functions means understanding the dynamics that flow between all members of the community. This includes being mindful of the institutional dynamics within which the work proceeds, and ensuring that in the process of individual treatment it is not forgotten or undermined when attention is turned to the group, the team or the organisation.

Institutional therapeutic communities started to spring up in Britain during the 1950s and were initially small, specialised units in institutions that only admitted selected patients deemed to be appropriate. Mental hospital superintendents, such as David Clark at Fulbourne Hospital, Denis Martin at Claybury Hospital, and Bertram Mandelbrote at Littlemore Hospital, championed the therapeutic community concept in its application to large psychiatric hospitals where patients, predominantly those with chronic schizophrenia, were housed (Gale, et al., 2008). These and similar units adapted the core values of shared responsibility and democratised decision making but maintained the practice of open communication, information sharing, informal relationships, and a culture of enquiry within the staff. The relevance of therapeutic community principles to the work with chronic mentally ill patients is closely related to its predecessor, moral treatment. The therapeutic community is principally a residential living environment adapted for psychiatric services where treatment is on a continuum with the more integrated or recovered psychotic patients participating in regular communal activities, such as running the household with their fellow residents (Kennard, 2004). Whereas with an individual whose symptoms prevent him or her from being actively involved, staff adopt a style of working beside the person, carefully facilitating a containing relationship. Sometimes it is difficult to say what patients will do well and who will fare poorly as most patients tend to move along a continuum from acute crisis to relative stability, and this is independent of diagnosis. As a consequence, it is important that patients have a choice regarding treatment and options that remain flexible.

Henderson hospital

The contribution of Maxwell Jones and Belmont Social Rehabilitation Unit (renamed by Jones in 1959 as Henderson hospital) has origins that were in parallel with the Northfield experiments and Tom Main's development of the therapeutic community at the Cassel Hospital. Of particular interest is the socio-anthropological and psychoanalytic study conducted there from 1953 to 1957 by Rapoport. During the Second World War, Maxwell Jones was a young psychiatrist at the Maudsley Hospital in South London under the guidance of the chief physician Sir Aubrey Lewis who exposed Jones to psychoanalytic ideas. Jones was given the opportunity to develop talking therapy approaches with his soldier patients as an alternative to the common treatments of Insulin Coma Therapy, ECT and Sodium Amytal (Winship, et al., 2009). Although Jones entered a training analysis with Melanie Klein, he gave it up after three years without qualifying as a psychoanalyst. By the latter years of the war Jones was made psychiatrist in charge of the Effort Syndrome Unit for military personnel at Mill Hill Hospital in North London with the aim of rehabilitating the social and psychological casualties of the Second World War (Jones, 2004).

From the experiment at Mill Hill Jones's ideas grew concerning the future task of the psychiatric hospital as a democratic therapeutic community and from 1947 the experiment progressed to the Social Rehabilitation Unit at Belmont Hospital in Sutton (Jones, 1982). The unit was created under the auspices of the Ministry of Health and the Ministry of Work and Pensions for the treatment of chronically unemployed "victims of the industrial society". These were adults with character disorders or psychopaths, usually with forensic histories, who were treated in the unit for an average of four to six months (Warren & Norton, 2004). In 1959 the diagnostic categorisation of the patients under the age of thirty years was: psychotic eleven per cent, personality disorder (weak ego-strength) fifty-four per cent, personality disorder (strong ego-strength) thirty-one per cent, and neurotic four per cent (Rapoport, 1960). Many patients had criminal records and experienced drug and alcohol abuse, added to this were histories of relationship and interpersonal problems. More recently, patients admitted to Henderson were described as character disorders, psychopaths, sociopaths, and anti-social personalities (Lees, Manning, & Rawlings, 1999).

Jones incorporated ideas from Stanton and Schwartz's 1954 study at Chestnut Lodge and others who worked with the institutional treatment of adolescents and delinquents; he wanted the mental hospital of the future to have open communication, a flattened staff hierarchy, and role blurring where the therapeutic input would not be restricted to professional staff (Jones, 2004). Eileen Skellern came to the Belmont in 1952 after several years nursing at the Cassel Hospital. She worked as sister-in-charge of the one hundred bed Social Rehabilitation Unit. This was an active period for Skellern in her collaboration with Jones and others in pioneering models of social rehabilitation and group methods. Skellerns leadership was noted in particular by Rapoport's team in his sociological research study, *Community as Doctor* (Rapoport, 1960). Skellern took her psychodynamic interest with her when she later worked at the Maudsley Hospital where she established a therapeutic community unit with Bob Hobson that offered a day program of dynamic psychotherapy where the nursing staff carried individual caseloads. The ideology at Henderson Hospital came out of its commitment to an experimental milieu that would be part of the work of the "third revolution in psychiatry" based on the inadequacies of the custodial system of psychiatric care (Rapoport, 1960). Treatment was seen as a collective venture and every member had an obligation to the community of working towards a common purpose. The community itself was invested with an important decision-making function and responsibility for the day-to-day running of the therapeutic community was shared among patients and staff; it was collaborative and democratically shared. A core expectation was that patients actively participate in their own treatment and that of their peers. All treatment at Henderson was in a group setting and the therapy was fundamentally social. The daily program was a series of group meetings and activities modelled on psychiatric principles of group therapy and workshops, and activity based work groups, in addition to the social group in the evening designed for socialising, interacting, and entertainment (Rapoport, 1960). A particular feature of the therapeutic community model is the attachments that patients make within the community; this is especially so when they are perhaps the first successful attachments a patient makes after repeated earlier failures (Whiteley, 2004). Patients are taught to analyse current social tensions in order to understand the effect that their words and actions have on others. Through this intensive process of social living, patients learn how to relate more effectively with others and to understand the obligations they have to others that could lead to genuine experiences of close human contact.

The success of a social movement depends on the nature of the belief system or ideology that gives the movement its *raison d'être*. "All utopian reformers think and act to some extent ideologically, using faith and conviction in the absence of demonstrated scientific principles"

(Manning, 1991, p. 90). Those who pledge allegiance to a particular ideology do not relinquish their beliefs easily; they tend to uncritically accept the teachings of the leader adhering to a moral commitment to the cause that rejects new perspectives. The quality of leadership that expresses these beliefs enables the membership to come together psychologically and materially. Maxwell Jones is an example of a charismatic narcissistic innovator; his enthusiasm was infectious for staff and patients alike creating a positive moral commitment to the community. Despite the warm feelings that charisma evokes, narcissists are typically uncomfortable with their own emotions and lack empathy for others (Maccoby, 2000). Equally, they do not listen to others nor do they learn from others very easily. The narcissist's faults tend to become even more pronounced the more successful they become. The result for the organisation is greater internal competitiveness. This is discussed further in chapter four with regard to leadership and authority.

Community as doctor

The first decade of Henderson Hospital's existence was characterised by the growth and development of ideas and opinions around the therapeutic community concept. Maxwell Jones invited Robert Rapoport, an American social anthropologist, to study the Henderson community from a participant/observer perspective because he wanted to establish a more theoretical foundation for their work based on scientific research. Rapoport and his team of sociologists, anthropologists, and psychoanalysts studied Henderson from 1953 to 1957. During this time similar research was being conducted in the United States at Chestnut Lodge and the Sonia Shankman Orthogenic school. The anthropologist literally takes up residence in the community and participates in its life with the aim of becoming accepted by its members, while making it very clear that the object of his or her presence is to study the group and its ways (Landy, 1961). The title of Rapoport's 1960 book *Community as Doctor* denotes the diffusion of the doctor's traditional authority to the collective whole and identifies ideological themes within the staff group.

Rapoport and his team explored what the therapeutic conditions were in the therapeutic community that facilitated change in an individual; so they asked patients to indicate what had been the most important factors for them in advancing their therapy. From these results and Rapoport's observations, four ideological themes were distilled: "permissiveness", "reality confrontation", "democracy", and "communality" (Rapoport, 1960). Permissiveness allows for individuals to express themselves freely and to tolerate a wide range of behaviours from others, including catharsis, self-disclosure, and the assumption of self-responsibility. Reality confrontation demands that the patient be continuously presented with feedback from others about their behaviour in order to break down denial, distortion, and withdrawal. This was said to promote self-awareness in the development of identity, a self-concept, and learning through interpersonal actions. Democracy was each community member's ability to share equally in the exercise of power in decision-making. It permitted self-management to emerge and altruism to flourish, as a resident was allowed to contribute meaningfully to the treatment of others. Communalism promoted interaction with others, the sharing of responsibility, the abandonment of fixed social roles and attitudes, and the development of new more intimate relationships.

Therapeutic community principles were frequently seen in dynamic tension with each other: for example, it was vital that all community members had a significant voice in decisions that affected their lives but there was a limit to democratic decision making when it came to the staff's responsibility to provide a safe environment. Likewise, permissiveness would be limited to the verbal expression of feelings only:

> In practice, power and authority is never truly relinquished by staff but "loaned" to clients under particular circumstances and conditions [...] a heavy burden is placed on the staff to balance the demands of the "medical model" with the promotion of a more democratic and power-sharing environment. As a result, the expected "community" norms of shared power and responsibilities must be clearly articulated through spoken and written communications, constantly repeated via community meetings, and non-verbally reinforced [...]. (Norton & Bloom, 2004, pp. 251–252)

An important observation of the study reflected on the emotional climate at Henderson and the repeated cycles of oscillations in the state of social organisation (Rapoport, 1960). The process of fluctuation was between two poles: from perfect equilibrium to disintegration. There were times of healthy functioning when residents were well able to manage responsibility and other times when high levels of disturbed behaviour meant that staff had to take a more active role, such as the reinstitution of authoritative leadership, the discharge of discordant members, the skilful use of interpretations or some form of external intervention.

Contradictions in the model

Rapoport pointed out a number of contradictory factors in the therapeutic community process at Henderson. The treatment ideology was manifest in the staff's conceptualisation of a patient's defective performance of social roles and of their personalities as malformed, in terms of abnormal ego growth. Here the idea was that ego weakness and poor social performance were indicative of psychiatric disorder for which the socio-environmental influence of the therapeutic community was the cure, as opposed to the evils of the conventional mental health system. On a continuum of ego strength to ego weakness the neurotic was at one end of the spectrum and the psychotic at the other, with an undifferentiated group of personality disorders in the middle. Rapoport judged each patient in the study according to their psychological adequacy in meeting life's problems by measuring their reality distortion, impulse control, and stability of role performance in order to ascertain the health of their egos. The community was said to be damaging to patients with weak ego functioning, which would probably indicate vulnerable or psychotic patients suggesting that this therapeutic community model may not be suitable for them. This idea has been contradicted by others who do recommend the therapeutic community approach in the treatment of psychosis but with some alterations to the organisational model (Gale, et al., 2008).

A reason for certain favourable and unfavourable patient outcomes was related to another tension in the community observed by Rapoport. Patients with better overall therapeutic outcomes were those who had better ego strengths and greater personal resources, accordingly patients with fewer deficits had a better prognosis. The outcomes were especially good for patients who formed close individual relationships with key staff figures. There was "[…] disproportionate improvement […] by patients with marked positive orientation to salient staff members, especially high-status staff" (Rapoport, 1960, p. 221). The emotional investment in the individual therapeutic relationship seemed to be associated with greater therapeutic success in comparison to the more diffuse emotional investment in group therapy and work groups. The uniqueness of the one-to-one therapeutic encounter that involved the development of a transferencial relationship with a staff member was an obvious and essential curative factor for these patients. Although individual therapy was not officially offered, certain healthier patients managed to find covert ways to establish exclusive relationships with staff. Patients with weaker ego strength were usually passive, socially withdrawn, and avoidant and, as such, unable to vie for the attention that the more assertive patients were able to obtain. Consequently, they were deprived of the much-needed opportunity to foster a therapeutic relationship and had poorer therapeutic outcomes. The avoidance of contact with psychotic patients in hospital settings was observed by Chiesa (1993) who explained that this may partly be due to the chronic frustration felt by nurses regarding the passivity of patients suffering from chronic mental illnesses, consequently they turn their attention towards less damaged patients who are more responsive to their efforts. There is a paradox here between the fundamentally democratic structure of the therapeutic community and a morally authoritative staff group.

The staff in the community had the duel demands of focusing on the community as a whole and the progress of individual residents. Dennie Briggs was on placement at Henderson for some time during the 1950s and reported that Maxwell Jones insisted that privileged communication between staff and members of the therapeutic community had largely been abandoned in the development of his treatment ideology:

> Staff members thus are not permitted to take confidences from the patients, and when a patient does succeed in getting a member of the staff to confide in him, he is encouraged to bring the material up at one of the various group meetings. (Briggs, 1959, p. 218)

The fostering of exclusive relationships with staff was in conflict with the unit's ideology of group solidarity, nonetheless, patients were significantly dependent on professional staff. This is reminiscent of a hidden collusion amongst staff at Chestnut Lodge where the existence of prestige was openly denied but was covertly promoted.

Another ambiguity was identified as a division between the goals of staff with a rehabilitative agenda to help patients return to their lives outside, and those staff with a therapeutic agenda of wanting patients to understand themselves better (Rapoport, 1960). Jones considered all treatment to be rehabilitation and this was interpreted by the staff as improvement in the patient's capacity for constructive interpersonal relationships in social life. In Jones's mind-set all patients were treated alike and received the same treatment, with no room for individuality in a patient's treatment process. If they did not fit the mould at admission they were rejected. Rapoport noted that patients deemed suitable for admission to Henderson had similar personality structures and were diagnosed by staff with personality disorders when, in fact, a sizeable proportion were neurotic or psychotic.

One of the obvious changes at Henderson since the Rapoport study was the incorporation of a more balanced treatment focus where equal attention is paid to the psychotherapy and the sociotherapy (Norton & Bloom, 2004). It still specialised in the treatment of patients with personality and character disorders and at the same time maintained a sociotherapeutic model within the framework of the therapeutic community. In order to maintain a twenty-four hour a day close collaboration with patients, staff had to be aware of the transference and countertransference effects in the relationship (Warren & Norton, 2004). To sustain this position, the staff needed an effective system of supportive and supervisory structures put in place so that they could reflect on their reactions in the process and minimise the risks of destructive inter-staff splitting and to promote a therapeutic culture. In 2007, Henderson Hospital was under threat of closure due to the withdrawal of government funding; it was out of step with an increasingly economic rationalist approach to mental health care and in 2008, the main gate was padlocked for good.

The Cassel hospital

The Cassel hospital in England clearly demonstrates how psychoanalysis was adapted and applied to the institutional treatment of patients in the context of a therapeutic community model. Ernest Cassel founded Cassel Hospital in 1919 as a treatment centre for shell-shocked soldiers of the First World War. Today Cassel Hospital is a psychiatric hospital located in Richmond, South West London; it is described as a national Tier four specialist service for the assessment and treatment of adults and young people with severe and complex personality disorders who have exhausted all other avenues of mental health support and care in their local communities. Patients present with long standing issues that may include: self harm and suicidal behaviour, depression and anxiety, eating disorders, alcohol and substance abuse, dissociation, transient psychotic states, severe relationship problems, or breakdown in everyday functioning. Cassel no longer calls itself a therapeutic community. From the time it was taken over by the West London Mental Health NHS trust, the treatment program became a living-learning therapeutic environment that offers psychosocial nursing, individual and group psychotherapy, as well as other services (The Cassel Hospital, 2015). It is hard to know how Cassel has changed with this takeover but since the closure of Henderson hospital Cassel is the only service of its kind in England.

Of patients admitted to the Cassel hospital during the 1990s two-thirds had a diagnosis of borderline personality disorder (Bell, 1997). Then it was described as an inpatient psychotherapy facility and therapeutic community that provided psychosocial treatment and individual psychoanalytically oriented psychotherapy in the setting of a therapeutic milieu (Lees, et al., 1999). The hospital was separated into three units offering treatment to adults, adolescents, and families; each unit had a psychoanalyst consultant, a senior nurse, nursing staff trained in psychosocial nursing and both medical and non-medical psychotherapists (Bell, 1997). The adult service provided inpatient accommodation with a length of stay from twelve to eighteen months within the therapeutic community where psychotherapy was conducted on a twice-weekly basis. Another option was a six month inpatient stay, followed by six months outreach nursing and twice weekly psychoanalytic group psychotherapy for eighteen months (The Cassel Hospital, 2005).

Tom Main was Cassel's first director who served there for thirty years following his Second World War experience as a psychiatrist for the armed forces and his participation in the experiments at Northfield (Hartnup, 1994). Main (1989) recommended long term psychoanalytically oriented treatment for patients with severe personality disorders that would require admission to a residential facility offering milieu therapy in the context of a therapeutic community. Since its inception after the Second World War, a tradition developed at Cassel Hospital where emphasis was placed on the psychoanalytic understanding of organisational dynamics in the development of the therapeutic community. They aimed at incorporating an awareness of unconscious processes in individual, group, and community situations in a setting that made institutional, social, and psychological dynamics a primary focus (Caldwell, 2001). The main ingredient of treatment at the Cassel Hospital was the socio-therapeutic program managed by the nursing staff, and the formal therapy between patient and psychotherapist. Individual twice-weekly therapy is orientated towards object relations theory with the principal influences drawn from clinicians, such as Winnicott and Balint (James, 1984). In the adult inpatient setting a special emphasis is placed on the work of Wilfred Bion (Bell, 1997). Psychotherapy focuses on the interpretation of internal conflicts, on the confrontation and clarification of dysfunctional behaviour and on the analysis of institutional transferences to the nurse, other staff, patients and the institution itself as they become apparent during the treatment (Skogstad, 2003).

One of the key features of inpatient psychotherapy, as opposed to patients in treatment off campus, is that the therapist knows the "others" that the patient refers to because they have a shared reality within the community. Therefore, the therapist interprets in the here and now, as well as in the context of what has been going on in the hospital community (Muir, 1987). The psychotherapist is part of the therapeutic team and has regular meetings with other members of the team, and for this reason the boundary between the psychotherapist and the rest of the institution can blur at times. All patients are allocated a doctor who is responsible for attending to physical illnesses, medication, and any administrative matters; this is to ensure that the role of psychotherapist is kept as uncontaminated as possible from other functions. A similar arrangement was in place at Chestnut Lodge, Maryland and is in place at Austin Riggs Center, Stockbridge in the United States.

The family inpatient unit

Psychotherapy at Cassel's family inpatient unit is theoretically influenced by British psychoanalysis: Anna Freud, Melanie Klein and her disciples and, in particular, the middle school clinicians, such as Winnicott and Balint. In the family unit there is a day unit, a school for children and adolescents, as well as an inpatient unit that can accommodate six or seven families and eight older adolescents without their parents. The family unit offers treatment for severe pathology in families through a prolonged admission of the whole family so that they can face their difficulties and restore functioning. A disturbed person is held more securely in the context of a whole family admission rather than if they were admitted alone, so patients are more commonly accepted according to their desire for treatment. The length of stay is usually around a year, in addition to an intensive assessment period of three to five weeks. From the outset it is obvious that, in the treatment at Cassel, attention is directed mainly towards adults rather than children, in particular on disturbances in mothering and parenting, and how this affects the child. While it is desirable that both parents are in treatment, especially in the case of a psychotic child, the treatment tries not to exclude the child's separate therapeutic needs. Treatment is based on four essential principles (Kennedy, et al., 1987, p. 2):

1. Patients are treated as independent subjects with an unconscious that needs to be respected and listened to.
2. The hospital structure functions as a holding and facilitating environment.
3. The hospital's therapeutic structures are the therapy, the psychosocial nursing in group and individual encounters, community and staff meetings, supervision of therapy and nursing, and the life of the community in general. Community life means actively participating in and taking responsibility for the daily running of the community.
4. The hospital provides a framework for psychoanalytic thinking and its applicability. Space is made for nursing and therapy as equal partners in the approach to the treatment of a patient and in supervision of the nurse-therapist relationship. In this way splits are exposed and countertransference feelings are explored.

The individual psychotherapy practiced on the family inpatient unit has a central focus on the potential for multiple transference phenomena with the therapist, the nurse, the family, the family unit, and the whole hospital. Therapy aims to improve reality testing and self control, produce a richer social and emotional life, to develop independence and adaptation to the realities of life.

The questions of confidentiality and privacy are significant issues that have to be worked out especially in the information exchange between therapist and nurse and in a community where most behaviour becomes public property. The drawing and redrawing of boundaries is central to the particular understanding reached between patient and therapist. Since the length of the hospital stay and duration of the psychotherapy are standardised, the treatment is considered to be short to mid-term so the therapeutic goals are focused on patients' most pressing symptoms. Transference to the therapist is likely to be false or compliant because therapy is entered into only as a condition of hospitalisation and not due to the patient's self motivation (Muir, 1987). Consequently, the therapist has to be aware of transferences both to him or her-self as well as the institution and the others in the institution in general.

Psychosocial nursing and psychotherapy

The psychosocial nursing practice at Cassel has been developed over fifty years and is based on psychoanalytic, psychological, and social theoretical frameworks (Hinshelwood & Skogstad, 1997). A dynamic model of practice that was called "psychosocial nursing" emerged during the early 1950s defining the idea of the nurse working alongside the patient by engaging in day-to-day activities and problem solving. In 1968 a book was published on the psychosocial nursing practiced at Cassel (Barnes, 1968). The key to this approach was the notion of the "therapeutic use of self" introduced by the matron, Doreen Wadell who later became a psychoanalyst (Winship, 2009). Wadell collaborated with Tom Main in running clinical supervision groups described in *The Ailment and Other Psychoanalytic Essays* (Main, 1989). Until recently the Cassel Hospital offered a post graduate Masters course in psychodynamic psychosocial nursing through the University of East London (The Cassel Hospital, 2008).

Nurses at Cassel have a patient caseload and the same nurse works with the same patient throughout the length of their stay. The nurse's prime role is to be beside the patient as they face their day-to-day tasks and responsibilities within the community. As well as the containing function, the nurse's job is to challenge the patient, mediating through meaningful and reflective talk the patient's physiological, psychological, and social experiences (Griffiths, Ord, Wells, & Barnes, 1998). To a large extent, nursing at Cassel involves working in groups from morning work groups, to group meetings, and group recreational activities. The aim is to encourage patients to be aware of themselves and others, in developing a sense of responsibility within the community, and in gaining real autonomy in their lives. Fellow patients are also very important in this way where relationships are encouraged, as reciprocal interdependence is central to the therapeutic communities' ethos. The boundary between therapist and nurse is dealt with flexibly and on a one-by-one basis, depending on the patient and the situation.

Confidentiality is important between therapist and patient because, in a hospital community, secrets and collusion create problems. As potential difficulties emerge, the main therapeutic aim of the consultant psychiatrist and senior nurse is to provide supervision for those who work with the patient from a model that can contain anxiety, and so obviate some of the pressures for countertransference enactments. The therapist and nurse work together in psychoanalytically oriented supervision and this keeps the therapist involved in the everyday life of the community. It is in the everyday experience of nurse and patient working together that situations arise and afford the patient the opportunity of questioning, learning and growing from the perspective of the community and this is fed back into the therapy.

The community and hospital culture

A typical day in a therapeutic community starts and finishes with a community meeting, usually chaired by a resident. The agenda is driven by the attempt to bring as much information into the large group as possible, so that it is accessible to everyone. The whole hospital community meets three times a week and each individual unit meets four times a week. Residents are actively involved in the day-to-day household running of the institution and are expected to take on tasks and responsibilities within the living and working environment of the community. Each unit has a representative who chairs meetings with residents and, with the help of the nurses, has important responsibilities in the organisation of the hospital. Nurses work alongside residents to help them make emotional sense of what they are doing, dealing not just with eruptions of disturbed behaviour but with their capacity to take on specific responsibilities and tasks. Ultimately, residents have responsibility for their own treatment. The aim of the work in the therapeutic community is to support the healthy part of the resident within the context of the responsibilities of everyday life; the work of the day (Kennedy, et al., 1987). A resident who is regarded as being capable of carrying a considerable degree of responsibility will be provided with enough support to do so in collaboration with the nurse who works alongside them. The "work of the day" comprises any ordinary activity from cleaning the bedroom to tasks that require significant responsibility, such as, helping to cook a meal for everyone or duties that involve major responsibility; this may take the form of, managing a work team, chairing meetings, caring for each other's wellbeing or providing a roster of support for someone in crisis (Hinshelwood, 2000). The community is a network of relationships for support and self-enhancement where all residents are expected to play a part as both supporter and supported.

A common regressive fantasy for patients is that of an all-providing mother figure who will take care of them and be responsible for them. The community aims to support the patient's ego-structure on the one hand and resist the pressure for severe regression on the other. In contradiction of this, at the first psychoanalytic hospital Schloss Tegel in Germany, it was thought that the protective milieu of the institution provided the patient with a symbol of the mother's womb, and patients were encouraged towards infantile regression (Simmel, 1929). It is uncertain as to the efficacy of this approach but at Cassel making the institution into an enclave was discouraged. Removing the patient from the reality of ordinary relationships, tasks and responsibilities means they could avoid, not only external difficulties, but the corresponding aspects of internal reality (Skogstad, 2003). The risk of creating an unhelpful refuge is ever present in any therapeutic setting, and even more so in an inpatient setting. The wish for removal may reflect the patient's avoidance of reality and of the frustrations that facing reality brings. It can foster an unhelpfully regressive culture in which patients and staff can collude in the omnipotent phantasy that reality, ordinary limitations and responsibilities can be avoided, and that infantile demands can be met. The hospital is a holding environment that requires constant assessment in each individual case for when holding and protecting the vulnerable can turn into dependency and avoidance.

The holding or containing function is attributed to the institution as a whole and its internal structures where the individual's experiences are integrated into an understanding of how they function within the microcosm of the hospital community (Coombe, 1996). The containment provided by the hospital milieu is felt to safeguard against the risk of suicide that is often present during the treatment of disturbed and psychotic residents as well as ensuring a degree of treatment compliance (Lees, et al., 1999). The Cassel demonstrates the use of Bion's concepts of container and reverie, referring to a mother's relationship to her infant in her ability to receive the infant's projections, allowing them to resonate within her and respond to the infant's distress having rendered the projections safe and less frightening. Thus, the mother is able to hold and contain the infant's projected frustrations, anxiety, hate, and destructiveness. The community at Cassel acts as the maternal container in the sense of the patient's experiences being held by various individuals, structures, and relationships, to be experienced and reflected back safely.

The "hospital in the mind" is described as the powerful influence that the multiple transferences have on the patient's functioning in the hospital and on the people around them (Hinshelwood & Skogstad, 1997). Within the community the therapist-nurse pair comes to represent the Oedipal couple and this is often the main transference event for the patient where distorted fantasies and strong feelings have the potential to be acted out. "A culture of enquiry" is revealed in the examination of issues surrounding the psychotherapeutic pair (Kennedy, et al., 1987). Here attention is focused on the nature of professional relationships through self-reflection and understanding, and this is why staff are encouraged to enter their own individual therapy or analysis. For an institution saturated in psychoanalytic ideas it is inevitable that a dynamic tension, both opposite and complimentary, pulls the psychoanalytic enquiry in two directions, towards the pair and towards the social system. The phenomenon of a "culture of anti-enquiry" is described as the avoidance of thinking or questioning, interdisciplinary rivalries, separating or distancing of oneself from others, developing a persecutory or "siege mentality" about patients, and an unwillingness to face the "unknown known" (Griffiths & Hinshelwood, 1995, pp. 12–15).

Main (1989) described the phenomenon of the "special patient" in his essay, *The Ailment* where from admission the special patient demands special attention. These patients appear to have considerable potential but when they do not improve it produces a sense of failure in the staff. This is followed by increasingly desperate attempts at a cure, which initiate a downward spiral in the patient. The staff begin to accuse each other, sedation is increasingly used to silence the patient and, eventually, the patient is discharged to another hospital. Failure to acknowledge the ambivalence in the relationship between staff and patients poisons the interaction (Hartnup, 1994). Main's approach was to view the larger system as troubled and this had important consequences for the organisation of the institution. The special patient at Cassel has striking similarities to the findings of the Chestnut Lodge study where the focus of the repeated problem of the special patient was fixed on the dual relation of the patient-nurse couple.

Main was aware that the whole hospital, both the patient and the staff, have to undergo psychoanalytic examination to ensure that the patient's treatment proceeds. Main (1989) set out to use the daily domestic and recreational aspects of life within the community in the service of the therapeutic work where the reasons for failures could be discussed and explored. He saw the therapeutic community as an extension of Freud's work because it involved the study of the unconscious within a culture of enquiry. The constant study of staff dynamics and the relationship between staff and patients requires a network of meetings in which staff regularly assess the treatment and progress of every patient, and discuss their own experiences of the patient and each other. The history of the institution thus becomes embedded in this pattern of staff meetings, in which the staff express their most acute and immediate concerns, without any awareness of the ancestry of the setting. Main recommended that psychiatry make use of psychoanalysis in the observation and study of the individual, the group and the institution. For him the scope for technical developments and the application of psychoanalysis in the various settings of psychiatry seemed limitless. He also emphasised that it was essential to submit to expert training in psychoanalysis and a personal analysis or, at the very least, basic psychotherapeutic training.

Outcome studies

The Research Unit at Cassel was established in 1995 with view to promoting and coordinating the research work within the hospital. The work of the research team has helped to establish and consolidate a research culture within the hospital and psychotherapy services in general. Amongst its objectives was the development of studies in the area of psychodynamic psychotherapy and its applied contributions to mental health as a way to contribute to the evidence-based health care developments within National Health Service (NHS) psychotherapy services. Over the years the Research Unit has forged working relationships with several Academic and NHS institutions including the Psychoanalysis Unit at University College London, Imperial College and the Centre for the Economics of Mental Health at the Institute of Psychiatry, London. The research team consists of Dr Marco Chiesa and one full-time equivalent of a research psychologist, a number of part-time voluntary assistants and a part-time personal assistant. Through collaboration with the Cassel Hospital Charitable Trust the research department has been given contributions from fund raising for the continuation and expansion of the hospital research activities. In one outcome study, patients who were admitted consecutively to Cassel's adult unit in 1977–1978 were followed up five years after discharge (Rosser, et al., 1987). Those who were found to improve at the end of treatment remained well at follow up. The characteristics of the improved group were correlated with a combination of the following: neurotic psychopathology, considerable depression, superior intelligence, lack of a chronic outpatient history and no psychotropic medication or illicit drug use. At admission around seventy per cent of patients who are likely to be long-term successes can be identified and these patients represent the best bets for a faster recovery and return to productivity. Not surprisingly, the less intelligent, chronically dependent patient who is socially isolated, but not necessarily depressed, with borderline personality organisation or psychosis does not respond immediately to the Cassel program, any more than to any other conventional psychiatric approach. It was concluded that the most severely disturbed patients may be discharged as failures at the very moment when they are becoming accessible to treatment, and consequently they are more likely to benefit from a longer treatment than is needed for less disturbed patients. Although this finding is consistent with other research worldwide it does not seem to have any impact on government expenditure for facilities that treat patients who suffer from conditions that incur a higher financial burden.

The Cassel Hospital provides an example of a clear treatment model that brings together inpatient psychotherapy and psychosocial nursing after many years of working and reworking it. The structural components that support the model are unambiguous role definitions, supervision of the therapist-nurse dyad, regular meetings within the individual units, including staff meetings, maintaining the idea of the hospital as a whole, and an ongoing commitment to research (Griffiths & Hinshelwood, 1995). The psychoanalytic milieu aims to be therapeutic and is founded on a guiding ethos, the hospital structure is considered as a whole and there is a common assumption of responsibility in the teamwork. The institution is examined and adapted to a purpose that is specifically psychoanalytic; principally in the way modifications are introduced to the analytic method. Importance is placed on staff training or education, and case conferences to clarify the treatment agenda on behalf of the institution and for each subject, one at a time. Tom Main described a culture of enquiry as the hallmark of the therapeutic community: "It both requires and sanctions instruments of enquiry into personal and interpersonal and intersystem problems, and the study of impulses, defences, and relations as these are expressed and arranged socially" (Main, 1989, p. 141).

Communities based on antipsychiatry

The activities of the anti-psychiatry faction provided the impetus for change that resulted in the therapeutic community as an alternative to the conventional institution. At around the same time biological psychiatry started to challenge psychoanalytic psychiatry claiming that psychoanalysis was unscientific, costly, and ineffective. The anti-psychiatry movement arose as a group of psychoanalysts and sociologists who organised themselves in opposition to what they perceived were biological psychiatry's abuses in the name of science. This protest was joined by a 1960s worldwide counterculture that was already rebelling against all forms of political, sexual, and racial injustice. Anti-psychiatry was internationally promoted through the efforts of Michel Foucault in France, R. D. Laing in England, Thomas Szasz in the United States, and Franco Basaglia in Italy, who was also anti-psychoanalysis. "All four championed the concept that personal reality was independent from any hegemonic definition of normalcy imposed by organised psychiatry" (Rissmiller & Rissmiller, 2006, p. 863).

Anti-psychiatry was a branch of psychiatry that recognised that the objectification of the mentally ill made psychiatry part of the problem rather than the solution. David Cooper (2003) coined the term "antipsychiatry" after the movement was already under way. Cooper believed that madness was a product of society and that its ultimate solution was revolution. This required positive non-action where, for recovery to occur, going mad was necessary. Joe Berke (1997) says that dehumanising mental health treatments are manifest in the over use and abuse of psychotropic medications, the resurgence of Electro Convulsive Therapy (ECT), involuntary hospitalisation, the absence of adequate funding, the deficiency in therapeutic training and expert supervision for staff who work with patients, and, in general, the lack of sophistication of mental health services in most areas. Franco Basaglia's radical Marxist views were directed at socio-political ideals in the liberation of psychiatric patients; he and others from the Radical Party formed a political support movement called *Psichiatrica Democratica* (Democratic Psychiatry) in 1976 that spearheaded radical changes to institutional psychiatry.

Since deinstitutionalisation the antipsychiatry movement has lost most of its broad based support and it changed from being an influential international movement dominated by intellectual psychiatrists, to an ex-patient consumerist coalition fighting against pharmacological treatment, coercive hospitalisations, and other authoritarian psychiatric practices (Rissmiller & Rissmiller, 2006). Critical psychiatry acknowledges the inevitable social dimension of psychiatric practice and that psychosocial perspectives have a long history in psychiatry in the development of community care. Interestingly, in 1967 Laing, Cooper, Berke, and Redler all met with Jacques Lacan in Paris where they lunched and shared ideas (Redler, 2000). Some mutual presentation of papers at conferences and publication of articles was also said to have taken place. Based on left wing politics, the counter culture revolution of the 1960s was a platform that demanded institutional reform. The antipsychiatry movement became intimately involved with concerns about institutional care in asylums and in the promotion of community care, producing such examples as Soteria House, The Arbours Centre, Villa 21, The Philadelphia Association, and Kingsley Hall.

The therapeutic community and group therapy models are both types of socially inspired therapy that might be described as therapeutic collectivism. Psychoanalytic theories of intersubjectivity, whether applied to individual, group or milieu, begin with a premise that the individual does not exist in isolation. Individualism and collectivism hold conflicting views of the nature of human beings, society, and the relationship between them in the context of balancing the needs of the individual against the needs of society. Freud saw the tendency individuals had of projecting their narcissism onto the group and of the detrimental effects the group can have on an individual's psychic functioning where they lose the capacity to think for themselves. Bion identified significant characteristics of the individual that he could not understand except in the context of the individual as a herd animal in the field of the study of groups. His explanations of group behaviour are derived from psychoanalysis from which he developed a framework for the study of group function. In analysing the psychiatric hospital as a community it was discovered that the social organisation of the group can have curative qualities. The original idea that the community itself might serve as an instrument of therapy was taken up widely in a modified form by psychiatric units and mental hospitals throughout many countries for many years. Social therapy will always be relevant wherever people with mental illness are gathered in residential institutions.

S.W. '13
Sonia Shankman Orthogenic School

CHAPTER NINE

Institutional approaches with children and adolescents

This chapter presents theoretical approaches to psychoanalytic treatment with children and adolescents, in particular those with psychosis, and their care and education in institutions. The impact of psychoanalytic theory in the establishment and operation of residential institutions for children and adolescents is demonstrated by examples that provide a picture of the influences and various outcomes of institutional care. Additional considerations for the successful functioning of these institutions were appropriate funding, government influence in decision-making, and parental involvement in the child's welfare. It is the analyst's holding function that creates a protective space within which private experience can safely be articulated; this is especially true in work with certain regressed or disturbed psychotic patients, and especially with children. For these patients to tolerate and to make use of the analytic process, the analyst's position is an emotionally responsive highly attuned presence that is an evenly available but a largely non-interpretive presence. As with many of the pioneers, a largely experimental approach to the analytic treatment of children inspired the work of many successful clinicians. It is therefore important to be inclusive of different views, approaches, and modifications to the analytic method until the efficacy of their use is better understood.

A Lacanian approach to the child is generally made from two different positions: that of the child as an object of their parent's desire, and the child as a subject in his or her own right who enters the analytic treatment with the capacity to participate (Laurant, 1990; Rodriguez, 1991). Psychoanalysis with children requires particular adjustments but this is the case in every analytic treatment because there is no homogeneous analytic technique. Psychoanalysis, whether with adults or children with or without a diagnosis of psychosis, is the subject's assumption of his or her own history as constituted by speech that is addressed to another in the form of the analyst (Lacan, 2002b, p. 48). A concern for family structure, genealogy, and language acquisition is central to an explanation of the subject's formation. In a note to Jenny Aubry, Lacan (1990a) described the child's symptom as answering something that is representative of the truth of the family structure, usually of the couple and more often the mother.

Psychoanalysis with children

Sigmund Freud did not treat children. He believed that psychoanalytic treatment with children was possible but required an adaptation or modification to the original analytic method designed for the treatment of adult neurotics:

> A child is psychologically a different object from an adult. As yet he possesses no super-ego, the method of free association does not carry far with him, transference (since the real parents are still on the spot) plays a different part. The internal resistances against which we struggle in adults are replaced for the most part in children by external difficulties. If the parents make themselves vehicles of the resistance, the aim of the analysis—and even the analysis itself—is often imperilled. Hence it is often necessary to combine with a child's analysis a certain amount of analytic influencing of his parents. (Freud, 1933a, p. 148)

In Freud's case of *Little Hans* (1909b) he had no actual contact with the five year old child; it was through the child's father, Max Graf, that the treatment was conducted providing the rich observational material gathered for Freud's case study. Freud (1933a) also identified the important work of applying psychoanalysis to education in the bringing up of the next generation when he referred to the work of his daughter, Anna, in compensating for his own neglect in the area. Anna Freud considered analytic techniques unnecessary in child analysis, preferring play and drawing in the observation of the child over sources of interpretable material (Glover, 2009). She relied more on the words of the child's parents and their wish for the child to be treated rather than the child's speech.

Donald Winnicott focused on the mother-infant dyad in the early stages of an infant's life and the impact of the encroachment of maternal depression (Winnicott, 1964). This sense of deprivation would lead the infant in the paranoid-schizoid position to regard its love as bad and destructive; there followed a withdrawal of emotional contact with the outer world and a disturbed sense of external reality. Winnicott (1960) asserted that there was no such thing as a baby separate from its mother prior to ego development and its ability to use word symbols. From the mother-infant bond comes the capacity to tolerate frustration through an interaction characterised by consistent availability, response to cueing and mutual attunement. The infant's progress relies on the mother's capacity to respond to its needs and to allow optimal frustration and separation as a baby matures and wishes to move away and explore. The mother functions as a container to protect the infant and for the projection of the infant's bad objects; it is this holding environment that allows the infant to transition at its own rate to a more autonomous position (Winnicott, 1960, p. 595). The concept of the "good-enough" mother is a mother who is physically and emotionally attuned to her infant, adapting appropriately to the baby during the stages of infancy depending on the growing infant's ability to deal with failure of adaptation and to tolerate the results of frustration (Winnicott, 1953). There is no infant independent of the care of the mother and it is for this reason that Winnicott emphasised the importance, in the very early stages of an infant's life, of the mother providing an environment that does not confront the infant with the fact of its own separateness.

In general, object relations theory places emphasis on the internalisation of interpersonal relationships for psychic development and mental health. An infant initially comprehends objects in terms of part-objects that represent the infant's subjective and repeated experience of his or her care-taking environment. Object relations theory focuses on the content of primitive, psychotic anxieties and proposes that psychotic mechanisms and processes are present throughout life. The roots of schizophrenia are firmly placed in ego impairments brought about by various kinds of deficiencies in the early mother-child dyad. Object relations begin with the creation of an attachment to the maternal object and a desire to sustain that attachment. Melanie Klein (1963) built on Abraham's reasoning that if psychotic patients were fixated at earlier oral and anal psychosexual stages, perhaps psychosis could also be linked with early infantile states of mind. Klein's analytic approach was alert to the interpretation of the patient's unconscious phantasy and the object relation to the mother and the interior of her body. She invented an analytic method of play technique that gave even very young children under three years of age a suitable medium for expressing their thoughts and feelings in language.

Klein (1946) viewed object relations as being present from the beginning of life with the first object being the mother's breast, which is split for the child into the good breast and bad breast that leads to a split between love and hate; its origins being in the interaction between introjection and projection, and internal and external objects. The object is split into good and bad as the child struggles to integrate the two primary drives of love and hate into constructive social interactions transitioning from the paranoid-schizoid position to the depressive position. The breast that feeds the hungry infant is the "good breast" and the frustrated infant that finds no breast is the "bad breast". Klein (1963) described the child's phantasy of attacking the inside of the mother's body, invading it sadistically. Projective identification is associated with the paranoid schizoid position where the phantasised split-off parts of the self are projected into the mother. She is supposed to contain these split-off parts and offer them back to the child in a more manageable form.

Melanie Klein's approach in the analytic treatment of psychosis involves the use of toys as symbols in the play, and her interpretations that invite the child into language. Klein's previous work at the Berlin Polyclinic taught her much about the structure of infantile psychosis preparing her for the treatment of a psychotic (probably autistic) four year old boy named Dick (Klein, 1930). This case paved the way for a new metapsychological framework for understanding psychosis and the analytic treatment of psychosis. Lacan (1975) maintained that the success of Dick's treatment lay less in the accuracy of Klein's interpretations than a speech act that required a reply, and engagement in a dialogical symbolising process that thrust him into language. Klein provided Dick with a set of linguistic symbolising tools for him to pick up and use in his relationship to others in his life. Thus, he could recognise himself, not only as a signifier in his dual relationships with each of his parents, but also as a witness, from a third position, to their relationship with each other.

The concept of projective identification arose from psychoanalytic treatments that the post-Kleinians were conducting with seriously disturbed schizoid patients. Herbert Rosenfeld claimed that some mothers of children who develop schizophrenia show a diminished tolerance toward the infant's projections, feeling disturbed and persecuted they withdraw their feelings from the child. Hence, a patient with schizophrenia never fully outgrows the earliest phase of development to which this object relationship belongs. Wilfred Bion (1963) highlighted the significance of the individual's relationship to their environment and the importance of the mother's ability to respond intuitively to her infant's needs. Derived from Winnicott's model of early psychic development, Bion created the idea of maternal reverie; this is the mother's capacity to sense and make sense of what is going on inside the infant. The infant needs maternal reverie in order to grow and develop; without it the infant cannot survive. According to Bion's theory, the infant projects beta (b) elements into the psyche of its mother. Beta elements are the infant's extremely archaic bodily feelings and emotional states linked to the very earliest sensory and relational experiences. The mother lends the child her own thinking apparatus to reshape, detoxify, and transform beta elements into alpha (a) elements that are then assimilated by the infant and integrated into its own mental functioning (Bion, 1961, 1962). The mother receives the child's projections and modifies them so that the infant is able to introject the fear in a detoxified form. Thus, the mother assists her child to cope with anxiety. This transformation is due to the mother's capacity for maternal reverie that fulfils a "de-saturating" function with regard to the beta elements that are produced and felt by the infant (Bion, 1963). The alpha function is the infant's first means of communication, based on Melanie Klein's concept of projective identification. Some analytic and organisational settings have adapted the function of containing anxiety by drawing on the psychic stance of both mother and father to provide containment and a thinking space that allows the patient to work through developmental stages.

Residential and education institutions

Contemporary social and child welfare policy regarding residential care for disturbed children has reflected ambivalence around the belief that a child's development would be enhanced within their family when some family environments are not conducive to a child's wellbeing (Cohler & Friedman, 2004). A psychiatric institution is a temporary solution that represents a breakdown in normal development that ought to take place in a child's life within a family unit for their physical, social, and mental health. The primary institution for any child is the family group into which they are born. However, frequently children who end up in residential treatment have used up all the available community treatment resources to become children that nobody wants; the family scapegoat. Problems such as divorce, abuse, poverty, drugs, alcohol, and other forces interfere with normal parenting and disrupt family life. Within these families, therapeutic efforts directed either at the troubled child, adult or the whole family often fails to resolve conflict. Traditionally, institutions for children with maladaptive and disturbed behaviour provide shelter and custody in the hope that they will eventually outgrow their problems, but this has merely served to exacerbate them (Milner, 1964). Residential education institutions that were influenced by psychoanalytic theory are discussed in this chapter with particular attention given to how psychoanalysis was interpreted and applied there. Reference also needs to be made to the treatment of children at Le Courtil in Belgium, discussed in chapter seven, and in chapter eight the family unit at Cassel hospital in England.

A psychodynamic milieu emphasises the nuances of relationships and meanings that the child derives from every interaction with the others in their environment. The placement of a child in a therapeutic milieu was a way of providing refuge for the child allowing the parent's time to gather their resources in an effort to restore their family life. The philosophy of these places was based on observation and self-discovery in a shared living situation where basic human values are privileged. Attention to a child's understanding of self and experiences, in addition to a focus on the interplay of dynamics between the child and the social milieu offer an important means for therapeutic change. This holds true today even at a time when there is pressure to mainstream children who have special needs, together with financial constraints and the reliance on psychopharmacology that have altered more traditional understandings of the provision of residential psychodynamic treatment for disturbed youth and children.

August Aichhorn was a Viennese teacher and psychoanalyst whose creative efforts were employed in treating children and youths in long-term milieu settings aimed at restructuring complex and ingrained pathological influences embedded in family dynamics. Aichhorn was responsible for setting up a number of educational centres for problem youth, and later he established the child guidance service for the Vienna Psychoanalytic Society. In his well-known book "Wayward Youth" (in German *Verwahrloste Jugend*), published in 1925, Aichhorn advised the removal of juvenile delinquent and disadvantaged youths from the home environment that had precipitated their antisocial behaviour, and recommended their relocation in a reform school or educational centre with the idea of applying psychoanalytic principles there (Aichhorn, 1984). Much of Aichhorn's experience was gained from an experiment in one of his educational centres involving a group of twelve adolescent boys described as outcasts, rebels, and malcontents who were all herded together. Aichhorn, known for his intuitive talents with teenagers, created an environment in one of the older buildings where the boys were left alone together to do as they liked. The staff interfered only when it was necessary to prevent injuries, never taking sides and always maintaining a consistent friendly attitude with repeated offers to engage in talking. The boys' aggressive acts became more frequent and more violent until most of the furniture was destroyed, the windowpanes broken and the doors kicked in. The local community was so alarmed that they sent for the police but Aichhorn remained firm. The boys' behaviour escalated becoming more and more destructive and, encountering no response, their violence soared until in the end it became a sort of shadow-boxing (Biddle, 1936).

A collapse of their morale was inevitable and this was accompanied by a strong outpouring of emotion, in which weeping was mingled with relief. Aichhorn believed that if aggression is not opposed it will reach a climax and then subside (Pines, 1999b). For three months alternating episodes of peace and rage followed as the boys began to develop an emotional connection between each other and the workers. The more life of the institution conformed to an actual social community the more certain was the social rehabilitation of the child. Aichhorn did not believe in imposing discipline and suppression on children and adolescents, and cautioned against making them adjust to rules that served the needs of the institution rather than those of the individual. When rules were broken or there was a disturbance Aichhorn sent for the participants to talk things over. This talking together combined with an attitude of forgiveness seemed to be their most valuable method of bringing the youth into contact with reality; providing them with experiences that would ready them for life outside rather than the artificial life of an institution. Aichhorn found that many of the youth he dealt with had suffered early maternal loss or deprivation. In comparing institutional children and those brought up in families he stressed the importance of early mothering on character development. This finding had an effect on Anna Freud's approach that was based on her conviction of the pathogenic effect of a child's separation from his or her mother (Hellman, 1983).

Hampstead War Nurseries

Anna Freud's key area of interest was the welfare of infants and young children as the result of two world wars. After the outbreak of the Second World War Anna and Dorothy Burlingham set up the Hampstead War Nurseries that provided foster care for single parent families, evacuees, and children separated from their parents during the Blitz. They accepted children from as young as two days to over five years of age, with some of the oldest staying until they were aged eight and nine. The experimental nurseries focused on how to assess the impact of deprivation at different developmental stages and how to supply what was missing or at least promote healthy adaptation. They worked at helping the children form attachments by providing continuity of relationships with the workers and by encouraging mothers to visit as often as possible and ensuring, where feasible, that separations from parents were gradual rather than abrupt. In the experimental nurseries in Hampstead, children were under close observation and details were recorded with particular attention to the effect of institutional life on a child's development of language and toilet training. The staff found that children with no close emotional bond to their mothers or the stimulus of maternal devotion had no wish to please their mother. These children were observed to have delayed speech, difficulty with anal sphincter control and developed autoerotic character traits at the expense of social traits, and were retarded in their intellectual and creative development as evidenced by the blunting of curiosity and the lack of identifications (Freud, 1988). The problem for young children without the mother's desire to indicate to them that they are a particular and unique being, is that they have no-one to show them which way to go towards language and to becoming a subject in their own right. Instead they become an undifferentiated child amongst all the others in an institution (Rodríguez, 1999, p. 178). The presence of the mother or her substitute is sufficient to compensate for all other deprivations, including the effect of continuous institutional care.

The residential nurseries were modelled, as nearly as was institutionally feasible, on the family unit with a substitute mother-carer available in a family like grouping that consisted of one staff member with up to five children. This arrangement was an immediate success but also produced anxiety in the children that was displayed in jealousy and sibling rivalry as they vied for the mother substitute's attention. This subsided after a number of weeks as the children came to trust the stability of the family group. Always the figure of the father was conspicuously absent. Visiting fathers were often rejected, especially if they had been abusive, and yet absent or dead fathers were often incorporated into the children's rich fantasies. Thus Anna Freud decided that men were needed in the nurseries as members of staff and recruited six young conscientious objectors (Hellman, 1983). They took on the maintenance tasks and gardening and were an important contribution to the development of young boys and girls.

At the weekly meetings, attended by Anna Freud, the teachers, students and staff members would report on a particular child, so that a careful evaluation was made of the child's condition and progress. These discussions would be followed by Anna Freud's advice on handling particular problems (Friedmann, 1988). The majority of staff who came to work at the war nurseries were enthusiastic but untrained. As a result, Anna and Dorothy initiated a training scheme and rotated them throughout their facilities so that they could gain a broad level of experience. Lectures on basic child care, nutrition, and anatomy were introduced as well as components on psychoanalytic theory (Freud, 1966). Over the years the training became more formalised as more psychoanalysts joined the venture. Recorded observations of children, much like a case presentation, were used as the basis for teaching and discussion. From the Hampstead War Nurseries came the Hampstead Clinic that opened in 1952. Its clinical services included psychoanalytic treatment on a five times weekly basis for some fifty children and adolescents. At the clinic Anna and her staff held weekly case study sessions that provided practical and theoretical insights into their work. The assessment technique they used was based on developmental lines where theoretical normal growth was charted from dependency to emotional self-reliance, and diagnostic profiles that enabled the analyst to separate and identify the case specific factors in the children that deviated from, or conformed to, normal child development.

Le Fondation Parent de Rosan

Le Fondation Parent de Rosan was a fifty bed public welfare institution in Paris, France that offered temporary asylum to children between the ages of one and four who had been abandoned by their mothers and were awaiting placement. The problem for such young children, without the mother's desire to indicate to them that they are a particular and unique being, is that there is no-one to show them the way to becoming a subject in their own right. Rosine Lefort carried out interviews at Parent de Rosan between 1951–1952 as part of a research project on hospitalism, investigating the effects of prolonged institutional care on young children (Lefort & Lefort, 1980). Parent de Rosan was not a psychoanalytic treatment facility although Jenny Aubry, a pediatrician and psychoanalyst, was its director at the time. Around fifty children resided in two villas and were lodged in dormitories of eight to ten beds. The children spent most days in bed and were fed individually by a nurse who went from bed to bed while children were crying as they waited their turn. Lefort's position with the children she met was that of a psychoanalyst with a subject. The work was observational in the form of progress notes recorded after Lefort's sessions with each child. Lefort considered these treatments with the children at Parent de Rosan to be psychoanalytic experiences because the principles that structure psychoanalytic discourse guided them (Rodríguez, 1999). The outcomes were discussed retrospectively from a Lacanian perspective and published as *The Birth of the Other* many years later in collaboration with her husband Robert Lefort (Lefort & Lefort, 1980). Lefort had to contend with the effects of hospitalism and the absence of parents in all the children she saw; she believed that the effect of the institution was superimposed rather than aetiological in the child's structure, a conclusion that was also borne out by Spitz. The place for a child in an institution is that of an object to be manipulated, available to the real and excluding any form of signifying representation (Lefort & Lefort, 1980, p. 48). No other comes to account in a lasting way for a signifier that might represent them. Nonetheless, even in an institution, at the very least, everyone has to deal with the signifier, even if only to answer to his or her own name.

Sonia Shankman Orthogenic School

After his release from Buchenwald concentration camp, Bruno Bettelheim immigrated to the United States and in 1944 he became director of the Sonia Shankman Orthogenic School of the Department of Education at the University of Chicago and stayed there for the next thirty years. Bettelheim was not a psychoanalyst; he was primarily a teacher who applied his passionate interest in and knowledge of psychoanalysis to his work in the treatment, teaching and research of delinquent, psychotic, and autistic children and youths. Bettelheim reshaped psychoanalysis under the influence of his admired mentors; Sigmund Freud, Anna Freud, and Erik Erikson, but it was August Aichhorn who was Bettelheim's greatest inspiration in his fashioning of the Orthogenic School (Zelan, 1993). Following Aichhorn's lead, Bettelheim maintained that severely disturbed youngsters should be removed from the environment that fostered their symptoms and housed in a specially designed treatment milieu based on psychoanalytic principles. Bettelheim was the chief administrator who made and enforced the rules at the Orthogenic School, leaving the counsellors, teachers, and therapists to foster empathic relationships with the students. Many of his publications deal with modifications to psychoanalysis in the creation of a milieu at the Orthogenic School that he and his staff pioneered over three decades.

Bettelheim felt strongly that education was the key to recovery for many, because children with learning difficulties or who refused to learn did so for a reason, and usually this was to avoid knowing something about their past history. He encouraged the teachers to cultivate a flexible curriculum for these children so that they not only succeeded in learning but that they enjoyed learning. This was in the belief that once emotional blocks are lifted the children would want to take advantage of every opportunity to learn. Teachers at the school were also members of the therapeutic team; they recognised that there was as much learning in therapy as there was therapy in learning (Milner, 1964). At the school the children were out of reach of their parents, and home visits were strictly regulated with the spacing and length of visits at the discretion of Bettelheim and the staff. During the initial stages of a child's orientation they were protected from experiences they were unable to manage until they gained enough security to face old sources of tension and tolerate a visit home. Bettelheim tried to work with families who had child rearing problems by attending to the parent-child interactions: he focused on the emotional and social benefits of play, especially those that develop into healthy parent-child relationships, viewing a child's play as their attempt to bridge their inner reality to the world around them (Bettelheim & Sylvester, 1949). Similarly fairy tales were used to cultivate a child's developing imagination providing a forum for emotional expression.

For Bettelheim, school was a laboratory for child development and an ideal setting for the observation of a child's development over time. The school did have some success in treating delinquent and psychotic children but was less successful in their results with autism (Jacobsen, 2000; Sutton, 1995). In 1956, the Ford Foundation awarded a grant to conduct a five year study on the positive outcomes of the residential treatment of autistic children at the school. The research outcomes were published in *The Empty Fortress* where Bettelheim claimed great success in treating autistic children and he probably did in certain cases (Bettelheim, 1967). The successful outcomes in the treatment of autism claimed by Bettelheim were drastically overstated (Cohler & Friedman, 2004). There were only ever a very small number of autistic children living at the Orthogenic School at any one time. He needed positive outcomes to ensure the continuation of the grant money because he feared that if funding dried up the school might have to close. It has to be said, that the treatment of autism can be protracted as in the case of Joey, the mechanical boy (Bettelheim, 1959).

Milieu therapy

Bettelheim hired child psychiatrist and psychoanalyst Emmy Sylvester who, like him, was a Viennese refugee. She headed the counselling program at the Orthogenic School and had a significant influence on Bettelheim, as did Fritz Redl another teacher and psychoanalyst Bettelheim met at University in Vienna. Redl pioneered the residential treatment of children, including psycho-educational interventions. The collaboration between Bettelheim and Emmy Sylvester, Fritz Redl, and David Wineman produced "milieu therapy":

> Milieu therapy [...] is no more than the application of psychoanalytical concepts to the specific task of creating a setting for emotionally disturbed children who are in need of residential treatment. At the Orthogenic School, which functions as a

> therapeutic milieu, the total frame of reference is one of psychoanalytic concepts in action, and has a therapeutic value which is greater than that of individual psychotherapeutic sessions. (Bettelheim & Sylvester, 1949, p. 54)

Milieu therapy was indicated for children whose relationship with their parents or carers had become irreparably damaged and for those children who lacked the tools for making contact in interpersonal relationships. At the Orthogenic School the milieu was the whole school environment where the entire staff were used for therapeutic interactions. Based on Aichhorn's ideas, the school had very few rules and encouraged the emergence of autonomous self-regulation in the children. Bettelheim felt that a coherent milieu allowed permissiveness to be experienced as freedom, and liberty to be enjoyed rather than as a license to misbehave.

Bettelheim administered the institution as a whole; he made rounds every evening at bedtime, he conducted daily staff meetings where he oversaw the child's "central persons", and he interrogated each child's behaviour for meaning. Foremost was Bettelheim's notion that children needed central people as ego supports to nurture, observe, and interpret what was going on in the child's life. Children were to be given a corrective emotional experience and the central persons were there to provide the love and understanding thought to be lacking in the child's early life. The staff at the school were expected to be utterly devoted to the cause: they worked long shifts on a one-to-one basis with the children, they lived on the premises and provided counselling on demand, they put the children to bed, got them up and ate with them. Staff discussions and case conferences were the forum for influencing the axis around which the child's experiences revolved. In the same way, it was considered essential that the relationships of staff members to each other were coherent and supportive.

Life was structured to promote the child's reach for autonomy and every child was expected to work hard to solve his or her own problems. Within the setting of the therapeutic milieu, importance was placed on personal security, adequate instinctual gratification, and group support so that each child was sensitive to interpersonal relationships. Bettelheim communicated a sense of safety in the milieu in the use of his position as director to highlight his protective authority and ability to look after everyone. He typecast himself as a domineering control freak on the one hand, and as a caring father figure on the other. He saw the benefits of a negative transference where his role was to be a screen onto which children, parents, and even staff could project their hate and vent their anger. This was meant to encourage the children to form a trusting attachment to their counsellor within the therapy. The school used no medication or physical restraints when children misbehaved or were out of control. It was reported that Bettelheim did at times lose his temper and resort to hitting children but more often than not he used therapeutic interventions. One resident spoke of Bettelheim's approach at the school in an interview:

> What [Bettelheim] did is stress that there is a moral component to deciding whether you're going to be nuts or not. He'd give you a lot of slack if you chose to get your act straightened out. But there was a really fearful contempt for anybody he perceived was not trying. He was the last high prophet saying that you choose and we'll give you some of the wherewithal to do something with your choice but ultimately the decision is yours. (Jacobson, 2000, p. 404)

An ethnographic observational study

Jules Henry was a noted anthropologist and professor of sociology at Washington University when he accepted Bettelheim's offer to conduct research at the Sonia Shankman Orthogenic School funded by a grant from the United States Public Health Service in association with the University of Chicago. Jules Henry's ethnographic observation study of daily life at the Orthogenic School between the years 1953 to 1954 resulted in around 700 hours of direct observation of interactions between staff and children, records of staff meetings and several hundred conversations, as well as a record of the school's daily life (Henry, 1957). Every institution develops its own culture of interpersonal relationships that depend on the formal properties of the social structure. Here emotionally toned ideas and beliefs (ideo-emotional (I-E) factors) govern the nature of interpersonal relations, and are expressions of a type of social system. Henry decided to investigate the extent to which the culture of the Orthogenic School was dependent on the formal properties of its social structure.

He classified the school as belonging to the "simple undifferentiated subordination" type of social structure (Henry, 1957). In this structure all participants form a dynamic part in the school system: one person (Bettelheim) is responsible for the direction of all the tasks at the school; the therapeutic task (the patient) is treated as a unit or as a whole individual; and is managed by one person (the counsellor). This was contrasted with the typical psychiatric hospital of the "multiple differentiated" type of social structure where there is more than one superior and the patient is split up and treated as parts of an object that is distributed among several departments and handled by different kinds of personnel. In most psychiatric hospital systems, patients and personnel are not usually part of the same social system:

> [...] if one wants workers to remain *uninvolved*, lacking in autonomy and dedication to the task, and *uninterested* in self-realisation, the formal structure of the contemporary psychiatric hospital is the social device par excellence for achieving these goals. (Henry, 1957, p. 734)

In contrast the Orthogenic School developed like a small republic or a large family with its own worldview where director, staff, and patients were mutually dependent and saw themselves as distinct from the others outside. Counsellors at the school, most of whom were in personal therapy, were given significant autonomy in how they conducted their roles. They were only responsible to the director, Bettelheim, who supervised them all intensively.

There were two counsellors who were responsible for approximately forty children and adolescents who were housed in each of the six dormitories. Children received individual therapy several times a week with their counsellor and attended their school lessons each day in a schoolroom in an adjacent building. The average length of a child's stay was three years with the maximum stay being six or seven years and staff stayed in their jobs on average for six or seven years. The combination of autonomy in the staff, delegation without renunciation, and active and intense supervision resulted in mutual dependence and support between counsellors and director with a consequent radical dilution of social distance between them. Henry observed that the prerequisite for a good counsellor was self-understanding, so he wondered where a counsellor's incentive came from to do such exacting work when there was little apparent reward (Henry, 1957). He surmised that the feeling of achieving autonomy was the reason and that their energy was derived from solving their own problems. This motivation was also shared by the children who were central to the therapeutic and emotional focus as dynamic parts of the same social system. Henry based these conclusions on observations and interviews that he had with the staff. The staff spoke of the need to prove that they had something of value to give, and some experienced a blurring of boundaries with the children as they identified with them in the meeting of their own emotional needs. This was encouraged by Bettelheim, who spoke about one of the counsellors as follows:

> Grace is really not giving affection to these children; she is giving everything to Sue [an exceedingly sick schizophrenic child], and Sue cannot give anything in return. She should give affection to Daisy, Mae and Rhoda, *who can give her something* in return [...]. She does not realize that the way she will gain ultimate satisfaction is by pleasing the children. (Henry, 1957, p. 732)

Henry observed that very few institutions in our culture offered this level of reward and involvement to staff. In his opinion the prohibition on staff-patient relationships in most therapeutic environments was problematic because the segregation of interpersonal relations only promoted myths and misconceptions, such as, that those in charge possess superior mental health. Such arrangements are problematic because they can lead to situations where staff deny the impact that a certain sets of rules governing interpersonal relationships has on therapeutic praxis, while at the same time, organise themselves around such rules. Without the guiding principles such as involvement, autonomy and self-realisation as part of the social organisation, Henry believed that the Orthogenic school would not have been able to function as it did. It is interesting to note that Henry's ethnographic observational study occurred in the same time period as Rapoport's 1953 research at Henderson Hospital in England and of Stanton and Schwartz's study at Chestnut Lodge in 1954.

Bonneuil-sur-Marne experimental school

Not far from Paris, Rose-Marie and Yves Guerinin established *Le Centre de Guénouvry* in 1974 starting with only three children. Then in 1969 Maud Mannoni came and put her psychoanalytically motivated ideas based on anti-psychiatry into practice and it became known as the *École*

Expérimentale de Bonneuil-sur-Marne (Mannoni, 1999). Bonneuil was a children's educational facility that specialised in the treatment of juvenile autism, mental retardation and psychosis, and as a research and training centre for young analysts in the areas of psychoanalysis and education. It was accredited as an outpatient service in 1975, with the capacity to accommodate twenty-six children and later up to forty children aged between six and eighteen years. Mannoni was inspired by the teachings of Jacques Lacan to examine the workings of the institution and believed that psychoanalytic discourse could be used to subvert the workings of these structures. Mannoni's approach was also in line with that of Françoise Dolto, a Lacanian analyst and paediatrician, who treated children predominantly with psychosis. Mannoni introduced to Bonneuil the model of institutional psychotherapy as recommended by Tosquelles and Oury. It is derived from elements in individual psychoanalysis to transform the hospital structure itself into a tool for treatment in (Mannoni, 1967).

Mannoni explained that the hospital was a place where the patient was caught in the midst of diverse influences, opposing interests, and divergent aims and that a significant obstacle to the functioning of an institution was the existence of transferences that were "diffuse, difficult to situate, and difficult to handle" (Mannoni, 1967, pp. 226–228). For a hospital to function effectively and therapeutically it needed to be alive and flexible, the staff needed to have a dynamic interest in their work with the opportunity for career advancement, and most of all, the structure of the facility had to operate smoothly so it needed to be governed properly. Mannoni rebelled against the prevailing psychiatric approaches to the operation of institutions where madness was managed by segregation and patients grouped into categories. As a result there was a principle of non-segregation at Bonneuil where one third of the children were autistic or psychotic, one third were mentally deficient or emotionally disturbed, and one third were suffering from neurosis with varying degrees of severity. This mode of operation made it possible to maintain a mix of symptomatologies that had the potential to open up dynamic perspectives.

Establishing the milieu

In the beginning at Bonneuil, children taken into analysis were seen separately so that their analysis had no connection to the institution; the same as being seen in private practice except that the analyst did see the child in the institution. Defining the context within which one is to function is important, so the analyst has to be careful that analytic discourse is given preference as the symbolic compass for a child's words. However, this is difficult in an institution where many specialists can have a confusing influence over a child, so it is inevitable that an institutional group would feel the analyst's presence as an intrusion, with the possibility of it producing persecutory anxiety. Here the analyst represents a confrontation with their unconscious Oedipal myth. "The analyst is for the other, the one who is deemed to know" (Mannoni, 1967, p. 230). Consequently, "If the analyst does not concern himself with the institution, the institution will concern itself with the analyst" (Mannoni, 1967, p. 231). Hinshelwood (1987) described this in terms of the denial and destruction of productive contact between people in an institution that can occur when an idealised form of human contact is amplified and preserved by splitting it off into suitable containing objects. The most suitable natural targets for these projections are psychoanalysts who are feared as dangerous and maddening. Thus they are denigrated and in turn idealised; they are condescended to and disparaged in a way that significantly reduces the effectiveness of the work of analysis in the institution.

With the opening of the Bonneuil experimental school, there was an aggressive struggle for prestige in the pecking order of the hierarchy and this resulted in serious communication problems. The teachers resented the analyst's position as the place of the observer in the group's imaginary fascination, and until the psychoanalysts joined the transference it remained a stalemate. This oppressiveness filtered down to the children as the anxiety escalated and is evocative of the impasse at Nonette discussed in chapter four. If the fantasy elements are not exposed then further defensiveness ensues with the possibility of understanding the meaning of what is going is lost, closing down an atmosphere of inquiry:

> Neurotically exercised authority has perverting effects, owing to the sadomasochistic relationships it sets up. When the functions of authority are perverted, there is no longer reference to the Law as the guardian of order; the relations of subjects to each other are reduced to the dimension of a duel relation. (Mannoni, 1967, p. 239)

Team research was undertaken in progress meetings with analysts and teachers where work and study subsequently became mediators in interpersonal links. This then paved the way for what might be possible between teachers and students who developed the task of working on a class project, thus diffusing the hierarchical location of authority. Progress occurred in a two steps forward and one step back manner as imaginary fears were more easily overcome, and the symbolic space was preserved, facilitating ongoing questioning and preventing acting-out. Psychoanalysts, Robert Lefort and Pierre Fedida, from the University of Paris VII, supervised the team in weekly meetings to managing themselves in the face of roles distortions in the institution.

It became clear to Mannoni that individual psychoanalysis at Bonneuil had no meaning unless it was integrated within the institution as a whole, requiring a rethink of the basic structure of the establishment. The aim was to ensure that the work done in analysis was not undone in the institution, because an institutional structure is closely related to the family structure from which the child has come. Mannoni proposed that the analysis of a child was not significantly different from that of an adult, but the child had first of all to be approached through the representation that the parents had of their child. The parents are always implicated in the child's symptom and the driving force of resistance to the treatment is their unconscious wish that nothing change. Accordingly it is of prime importance to have the child's parents involved in the treatment, and no treatment was undertaken at Bonneuil if parents refused to see the analyst. For Mannoni the disturbed child is the spokesperson for the dysfunctional family, whose history is expressed in the child's symptoms and reinforced by social exclusion.

Activities at the school

Originally the team members at Bonneuil were all volunteers who worked in exchange for psychoanalytic training and clinical work under supervision because there were not enough funds to pay specialist wages. The work proceeded with guidelines for a framework that would provide them with their bearings so that the venture would survive. These guidelines had to guarantee the law at Bonneuil, otherwise the structure would fail and order would be lost. It is around certain laws that human (symbolic) order is established so that an individual can locate him or herself with regard to their own desire and the Other's desire. The aim in the beginning of this institution was to listen to the children and to work with them on the rules for communal life. The children were encouraged to give voice to their fears, destructive feelings, and fantasies. Central to Mannoni's therapeutic approach was the cultivation of the capacity to play that makes loss bearable. She sought to free the child from the smothering effect of the anxiety generated by the Other by helping him or her to find a personal language in the symbolic. An example of this was the grumbles book where the children wrote down all their complaints, ideas, and suggestions in a book that was studied, read, and discussed at a general meeting at the end of each week. At meetings everyone spoke without fear of being judged or punished and this purging of oneself through expression in words had the effect of binding the group together. A cooperative council made up of adults and children was created at Bonneuil to arrange the daily program, the allocation of jobs and the making of decisions about the running of the community:

> The importance accorded to the child's speech in a collective prevents the institution from becoming rigid [...]. The patient spontaneously offers resistance to change, as if seeking firm boundaries to control the part of himself that feels endangered by the dynamism and movement of a changing world. The framework of institutional activities is the repository of the patient's fantasmatic world and must become the object of analysis in order to undo the patient's psychotic bonds with the institution. The inertia of the institutional framework protects against anxiety. (Mannoni, 1999, p. 113)

One of the first structuring points of reference at Bonneuil was "the studio". The framework that the studio provided for creative expression worked as a container for anxiety and an outlet for aggressively, without which a child would be left alone in his or her fantasy world where they would be more likely to act out. Another guideline was respect for the equipment used in the studios, and yet another significant one was a prohibition of sexual contact between the children and adolescents. "Speech can arise from a field of language, but not from a cacophony" (Mannoni, 1999, p. 106). Throughout life an individual is exposed to restrictions that are imposed, generating the symbolic value of castration. Mannoni stressed that desire depends on prohibition and the acceptance of one's own castration creates the lack from which desire proceeds.

The creative life at Bonneuil was centred in the studios and took the form of theatre, painting, music, storytelling, pottery, sculpture, and creative movement, dance and play, and it thrived. Every day started with chat time in small groups followed by schoolwork and then studio time or outside activities. A particular concern was how to introduce autistic children to ways of speaking with their bodies when words were absent, but still give them the right to refuse to participate. "The body in analysis is the body of which one speaks" (Mannoni, 1999, p. 118). Mannoni drew upon the work of Margaret Mahler, Piera Aulagnier, R. D. Laing, and D. W. Winnicott in the areas of a child's body representation, alienation in the body, the child's place in the mother's fantasy, and the function of transitional objects in autism and psychosis. The double failure in psychosis, in particular autism and schizophrenia, is located on one hand in the symbolic domain with problems in language and on the other in the imaginary domain with problems with the body. The psychotic subject's ego-image excludes a realistic concept of their body, making certain signifiers rooted in bodily experience inaccessible. In the first instance, clay (painting or music could be substituted) was used for the children to explore their hands and they chose whether to explore alone or collectively. Art aims at disrupting ordinary life where despair and madness become concerns for all. To be a true painter the materials, the mixing of colour, the cleaning of brushes, and the paper are all considerations in the overall product. "For there are many symptoms that have to be integrated into the painting by finding the right words that will enable the child to displace a crisis" (Mannoni, 1999, p. 133). The temptation to restore order based on a reflex action that leads to punishment and rejection misses the opportunity of naming the child's suffering and integrating it with the symptom in the painting. Children were introduced to the studio with great care and maternal attention so that they felt safe and could choose when they felt able to take their place and participate.

The stage was thought to be a way to enable the mute language of autistic children to find expression in removing the inhibitions of the body by creating a physical presence, and so Antonin Artaud and Jerzy Grotowski (Actor and Director) introduced theatre to Bonneuil. This is reminiscent of the annual theatre performances by the residents at La Borde and other places. Learning to be an actor requires the discipline of physical exercise and body movement, breath and voice training, improvisation and miming to release resistances and overcome fear. Artaud and Grotowski made use of everything a child produced, and from their gestures, sounds, and cries they constructed language. In a play or a piece of theatre, freed from a rigid script, the children could use their own imagination to translate a message into language and send it to each other and to the audience. Care has to be taken because signification of the body produces a fragmentation or the potential for fragmentation of the subject because the body is not represented as a whole but as separate components in the real. In psychosis the body is untrustworthy; it loses its boundaries, its corporeal nature and its singularity, or else it acquires incomprehensible characteristics.

Another workshop at Bonneuil was storytelling by a student of Fedida, an African woman, who told to the children tales and myths about her childhood and village life in Africa. Because the story being told was the storyteller's own story they were personally implicated in their own narrative and the children were also agents in a story that at various points converged with their own. The stories introduced taboos, rites of passage, and consequences for breaking the law with symbolic messages about sexuality, marriage, birth, and death, and an orientation to the previous generation. While they listened to the stories the children handled and moulded clay, working and reworking it as the narrative was reflected in as a bodily experience. Mannoni described how easy it was to lapse in the priority placed on a child's speech when in 1975 an intrusion came from outside meaning that the original constitution of Bonneuil had to be altered to conform to government legislation regarding child welfare and education. In the restructure the regular meetings chaired by the children stopped, visits to artisans in the town stopped, the approach to schooling changed etc. So when they became aware of this they had to safeguard making room for a place for the child's speech and for analytic listening. The theme of making and remaking space for speech over and over is a central one, as is the ease with which it is forgotten. *Vivre* à *Bonneuil* is a documentary film about life at Bonneuil made in 1975; directed by Guy Séligmann it featured Roger Gentis, Robert Lefort, and Maud Mannoni.

The exploded institution

To combat the unconscious law within the institutional group that can, at times, be under the pressure of a threatening superego, the community's focus was directed towards external life outside. What became central to the experiment of Bonneuil was the idea of the "exploded or burst institution" (in French *institution éclaté*), an institution open to the outer world, but at the same time staying in a protected space (Mannoni, 1999, p. 112). It is a place that opens up and spreads out so that different perspectives and levels of complexity can be examined. When attention is directed to what is going on in the outside world it acts as a counterbalance to what the group internalises. For example, children who graduated from Bonneuil were encouraged to come back to visit and speak about what they were doing since leaving, including others who were invited in from outside to contribute something to the daily activities. In addition, each week the children went to the local town to call in at the workshop of a local craftsman or artisan, to visit someone, go shopping or to just have an outing.

What determined the analyst's role in this setting was the specific place occupied with and for the children on their journey. This could be in cooking, cleaning, working alongside artisans or farmers, the studio activities or schoolwork. The analyst mediates in all these activities making it possible to avoid an imaginary construction where relations between adult and child are built without reference to a third party. However, the third party, the Other, is always present but the analyst facilitates its emergence. The analyst attends to the fact that the transference is revealed in every imaginary relation that appears when speech is manifest and directed to the Other. In this context, analysts need to be mindful of their own aggressive potential and so avoid acting out from a position of dominance. The theory at Bonneuil was based on the work of retrospective interpretation that examines individual pathways in the context of institutional life. The constant oscillation between theory and praxis, especially in activities of the many studios and work groups, came to characterise the analyst's paradoxical place in the institution.

One of the intentions of the pioneers of group residential care was to advocate the need to simplify the lives of children and youths who had known only chaos and to create an atmosphere in which everything had a purpose and where predictable positive responses were given unconditionally. "Going through life with some psychological limp need not be a serious impairment when one is helped to make the best of it" (Milner, 1964, p. 102). The therapeutic relationship with children necessitates special qualities in the therapist, and particular training is required for working in residential treatment centres, whether it is a school, orphanage, psychiatric unit, therapeutic community, or community service.

CONCLUSION

The purpose of this book was to explore the possible contributions psychoanalysis makes to the treatment of psychosis in today's institutional structures. Thus, consideration has been given to the influence of psychoanalysis in both the treatment of psychosis and to an understanding of how institutions function. The institutional environment considered in this book goes beyond the bricks and mortar of a hospital complex to include community and hospital health care, its services to patients and staff, its history, traditions, and social organisations. Although, in the last few decades, the psychiatric management of people with psychosis has reduced its reliance on institutional types of care, a certain level of institutional care will always be needed. Deinstitutionalisation led to the construction of alternate networks for social and psychiatric services that do not fulfil the function of asylum, shelter and protection that institutions did provide at one time. Even an ideal community service will fall short of a reality that is characterised by disenfranchised, alienated people who are often homeless or isolated in boarding houses, and who are repeatedly hospitalised for short stays with little or no improvement over time. It is not institutions in themselves that were the problem in institutionalisation, but the human beings responsible for managing these institutions that perpetuated mindlessness and neglect. A plea is made for retaining the asylum function of the institution:

> Until we can cure psychotic illnesses, some of our patients will require asylum, and we need to pursue reimbursement mechanisms that will enable us to provide it. What we call the places where these patients reside—asylums, sheltered settings or long term residences—is immaterial. What is important is that we find ways to offer humane asylum in our communities for the frail, inadequate, and inept mentally ill who need it. (Talbot, 2004, p. 1127)

In recent times, the same criteria believed to be useful in running a business are now applied to all institutions regardless of the type of business. In health systems, the nexus between patient and medical services has become an economic one for the reason that the organising metaphor of the provider has taken over, and economic realities tend to supersede the primary task of the delivery of health care. They have become dominated by budgetary restrictions and the demands of the market place with token attention paid to the nature of the treatment the patient requires beyond the expediency of brief, cost-effective therapies, and pharmacological cures. The obligation for a caring asylum, where people are able to express themselves, engage in fulfilling activity and participate in decisions that affect their lives will not go away.

Applied psychoanalysis is the extension of the work of psychoanalysis into the institutional arena. When psychoanalysis is applied in an institution it takes place within a complex structure that comprises a network of relationships and it offers an effective integrating function. Generally, a psychoanalytic model is best understood as providing care that varies along a continuum. This would include a basic structure that responds to crisis and fragmentation but is flexible enough to also place importance on listening to the patient and trying to decode what is going on for them and their family or carers. From this a formulation could be made about a treatment approach that may or may not include a secure and protective institutional system where the patient and the treatment team determine a multifaceted interactive field. The adoption of a psychoanalytic orientation to the psychiatric field affords a way for complex dynamics and processes to be understood, monitored and used therapeutically in a wide range of settings with a variety of people.

The origin of many problems in institutions is due to the failure of practitioners to question their own practices. This can be the result of poor clinical leadership and management where personnel do not maintain professional standards and supervision, or when they have had inadequate training for the job they are required to perform. When this occurs in a work setting the cumulative effects of staff shortages, recruiting difficulties or a restricted labour pool can lead to serious problems in morale, a lack of commitment to the project and staff who will have no desire for the work they are doing. As always, poor patient outcomes are the result. An institution is a social system within which any action can have meaning. Potential knowledge will only become known if systems are put in place to study the institution, and this means relinquishing power and control. This control is built into the fundamental workings of a service structure or a hospital's policies, procedures, techniques, and even in its use of language where patients are objects of care. Sociological research indicates that little overall change is likely to occur in response to institutional problems when there is resistance to social change and this is more likely in institutions whose social defence systems are dominated by primitive psychic defence mechanisms.

The presence of psychoanalysis in psychiatric institutions takes on different connotations and meanings according to the psychoanalyst's position and role. To work effectively in an institution, the analyst needs to be cognisant of the institutional dynamics within which the work proceeds. The "institution-in-the-mind" is a concept used in organisational consultancy to deliberate on the relevance of psychoanalytic knowledge in institutional settings as a method of attention to and interpretation of emotional experience (Armstrong, 1996). One of the principles of the therapeutic community is for the institution to examine and treat itself as a living and learning situation. A contribution of psychoanalysis to this perspective is a "culture of enquiry" where the dynamics of the institution's culture welcomes an attitude of openness to questioning so that understanding is owned by all and not seen as solely residing in a few professionals (Griffiths & Hinshelwood, 1995). All those involved in the institution are encouraged to be curious about themselves, each other, the institution, the staff, the management structure, psychological processes, group function, and everything else relevant to events and relationships within the community. The capacity to sustain a culture of enquiry needs support, and one of the most important ways of sustaining this level of enquiry is to be clear about the central focus of the work.

The experiment at Le Courtil was aimed at finding out if it was possible to lodge psychoanalytic discourse at the heart of the institution by subverting the institution through psychoanalysis. The ethical response of psychoanalysis is to the singularity of each patient's discourse and this is where the institution becomes particular and different for each individual. For a psychoanalyst to operate in an institution it can only be from a position outside of that of specialist by making a particular choice to avoid the usual traps associated with groups, organisations, and institutions. Mannoni (1999) believed that psychoanalytic discourse could be used to subvert the workings of institutional structures. The organisation of the institution functions as the "exploded" or "burst" institution where the community develops the capacity to open up and spread out, allowing different perspectives and levels of complexity. The back-and-forth movement between theory and praxis characterises the paradoxical position of the analyst in the institution. When attention is directed to what is going on in the outside world, it acts as a counterbalance to what is being internalised by the group.

Emergent themes

The themes that emerged most strongly in the book were, firstly the importance of conceptual models to orient the work with patients and to guide how the institution functions, and secondly was the significance of how effective an institution was at examining itself ethically and psychoanalytically.

Most institutions make use of institutional models that are derived from various theoretical sources. Institutions oriented to psychoanalytic are usually contributed to by particular schools of thought, such as: object relations, post-Kleinian psychoanalysis, ego psychology, interpersonal psychotherapy, and Lacanian psychoanalysis. Four institutional models that were identified show how psychoanalytic models were adapted in psychiatric institutions in the United States, France, Italy, and the United Kingdom (Vigorelli, 1998). Interestingly, many of the models of institutional care that prevailed were an amalgam of other theoretical orientations that were merged to produce a unique approach that suited their particular needs. An institutional model of healthcare ought to consider a range of approaches and services that are flexible enough to adjust to the needs of patients as they enter and recover from psychosis and give support to them continuing with individual psychoanalysis or any other kind of therapy if they so choose. The institutional field model is an example of this as it provides a global outlook in the investigation of institutional life by offering a bridge between the individual and the group where teamwork is representative of the group work of an institution (Correale & Di Leone, 2001). The first purpose of this model is the provision of an environment that holds and contains, thus offering the patient protection from dislocation and further fragmentation. The second purpose is the way the team facilitates the creation of a significant personal relationship with the patient that evolves and opens up a space for their speech. The attitude and position of the team is therefore the equivalent of a structuring function that offers protection, asylum, and the potential for gradual integration. The psychoanalytic milieu orients the institutional work with patients and therefore guides how the institution functions.

Careful consideration is given to the practice of psychoanalysis at Le Courtil where the primarily focus is at the level of the training of the team who can have an effect within the institution (Stevens, 2002a). The intention is to disrupt the development of institutional ideals through analytic discourse that is constitutive of the institution. Central to this model is the wish to avoid the pitfalls of the psychoanalyst becoming a specialist in the institution; hence the decision not to practice individual psychoanalytic treatments. At Le Courtil it is the institution that operates psychoanalytically to support the work with psychosis in a specific way by allowing a space for the person without a treatment agenda. It is here that the institution operates as a place of asylum, a guarantee of order, and as a limit in the face of an intrusive, uncontrolled Other that harasses the psychotic subject.

In general, institutional models utilise a particular kind of knowledge that is adopted and directed to the whole institution making it possible to understand previously unexplored events. An institution's attitude to examining itself psychoanalytically can be seen in the example of Cassel Hospital in England where a culture of enquiry was aimed at preserving the uniqueness of each individual and thwarting the temptation to idealise psychoanalysis or the institution. Institutions that operate psychoanalytically do so in a specific way by allowing a space for the patient to emerge. To succeed in applying psychoanalysis in an institution, the model has to be constantly questioned by staff on all levels. To do this it is necessary to acknowledge and confront what will always be a symptom there in the determinants of the master's discourse. In order to work in an institution, staff, and patients have to deal with the effects of the master's discourse because each person has to take responsibility for how they face the specificity of how this is manifest in the transference. This stems from the knowledge that the transference in psychosis is problematic and it is here that a major difficulty occurs in the work with psychosis. The institutional psychotherapy practiced at La Borde requires permanent analysis of the institutional countertransference (Guattari, 1984). The emotional reactions of the staff, their interrelations, and the social and administration relations of the institution determine the therapeutic action of the institution. The containment of severe disturbance brings relief to both patients and staff since what is experienced as unbearable in institutional responses needs to be continually monitored and considered. The organisation has to integrate the individuality and uniqueness of each member with a collective agreement on the therapeutic aim of the work.

What makes an organisation a healthy place to work is the number of "well-functioning" individuals with stable senses of identity who work there (Kets de Vries, 2001). These individuals are capable of reality testing, can take responsibility for their actions, are resourceful and can manage anxiety effectively. The culture of an organisation is based on accumulated collective learning, a shared history and a pattern of common basic assumptions (Schein, 2010). The effective articulation by the leader of a vision that is possible for the group to achieve, and a mission that gives the group direction is fundamental for a successful organisational culture. An authentic organisation "has a compelling connective quality for its employees in its vision, mission, culture, and structure" (Kets de Vries, 2001, p. 108). Such organisations have an ethos that is carried by the institution's leaders who are able to communicate clearly and convincingly the importance and meaning in each person's task within the work place. To create an authentic and effective institution, leaders need to generate a sense of purpose for the people who work there. A group will pass elements of its culture on to new generations of group members as they enter the institution.

The subjective truth that underlies organisational problems needs to be approached through peoples' discourse, which is thought to determine most of the problems in the first place. In order to break the cycle of repetition, clinicians, as subjects, have to set in motion a process of symbolisation aimed at modifying their relationship to the signifiers that closely condition them professionally and this means they recover a new scope for action. To do this it is incumbent on the professional to refrain from occupying a position as expert but rather "[...] to adopt the position of an analyst who questions practices, encourages symbolisation, and pays attention to peculiarities in people's accounts of their work" (Arnaud & Vanheule, 2007, p. 364). Accordingly, the professional must agree to constantly throw into question their perceptions and attitudes, and their own relation to the role they occupy in the organisation. The subject in divided by its very nature and its constitution is conflictual in its organisation.

Strategies for clinical practice in institutions

A number of other themes emerged during the course of researching the topic of the influence psychoanalysis has in understanding institutions and the treatment of patients with psychosis. A historical perspective allows reflection on the discoveries of Freud and the pioneer analysts in the early years of research and experimentation in the application psychoanalysis. The pioneers had no way of knowing what kind of patients would be suitable for the psychoanalytic method. These early researchers made discoveries that still have influence on psychoanalysts today who benefit from a rich inheritance. With the decline in psychoanalysis has come an upsurge in the popularity of short-term psychological treatments and the proliferation of biological approaches, specifically, psychotropic medications.

Concepts derived from psychoanalytic research help to develop strategies for the clinical work with psychosis. A greater contribution from psychoanalysis in the areas of training for mental health professionals, especially allied health professionals would include supervision, theoretical, and clinical studies in conjunction with multi-disciplinary clinical discussion. Psychoanalysis is invaluable in the supervision of students and staff as a means of investigating and understanding the dynamics that influence a patient, a group, a team or the whole hospital or service. A position of seniority in the bureaucratic hierarchy is not enough to guarantee that adequate expert supervision is being offered to staff. The level of skill and training of an individual should determine the role of a supervisor and preferably that they come from outside the structure rather than from within. Undertaking one's own personal therapy or analysis is considered to be the cornerstone of ethical analytic practice.

The aim of the treatment of psychosis is the introduction of a space for containment of disruptive elements so that a form of stabilisation has an opportunity of occurring. The basis for this is established via the transference within the frame of the analytic discourse, and this can be achieved within or outside of an institutional structure. An understanding of psychoanalytic theory can help inform the management of the transference and the logic behind certain interventions, including the design of psychiatric treatment plans and approaches to community care, how to deal with family and relationship issues, and other matters, such as occupational and social needs. The patient and the treatment team come together to determine a complex interactive field. In order for rich and productive work to occur in an institution and its services, rather than just applying a technique, psychoanalysis has to be a mental attitude that is coupled with an ability to listen.

The dominant ethos of a psychoanalytically informed institution is its potential for the provision of asylum, care, and management of behaviourally disorganised and psychotic individuals, including the possibility of psychoanalytic treatment. But the role of psychoanalysis in an institution is not solely the treatment of the patient, more importantly it is the provision of a space for psychoanalytic listening so that all the others in the institution have an opportunity of being involved in a collective discourse. Institutions that are truly psychoanalytic can be identified by the way the whole service is set up and organised according to a shared ethos or culture analogous to that which characterises the theoretical model of reference. Difficulties with collaboration arise if the orientation of an institution is not clearly defined at the outset. For an institution to be viable patients and staff need to be able to find the means of making progress within it, so it is very important that the staff are aligned with the institution's philosophical orientation or *reason d'être*. Transformational leaders build on the assumption that all members of the organisation should be allowed to develop to their full potential.

The focus on social processes in the institutions highlights the impact that staff attitudes have in creating a therapeutic atmosphere and how the idea of "the hospital as a whole", initiated by the therapeutic community model, can act as a re-socialising agent with the patient as an active participant in the process. However, phenomena such as the "revolving door", brief admissions policy and inconsistency in the presence and dependability of key staff promote insecure attachment. The move from institutional care to community-based services took place without adequate recognition of the continuing need for a stable hospital home base or the back up of a close-knit community to provide institutional care of the right kind. It is unlikely that an institution would incorporate a particular space in its structure for the therapeutic relationship unless it was an institution that examined itself and made a decision to place importance on the therapeutic relationship as a vital ingredient to the success of a patient's treatment. To achieve this, an institution would need to make a conscious effort to integrate a theoretical model of treatment and apply it at its heart. Psychoanalysis is a deliberate act, a choice that has to be sustained and maintained for it to endure. To continue to keep the momentum going a series of ongoing acts need to occur so that a psychoanalytic approach to institutional life can persist.

APPENDIX

List of institutions

	Institution	*Country*	*Psychoanalytic influence*	*Associated leaders*	*Type*
1	Austen Riggs Center	USA	Erikson, Lacan, & object relations	Erikson, Knight	Psychiatric hospital & TC
2	Bellevue Sanatorium	Switzerland	Freud & Existential analysis	Binswanger	Psychiatric hospital
3	Henderson Hospital (Belmont Social Rehabilitation Unit)	UK	Klein & Social theory	Jones	Psychiatric hospital & TC
4	Bonneuil-sur-Marne	France	Lacan & institutional psychoanalysis	Mannoni	Residential school
5	La Borde Clinic	France	Freud & Lacan	Oury, Aubry, Guattari	Psychiatric hospital
6	Burghölzli Clinic	Switzerland	Freud	Bleuler, Jung, Abraham, Binswanger	Psychiatric hospital

(*Continued*)

	Institution	*Country*	*Psychoanalytic influence*	*Associated leaders*	*Type*
7	Cassel Hospital	UK	Anna Freud, Klein, & object relations	Main	Psychiatric hospital & TC
8	Chestnut Lodge Sanatorium	USA	Ego psychology & interpersonal psychotherapy	Bullard, Fromm-Reichmann	Psychiatric hospital
9	Le Courtil	Belgium	Freud & Lacan	Stevens	Psychiatric hospital
10	Le Fondation Parent de Rosan	France	Lacan	Le Fort, Aubry	Orphanage
11	GIFRIC Centre	Canada	Freud & Lacan	Apollon, Catin Bergeron	Psychiatric hospital
12	Hampstead War Nurseries	England	Anna Freud	Dorothy Burlingham	Nurseries
13	Hollymoor Military Hospital	England	British object relations school, Tavistock	Bion, Foulkes, Rickman, Bridger, Main	Army hospital Northfield
14	Menninger Clinic	USA	Ego psychology	Menninger, Wallerstein	Psychiatric hospital
15	Nonette	France	Freud & Lacan	Tosquelles	Psychiatric hospital
16	Schloss Tegel Sanatorium	Germany	Freud	Simmel	Psychiatric hospital
17	Sheppard and Enoch Pratt Hospital	USA	Interpersonal psychotherapy	Sullivan	Psychiatric hospital
18	Sonia Shankman Orthogenic School	USA	Anna Freud, Erikson, & Aichhorn	Bettelheim, Sylvester, Redl	Residential school

REFERENCES

Abraham, K. (1949a). Notes on the psycho-analytical investigation and treatment of manic-depressive insanity and allied conditions. D. Bryan & A. Strachey (Trans.). In: E. Jones (Ed.), *Selected Papers of Karl Abraham* 13; London: The Hogarth Press & the Institute of Psycho-analysis, pp. 137–156.

Abraham, K. (1949b). Development of the libido: The psycho-analytic therapy of manic-depressive states. D. Bryan & A. Strachey (Trans.). In: E. Jones (Ed.), *Selected Papers of Karl Abraham* (13; London: The Hogarth Press & the Institute of Psycho-analysis), pp. 476–480.

Aichhorn, A. (1984). *Wayward Youth*. New York: Northwestern University Press & Viking Press.

Alanen, Y. (1997a). *Schizophrenia: Its origins and need-adapted treatment*. London: Karnac.

Alanen, Y. (1997b). Vulnerability to schizophrenia and psychotherapeutic treatment of schizophrenic patients: Towards an integrated view. *Psychiatry, 60(Summer)*: 142–157.

Alanen, Y., Räkköläinen, V., Rasimus, R., Laakso, J., & Kaljonen, A. (1985). Psychotherapeutically oriented treatment of schizophrenia: Results of 5-year-follow-up. *Acta Psychiatrica Scandinavica, 71*(S319): 31–49.

Amado, G. (1995) Why psychoanalytical knowledge helps us understand organisations; A discussion with Elliott Jacques, *Human Relations, 48*(4): 351–358.

American Psychiatric Association (Eds.) (2013). *Diagnostic and Statistical Manual of Mental Disorders DSM-V.* 5: Washington, DC: American Psychiatric Association.

Andreasen, N. (1999). Understanding the causes of schizophrenia. *The New England Journal of Medicine, 340*(8): 645–648.

Anzieu, D. (1984). *The Group and the Unconscious.* B. Kilbourne (Trans.). London: Routledge & Kegan Paul.

Apollon, W. (1991). Theory and tractice in the tsychoanalytic teatment of psychosis. In: R. Bracher (Ed.), *Lacan and the Subject of Language.* New York: Routledge, pp. 116–140.

Apollon, W., Bergeron, D., & Cantin, L. (2002). *After Lacan: Clinical Practice and the Subject of the Unconscious.* New York: SUNY Press.

Armstrong, D. (1995). The "institution in the mind": Reflections on the relation of psycho-analysis to work with institutions. In: D. Armstrong, W. G. Lawrence, & R. M. Young (Eds.), *Group Relations: An Introduction.* London: Process Press.

Armstrong, D. (1996). The recovery of meaning. Paper presented at the 13th Annual Meeting of the International Society for the Psychoanalytic Study of Organizations, New York.

Arnaud, G., & Vanheule, S. (2007). The division of the subject and the organization: A Lacanian approach to subjectivity at work. *Journal of Organizational Change Management, 20*(3): 359–369.

Austen Riggs Center (2015). The Austen Riggs Center Web Site Retrieved 16/3/2015, 2015, from www.austenriggs.org/about-austen-riggs-center

Avila, L. A. (2003). Georg Groddeck: Originality and exclusion. *History of Psychiatry, 14*(1): 83–101.

Bachmann, S., Resch, F., & Mundt, C. (2003). Psychological treatments for psychosis: History and overview. *Journal of The American Academy of Psychoanalysis and Dynamic Psychiatry, 31*(1): 155–176.

Bain, A. (1998). Social defenses against organizational learning. *Human Relations, 51*(3): 413–430.

Banet, A. G., & Hayden, C. (1977). A Tavistock primer. In: J. E. Jones & J. W. Pfeiffer (Eds.), *The 1977 Annual Handbook for Group Facilitators.* La Jolla, CA: University Associates, pp. 155–167.

Barnes, E. (1968). *Psychosocial Nursing.* London: Tavistock.

Barton, R. (1972). Institutional Neurosis. *British Medical Journal, 1(5798)*: 505.

Barzilai, S. (1997). History is not the past: Lacan's critique of Ferenczi. *Psychoanal Review, 84*(4): 553–572.

Basaglia, F. (1964). The destruction of the mental hospital as a place of institutionalisation (Direttore Ospedale Psichiatrico Provinciale di Gorizia). Paper presented at the First international congress of social psychiatry, London, pp. 1–5.

Bechgaard, B. (2003). Lessons in how to ruin a study in psychotherapy effectiveness: A critical review of the follow-up study from Chestnut Lodge. *Journal of the American Academy of Psychoanalysis and Dynamic Psychiatry*, *31*(1): 119–140.

Bell, D. (1997). Inpatient psychotherapy: The art of the impossible. *Psychoanalytic Psychotherapy*, *11*(1): 3–18.

Bergeron, D. (2002). The work of the dream and jouissance in the treatment of the psychotic. In: W. Apollon, D. Bergeron, & L. Cantin (Eds.), *After Lacan: Clinical Practice and the Subject of the Unconscious*. New York: SUNY Press, pp. 71–86.

Besserer, P. (2002). When the surprise makes the clinic. *Courtil Papers*, pp. 1–8.

Berke, J. (1997). Anti-Psychiatry: The ethical and practical alternatives to traditional treatment. In: B. Davidson & P. Barker (Eds.). *Psychiatric nursing: Ethical strife (Vol. Chapter 6)*. London: Hodder Arnold, p. 384.

Bettelheim, B. (1959). Joey: A "mechanical boy", *Scientific American*, *200* (March), pp. 116–20.

Bettelheim, B. (1967). *The Empty Fortress: Infantile Autism and the Birth of the Self*. New York: The Free Press.

Bettelheim, B., & Sylvester, E. (1949). Milieu therapy: Indications and illustrations. *Psychoanalytic Review*, *36*: 54–68.

Biddle, S. (1936). Wayward Youth. *Psychoanal Quarterly*, *5*: 119–31.

Binet, E. (1999). Françoise Dolto (1908–88). *Prospects: The Quarterly Review of Comparative Education*. Paris, UNESCO: International Bureau of Education, pp. *XXIX*(3), 445–454.

Binswanger, L. (1958–1959). Existential analysis and psychotherapy. *Psychoanalytic Review*, *45C*: 79–83.

Bion, W. R. (1952). Group dynamics: A re-view. *International Journal of Psycho-Analysis*, *33*: 235–247.

Bion, W. R. (1955). Language and the schizophrenic. In: M. Klein, P. Heimann, & R. Money-Kyrle (Eds.), *New Directions in Psychoanalysis*. London: Tavistock Publications, pp. 220–239.

Bion, W. R. (1961). *Experiences in Groups and Other Papers*. London: Tavistock.

Bion, W. R. (1962). A theory of thinking. *International Journal of Psycho-Analysis*, *43*.

Bion, W. R. (1963). *Elements of psycho-analysis*. London: William Heinemann.

Bion, W. R. (1967). Differentiation of the psychotic from the non-psychotic part of the personalities *Second Thoughts*. New York: Jason Aronson.

Bion, W. R. (2007). *Second Thoughts*. London & New York: Karnac.

Bion, W. R. (1980). *Experiences in groups and other papers*. London: Human Relations.

Bion, W. R., & Rickman, J. (1943). Intra-group tensions in therapy their study as the task of the group. *The Lancet, 242*(6274): 678–82.

Bleger, J. (1967). Psycho-analysis of the psycho-analytic frame. *International Journal of Psycho-Analysis, 48*: 511–519.

Bleuler, E. (1950). *Dementia praecox or the group of schizophrenias*. J. Zinkin (Trans.). 1911 Edition. New York: International Universities Press.

Bloch, S., & Singh, B. S. (Eds.) (2001). *Foundations of Clinical Psychiatry*. Melbourne: Melbourne University Press.

Bott-Spillius, E. (1990). The unconscious in culture and society: Asylum and society. In: E. Trist & H. Murray (Eds.). *The Social Engagement of Social Science: A Tavistock Anthology*. 1: University of Pennsylvania Press, pp. 586–613.

Briggs, D. (1959). Social psychiatry in Great Britain. *The American Journal of Nursing, 59*(2): 215–220.

Brill, A. (1934). Remarks introductory to the symposium on the relation of psychoanalysis to psychiatry. Paper presented at the *Ninetieth Annual Meeting of the American Psychiatric Association, Section on Psychoanalysis*, May 28–June 1. New York: APA, pp. 1089–1092.

Brody, E., & Redlich, F. (Eds.). (1952). *Psychotherapy with Schizophrenics*. New York: International Universities Press.

Bullard, D. (1939). The application of psychoanalytic psychiatry to the psychoses. *Psychoanalytic Review, 26*: 526–534.

Bullard, D. (1954). Foreword: *The mental patient: A study of institutional participation in psychiatric illness and treatment*. London: Tavistock Publications Limited, pp. v–vii.

Bullard, D. M. (1952). Problems of clinical administration. *Bulletin of the Menninger Clinic, XVI*: 193–201.

Caldwell, L. (2001). Continuities and discontinuities at the Cassel Hospital Richmond 1977–1982. *Psychoanalytic Studies, 3(3/4)*.

Callaway, B. J. (2002). *Hildegard Peplau: Psychiatric Nurse of the Century*. United States: Springer Publishing Comapny, p. 488.

Campling, P. (2001). Therapeutic communities. (The Royal College of Psychiatrists). *Advances in Psychiatric Treatment, 7*(5): 365–372.

Cantin, L. (2009). An effective treatment of psychosis with psychoanalysis in Québec City, since 1982. *Annual Review of Critical Psychology, 7*: 286–319.

Cassel Hospital (2005). The Cassel Hospital, 2005. Retrieved 2005 from www.thecasselhospital.org/

The Cassel Hospital (2008). Psychodynamic Psychosocial Nursing. Available at: www.uel.ac.uk/programmes/tavistock/postgraduate/psychodynamic-psychosocial.htm

Cassel Hospital (2015) NHS Choices: The Cassel Hospital, Website: www.wlmht.nhs.uk/

Charles, M. (2008). A view from Riggs: Treatment resistance and patient authority-VIII. Standards of care and patient autonomy. *Journal of the American Academy of Psychoanalysis and Dynamic Psychiatry*, *36*(3; Health & Medical Complete): 547–561.

Chateline, K. L. (2001). Sullivan the clinician. (United States Chapter of the International Society for the Psychological treatment of Schizophrenia and other psychoses). *ISPS—US Newsletter*, *2*(2): 7–10.

Chiesa, M. (1988). Intensive psychotherapy with in-patients at Chestnut Lodge Hospital. *Psychiatric Bulletin*, *12*: 323–327.

Chiesa, M. (1993). At the border between institutionalization and community psychiatry: Psychodynamic observations of a hospital admission ward. *Free Associations*, *4B*: 241–263.

Cohler, B. J., & Friedman, D. H. (2004). Psychoanalysis and the early beginnings of residential treatment for troubled youth. *Child Adolesc Psychiatr Clin N Am*, *13*(2): 237–254.

Colucci, M., Norcio, B., & Sindici, C. (2000, 7–10 March). De-institutionalisation in Italy: Between ethics and politics. Paper presented at the European Conference on Mental Health, Rotterdam.

Coombe, P. (1996). The Cassel Hospital, London. *Australian and New Zealand Journal of Psychiatry*, *30*: 672–680.

Cooper, D. (2003). *Psychiatry and Anti-Psychiatry*. London: Routledge.

Copolov, D. L. (2003). Psychoses: A primary care perspective. *Medical Journal of Australia* (178).

Correale, A. (2006). Public paths of interiority: Psychoanalysis and psychiatric institutions. *European Journal of Psychotherapy and Counselling*, *8*(1): 9–19.

Correale, A., & Di Leone, G. (2001). Contribution from Italy: Psychoanalytical approaches to the study of institutions in Italy. In: R. Hinshelwood & M. Chiesa (Eds.), *Organisations, Anxieties and Defences*. New York: Brunner-Routledge, pp. 77–96.

Cottes, J. -F. (2002). Psychosis and the child in the teachings of Jacques Lacan: Consequences for an institution. *Courtil Papers*: 1–13.

Cullberg, J., Levander, S., Holmqvist, R., Mattsson, M., & Wieselgren, I.-M. (2002). One-year outcome in first episode psychosis patients in the Swedish Parachute project. *Acta Psychiatr Scand*, *106*: 276–285.

Danto, E. (1998). The Ambulatorium: Freud's free clinic in Vienna. *International Journal of Psycho-Analysis*, *79*: 287.

Danto, E. (1999). The Berlin Poliklinik: Psychoanalytic innovation in Weimar Germany. *Journal of the American Psychoanalytic Association*, *47*(4): 1269–1292.

Danto, E. (2005). *Freud's Free Clinics: Psychoanalysis & Social Justice, 1918–1938*. New York: Columbia University Press.

de Waelhens, A., & Ver Eecke, W. (2001). *Phenomenology and Lacan on Schizophrenia, after the Decade of the Brain*. Leuven, Belgium: Leuven University Press.

Deleuze, G., & Guattari, F. (2004). *Anti-Oedipus: Capitalism and Schizophrenia*. London: Continuum International Publishing Group.

Deri, F., & Brunswick, D. (1964). Freud's letters to Ernst Simmel. *Journal of the American Psychoanalytic Association*, *12*: 93–109.

DeSisto, M., Harding, C., McCormick, R., Ashikaga, T., & Brooks, G. (1995). The Maine and Vermont three-decade studies of serious mental illness I: Matched comparison of cross-sectional outcome. *British Journal of Psychiatry*, *167*: 331–342.

Dolto, F. (1973). *Dominique. Analysis of an Adolescent*. Ivan Kat (Trans.). New York: Outerbridge & Lazard.

Drake, R. E., Green, A. I., Mueser, K. T., & Goldman, H. H. (2003). The history of community mental health treatment and rehabilitation for persons with severe mental illness. *Community Mental Health Journal*, *39*(5): 427–440.

Ellen, E. F. (2003). Psychiatry's hottest niche markets. *Psychiatric Times*, *XX*(4).

Eros, F. (2003). The Ferenczi cult: Its historical and political roots. *International Forum of Psychoanalysis*, *13*: 121–128.

Evans, J. (1997). An explanation of Jacques Lacan's use of cartels in organisational structure. *Lacanian Works*. Available at: www.lacanianworks.net/?p=81. Retrieved Nov 1, 2013.

Fairbairn, W. (1963). Synopsis of an object-relations theory of the personality. *International Journal of Psycho-Analysis*, *44*: 224–225.

Falzeder, E. (2004). The Significance of Ferenczi's clinical contributions for working with psychotic patients. *International Forum Psychoanalysis*, *13*: 26–30.

Falzeder, E., & Haynal, A. (2002). Introduction to the complete correspondence of Sigmund Freud and Karl Abraham *The Complete Correspondence of Sigmund Freud and Karl Abraham 1907–1925*, pp. xix–xxx.

Federn, P. (1943a). Psychoanalysis of psychosis: I Errors and how to avoid them. *The Psychiatric Quarterly*: 4–21.

Federn, P. (1943b). Psychoanalysis of psychoses: II Transference. *The Psychiatric Quarterly*: 246–258.

Federn, P. (1943c). Psychoanalysis of psychoses: III The Psychoanalytic Process. *The Psychiatric Quarterly*: 470–487.

Federn, P. (1953). *Ego psychology and the psychoses*. London: Imago Publishing Co Ltd, p. 375.

Felix, A. D., & Wine, P. R. (2001). From the couch to the street: Applications of psychoanalysis to work with individuals who are homeless and mentally ill. *Journal of Applied Psychoanalytic Studies*, *3*(1): 17–32.

Fenton, W., Blyler, C., & Heinssen, R. (1997). Determinants of medication compliance in schizophrenia: Empirical and clinical findings. *Schizophrenia Bulletin, 23*(4): 637–651.

Ferenczi, S. (1931). The principle of relaxation and neocatharsis. *International Journal of Psycho-Analysis, 11*: 428–443.

Fine, R. (1979). *A History of Psychoanalysis*. New York: Columbia University Press.

Freud, A. (1966). A short history of child analysis. *Psychoanalytic Study of the Child, 21*: 7–14.

Forrester, J. (1987). The seminar of jacques lacan: in place of an introduction—book i. Freud's papers on technique, 1953–1954. *Free Associations, 1K*: 63–93.

Freud, A. (1988). The nursery school of the Hampstead child-therapy clinic. *Bulletin of the Anna Freud Centre, 11*: 265–69.

Freud, S. (1894a). The neuro-psychoses of defence. In: J. Strachey (Ed.), *The Standard Edition of the Complete Psychological Works of Sigmund Freud III (1893–1899): Early Psycho-analytic Publications*. London: Hogarth, pp. 41–61.

Freud, S. (1896b). Further remarks on the neuro-psychoses of defence. In: J. Strachey (Ed.), *The Standard Edition of the Complete Psychological Works of Sigmund Freud III (1893–1899): Early Psycho-analytic Publications*. London: Hogarth, pp. 157–185.

Freud, S. (1905a). On psychotherapy. In: James Strachey (Ed.), *The Standard Edition of the Complete Psychological Works of Sigmund Freud VII (1901–1905): A Case of Hysteria, Three Essays on Sexuality and other works*. London: Hogarth, pp. 255–268.

Freud, S. (1909b). Analysis of a Phobia in a Five-Year-Old Boy. In James Strachey (Ed.), *The Standard Edition of the Complete Psychological Works of Sigmund Freud X (1909): Two Case Histories (Little Hans and the Rat Man)*. London: Hogarth, pp. 1–150.

Freud, S. (1911). Psycho-analytic notes on an autobiographical account of a case of paranoia (dementia paranoides). In: J. Strachey (Ed.), *The Standard Edition of the Complete Psychological Works of Sigmund Freud XII (1911–1913): The Case of Schreber, Papers on Technique and Other Works*. London: Hogarth, pp. 1–82.

Freud, S. (1911). Letter from Freud to Ludwig Binswanger, January 30. In: Alex Strachey (Ed.), *The Sigmund Freud-Ludwig Binswanger Correspondence 1908–1938*. London, pp. 59–61.

Freud, S. (1912b). The dynamics of transference. In: J. Strachey (Ed.), *The Standard Edition of the Complete Psychological Works of Sigmund Freud XII (1911–13): The Case of Schreber, Papers on Technique and Other Works*. London: Hogarth, pp. 97–108.

Freud, S. (1912–1913). *Totem and Taboo: Resemblances Between the Mental Lives of Savages and Neurotics.* J. Strachey (Trans.). In: J. Strachey (Ed.), *The Standard Edition of the Complete Psychological Works of Sigmund Freud XIII (1913–1914): Totem and Taboo and Other Works.* London: Hogarth, pp. vii–162.

Freud, S. (1914c). On narcissism: An introduction. J. Strachey (Trans.). In: J. Strachey (Ed.), *The Standard Edition of the Complete Psychological Works of Sigmund Freud XIV (1914–1916): On the History of the Psycho-Analytic Movement, Papers on Metapsychology and Other Works.* London: Hogarth, pp. 67–102.

Freud, S. (1914d). On the history of the psycho-analytic movement. A. A. Brill (Trans.). In: J. Strachey (Ed.), *The Standard Edition of the Complete Psychological Works of Sigmund Freud XIV (1914–1916): Metapsychology and Other Works.* London: Hogarth, pp. 1–66.

Freud, S. (1917a). Mourning and melancholia. J. Strachey (Trans.). In: J. Strachey (Ed.), *The Standard Edition of the Complete Psychological Works of Sigmund Freud XIV (1914–1916): On the History of the Psycho-analytic Movement, Papers on Metapsychology and Other Works.* London: Hogarth, pp. 237–258.

Freud, S. (1919a). Lines of advance in psycho-analytic therapy. In: J. Strachey (Ed.), *The Standard Edition of the Complete Psychological Works of Sigmund Freud XVIII (1920–22): Beyond the Pleasure Principle, Group Psychology and other Works.* London: Hogarth Press & the Institute of Psycho-analysis.

Freud, S. (1921c). Group psychology and the analysis of the ego. In: J. Strachey (Ed.), *The Standard Edition of the Complete Psychological Works of Sigmund Freud XVIII (1920–22): Beyond the Pleasure Principle, Group Psychology and other Works.* London: Hogarth, pp. 65–144.

Freud, S. (1923a). Two encyclopedia articles. In: J. Strachey (Ed.), *The Standard Edition of the Complete Psychological Works of Sigmund Freud XVIII (1920–1922): Beyond the Pleasure Principle, Group Psychology and Other Works.* London: Hogarth Press & the Institute of Psycho-analysis, pp. 233–260.

Freud, S. (1923b). The Ego and the Id. *The Standard Edition of the Complete Psychological Works of Sigmund Freud XIX (1923–1925): The Ego and the Id and Other Works.* London: Hogarth Press, pp. 1–66.

Freud, S. (1924b). Neurosis and psychosis. In: J. Strachey (Ed.), *The Standard Edition of the Complete Psychological Works of Sigmund Freud XIX (1923–1925): The Ego and the Id and Other Works.* London: Hogarth, pp. 147–154.

Freud, S. (1924e). The loss of reality in neurosis and psychosis. In: J. Strachey (Ed.), *The Standard Edition of the Complete Psychological Works of Sigmund*

Freud XXIX (1923–1925): The Ego and the Id and Other Works. London: Hogarth & the Institute of Psycho-analysis, pp. 181–188.

Freud, S. (1924f). A short account of psycho-analysis. In: J. Strachey (Ed.), *The Standard Edition of the Complete Psychological Works of Sigmund Freud XIX (1923–1925): The Ego and the Id and Other Works*. London: Hogarth, pp. 189–210.

Freud, S. (1925d). An autobiographical study. In: J. Strachey (Ed.), *The Standard Edition of the Complete Psychological Works of Sigmund Freud XX (1925–1926): An Autobiographical Study, Inhibitions, Symptoms and Anxiety, the Question of Lay Analysis and Other Works*. London: Hogarth, pp. 1–74.

Freud, S. (1926a). The question of lay analysis, In: J. Strachey (Ed.), *The Standard Edition of the Complete Psychological Works of Sigmund Freud XX (1925–1926): An Autobiographical Study, Inhibitions, Symptoms and Anxiety, the Question of Lay Analysis and Other Works*. London: Hogarth, pp. 179–258.

Freud, S. (1926b). Letter from Sigmund Freud to Oskar Pfister September 14. *The International Psycho-Analytical Library, 59*: 105–106.

Freud, S. (1930a). *Civilisations and its Discontents*. In: J. Strachey (Ed.), *The Standard Edition of the Complete Psychological Works of Sigmund Freud XXI (1927–1931): The Future of an illusion, Civilization and its Discontents, and Other Works*. London: Hogarth, pp. 57–146.

Freud, S. (1933a). New introductory lectures on psycho-analysis In: J. Strachey (Ed.), *The Standard Edition of the Complete Psychological Works of Sigmund Freud XXII (1932–1936): New Introductory Lectures on Psycho-analysis, and Other Works*. London: Hogarth, pp. 1–182.

Freud, S. (1940a [1938]). An outline of psycho-analysis. In: J. Strachey (Ed.), *The Standard Edition of the Complete Psychological Works of Sigmund Freud XXIII (1937–1939): Moses and Monotheism, An Outline of Psycho-Analysis and Other Works*. London: Hogarth, pp. 139–208.

Friedmann, M. (1988). The Hampstead clinic nursery: The first 20 years (1957–1978), *Bulletin of the Anna Freud Centre, 11*: 277–87.

Fromm-Reichmann, F. (1947). Problems of therapeutic management in a psychoanalytic hospital. *The Psychoanalytic Quarterly, 16*: 325–355.

Fromm-Reichmann, F. (1950). *Principles of Intensive Psychotherapy*. Chicago: Phoenix Books & University of Chicago Press.

Fromm-Reichmann, F. (1954). Psychotherapy of schizophrenia. *American Journal of Psychiatry, 111*: 410–419.

Fromm, M. G. (2006). A view from Riggs: Treatment resistance and patient authority-II. Transmission of trauma and treatment resistance. *Journal of the American Academy of Psychoanalysis and Dynamic Psychiatry, 34*(3; Health & Medical Complete): 445–460.

Frosh, S. (2003). Psychoanalysis, Nazism and Jewish science. *International Journal of Psychoanalysis, 84*: 1315–1332.

Fuller-Torrey, E. (1997) Taking Issue: "Psychiatric survivors" and non-survivors. *Psychiatric Services, 48(2)*: 143.

Gale, J., Realpe, A., & Pedriali, E. (Eds.). (2008a). *Therapeutic Communities for Psychosis: Philosophy, History and Clinical Practice*. London & New York: Routledge, p. 272.

Gallano, C. (2002). Possible treatment of schizophrenia: Stabilisation and suppletion. Paper presented at the Australian Centre for Psychoanalysis Lacan Seminar, August 4th, Royal Society: Melbourne.

Gardner, D., & Teehan, M. (2011). *Antipsychotics and their Side Effects*. New York: Cambridge University Press.

Garety, P. A. (2003). The future of psychological therapies for psychosis. *World Psychiatry*, *2*(3): 147–152.

Garrido, P., & Saraiva, C. B. (2012). Understanding the revolving door syndrome, *European Psychiatry*, 27(1): 1.

Geller, J. L. (2006). Avoiding extinction: Successful private psychiatric hospitals in the opening decade of the twenty-first century. *Psychiatric Quarterly*, *77*(2): 189–201.

Gibbs, P. (2007). The primacy of psychoanalytic intervention in recovery from the psychosis and schizophrenias. *Journal of the American Academy of Psychoanalysis and Dynamic Psychiatry*, *35*(2): 287–331.

GIFRIC (2009). Groupe Interdisciplinaire Freudien de Recherches et d'Interventions Cliniques et Culturelles Retrieved March, 2009 from www.gifric.com/

Gittelman, M., Dubuis, J., & Gillet, M. (1973). Recent developments in French public mental health. *Psychiatric Quarterly*, *47*(4): 509–520.

Gleeson, J., & McGorry, P. (Eds.). (2004). *Psychological Interventions in Early Psychosis: A Treatment Handbook*. Chichester, WS, England: John Wiley & Sons Ltd.

Glover, N. (2009). *Psychoanalytic aesthetics: An introduction to the British school*. London: Karnac.

Goffman, E. (2007). *Asylums: Essays on the Social Situation of Mental Patients and Other Inmates*. New Brunswick & London: Aldine Transaction.

Goode, E. (2003). Famed psychiatric clinic abandons prairie home. *The New York Times, Saturday, May 31*.

Gottdiener, W. (2004). Psychodynamic psychotherapy for schizophrenia. In: L. M. John Read & R. Bentall (Ed.). *Models of Madness: Psychological, Social and Biological Approaches to Schizophrenia*. New York: Brunner-Routledge.

Gottdiener, W., & Haslam, N. (2002). The benefits of individual psychotherapy for people diagnosed with schizophrenia: A meta-analytic review. *Ethical Human Sciences and Services*, *4*(3): 163–187.

Gottdiener, W., & Haslam, N. (2003). A critique of the methods and conclusions in the Patient Outcome Research Team (PORT) report on psychological treatments for schizophrenia. *Journal of the American Academy of Psychoanalysis and Dynamic Psychiatry, 31*(1: Health & Medical): 191–209.

Grasser, F. (2003). The error of the Other. *International Journal of Mental Health and Applied Psychoanalysis (Mental Online),* (Analysis in the age of globalization): 89–93.

Green, D. (2003). The end of institutions, housing and homelessness. *Journal of the Council to Homeless Persons, After Deinstitutionalisation* (April): 1–7.

Griffiths, P., & Hinshelwood, R. (1995). A culture of enquiry: Life within a hall of mirrors. Paper presented at the conference of the International Society for the Psycho-Analytic Study of Organisations, July ISPSO: London.

Griffiths, P., Ord, J., Wells, D., & Barnes, E. (Eds.). (1998). *Face to Face with Distress: The Professional use of Self in Psychosocial Care.* London: Elsevier Health Sciences, p. 232.

Guattari, F. (1984). *Molecular Revolution: Psychiatry and Politics.* R. Sheed (Trans.). Harmondsworth: Penguin.

Guattari, F., & Genosko, G. (1996). *The Guattari Reader: Pierre-Félix Guattari.* G. Genosko (Trans.). Oxford: Blackwell publishing, p. 281.

Gunderson, J., Frank, A., Katz, H., Vannicelli, M., Frosch, J., & Knapp, P. (1984). Effects of psychotherapy in schizophrenia II: Comparative outcome of two forms of treatment. *Schizophrenia Bulletin, 10*: 564–598.

Haarscher, D. (2001). From beforehand to the preliminaries. *Courtil Papers.*

Harding, C. (2003). Changes in schizophrenia across time: Paradoxes, patterns and predictors. In: C. I. Cohen (Ed.), *Schizophrenia Into Later Life: Treatment, Research, and Policy.* Arlington, VA: American Psychiatric Publishing, p. 344.

Harding, C., Brooks, G., Ashikaga, T., & Breier, J. S. A. (1987). The Vermont longitudinal study of persons with severe mental illness, I: Methodology, study sample and overall status 32 years later. *American Journal Psychiatry, 144*(6): 718–735.

Harrison, T. (2000). *Bion, Rickman, Foulkes, and the Northfield experiments: Advancing on a different front.* London: Jessica Kingsley.

Hartmann, H. (1950). Comments on the psychoanalytic theory of the ego. *Psychoanalytic Study of the Child, 5*: 74–96.

Hartnup, T. (1994). The state, the institution, and the patient: A three-way collison at the crossroads as a hospital fights closure. *Psychoanalytic Psychotherapy, 8*(1): 3–15.

Harvey, C. A., & Fielding, J. M. (2003). The configuration of mental health services to facilitate care for people with schizophrenia. *Medical Journal of Australia* (178): S49–S52.

Hasnaina, M., Vieweg, W. V., Fredrickson, S. K., Beatty-Brooks, M., Fernandez, A., & Pandurangi, A. K. (2008). Clinical monitoring and management of the metabolic syndrome in patients receiving atypical antipsychotic medications. *Primary Care Diabetes*: 1–11.

Hellman, I (1983), Work in the Hampstead war nurseries. *International Journal of Psycho-Analysis*, *64*: 435–439.

Henry, J. (1957). The culture of interpersonal relations in a therapeutic institution for emotionally disturbed children. *American Journal of Orthopsychiatry*, *27*(4): 725–734.

Hinshelwood, R. (1987). The psychotherapist's role in a large psychiatric institution. *Psychoanalytic Psychotherapy*, *2*(3): 207–215.

Hinshelwood, R. (1988). Models of demoralisation. *British Journal of Psychotherapy*, *5*: 218–227.

Hinshelwood, R. (1994). The relevance of psychotherapy. *Psychoanalytic Psychotherapy*, *8*(3): 283–294.

Hinshelwood, R. (2000). Alienation: Social relations and therapeutic relations. *Psychoanalytic Studies*, *2*: 21–30.

Hinshelwood, R. (2001). Group mentality and "having a mind": Reflections on Bion's work on groups and on psychosis. *Psyche matters*: 1–13.

Hinshelwood, R., & Skogstad, W. (1997). The hospital in the mind: In-patient psychotherapy at the Cassel hospital. In: J. Pestalozzi, S. Frisch, R. D. Hinshelwood, & D. Houzel (Eds.), *Psychoanalytic psychotherapy in Institutional Settings*. London: Karnac Books, pp. 59–73.

Hoffman, K. (2002). Psychoanalysis in psychiatric institutions: Theoretical and clinical approaches. *International Forum of Psychoanalysis*, *11*: 237–243.

Hoornaert, G. (2002). The problem of the superego in the treatment of psychosis. *Courtil Papers*: 1–6.

Hornstein, G. A. (Ed.). (2000). *To Redeem One Person is to Redeem the World: The Life of Frieda Fromm-Reichmann*. New York: The Free Press, pp. xxxii + 477.

Hughes, R., & Malone, K. R. (2002). Introduction: The dialectic of theory and clinic. In: R. Hughes & K. R. Malone (Eds.), *After Lacan: Clinical practice and the Subject of the Unconscious*. New York: State University of New York Press, pp. 1–35.

Jackson, M. (1995). Learning to think about schizoid thinking. In: J. Ellwood (Ed.), *Psychosis: Understanding and Treatment*. London: Jessica Kingsley Publishers, pp. 10–22.

Jacobsen, K. (2000). Blaming Bettelheim. *Psychoanalytic Review*, *87*(3): 385–417.

James, O. (1984). The role of the nurse-therapist relationship in the therapeutic community. *International Review of Psycho-Analysis*, *11*: 151–159.

Jaques, E. (1995). Why the psychoanalytical approach to understanding organizations is dysfunctional. *Human Relations*, *48*(4): 343–350.

Jaques, E. (2003). Work and the unconscious. *Psychoanalytic Psychology*, *20*: 236–244.

Jarrett, M., Bowers, L., & Simpson, A. (2008). Coerced medication in psychiatric inpatient care: Literature review. *Journal Advanced Nursing, 64*(6): 538–548.

Jones, E. (1957). *Sigmund Freud life and work: The Last Phase 1919–1939* 3: London: Hogarth Press.

Jones, E. (2004). War and the practice of psychotherapy: The UK experience 1939–1960. *Medical History, 48*: 493–510.

Jones, M. (1956). The concept of a therapeutic community. *Am J Psychiatry, 112*: 647–650.

Judd, P. Hoffman, Aronson, D. L., & McGlashan, T. H. (2002). *A developmental model of borderline personality disorder*. New York: American Psychiatric Pub, p. 231.

Jones, M. (1982). *The Process of Change: From a Closed to an Open System in a Mental Hospital*. Boston: Routledge & Kegan Paul.

Jung, C. G. (1906). Letter from C. G. Jung to Sigmund Freud. *The Freud/Jung Letters: The Correspondence Between Sigmund Freud and C. G. Jung, December 29, 1906, 13–16*(9J).

Jung, C. G. (1960). *The Psychogenesis of Mental Disease*. R. F. C. Hull (Trans.). London: Routledge & Kegan Paul.

Kächele, H. (2001). Are there pillars of therapeutic wisdom for psychoanalytic therapy? *Journal of European Psychoanalysis, 12–13*: 1–12.

Karon, B., & Vandenbos, G. (1981). *Psychotherapy of Schizophrenia: The Treatment of Choice*. Northvale, N J: Jason Aronson Inc.

Keks, N. A., Altson, B. M., Sacks, T. L., Hustig, H. H., & Tanaghow, A. (2003). Collaboration between general practice and community psychiatric services for people with chronic mental illness. *Medical Journal of Australia* (178).

Kennard, D. (2004). The therapeutic community as an adaptable treatment modality across different settings. *Psychiatric Quarterly, 75*(3): 295–308.

Kennedy, M., Helms, P., & Dykstra, M. (1936). The sedative wet sheet pack *The American Journal of Nursing, 36*(1): 53–60.

Kennedy, R., Heymans, A., & Tischler, L. (Eds.). (1987). *The Family as In-patient: Working with Families and Adolescents at the Cassel hospital*. London: Free Association Books.

Kernberg, O. (1973). Psychoanalytic object-relations theory, group processes, and administration: Toward an integrative theory of hospital treatment. *Annual of Psychoanalysis, 1*: 363–388.

Kernberg, O. (1975). *Borderline Conditions and Pathological Narcissism*. New York: Jason Aronson, p. 361.

Kernberg, O., et al. (1989). *Psychodynamic psychotherapy of borderline patients*. New York: Basic Books.

Kernberg, O. (1997). Psychoanalysis in America. *Journal of European Psychoanalysis*, (5): 1–11.

Kets de Vries, M. (2001). Creating authentizotic organizationa: Well-functioning individuals in vibrant companies *Human Relations 54*(1): 101–112.

Kirsner, D. (1998). *Unfree Associations Inside Psychoanalytic Institutes*. Melbourne: Academy for the Study of the Psychoanalytic Arts, pp. 1–114.

Kirsner, D. (2004a). Psychoanalysis and its discontents. *Psychoanalytic Psychology, 21*(3): 339–352.

Klein, M. (1930). The importance of symbol-formation in the development of the ego, *International Journal of Psycho-Analysis, 11*: 24–39.

Klein, M. (1935). *A Contribution to the Psychogenesis of Manic-depressive States*. New York: Macmillan, Inc.

Klein, M. (1946). Notes on schizoid mechanisms. *International Journal Psychoanalysis, 27*: 99–110.

Klein, M. (1963). *The Psycho-Analysis of Children*. London: Hogarth Press.

Klerman, G. (1990). The psychiatric patient's right to effective treatment: Implications of Osheroff v. Chestnut Lodge. *American Journal of Psychiatry, 147*(4): 409–418.

Kohut, H. (1971). *The Analysis of the Self*. New York: International Universities Press.

Kohut, H., & Wolf, E. S. (1978). The disorders of the self and their treatment: An outline. *International Journal of Psycho-Analysis, 59*: 413–425.

Kraepelin, E. (1883). *Compendium der Psychiatrie*. Leipzig: Abrm. Abel.

Kraepelin, E. (2002). *Dementia Praecox and Paraphrenia* R. M. Barclay (Trans.). Bristol: Thoemmes Press.

Krim, M. (1994). The psychoanalyst: On becoming more human than otherwise. *Journal of Religion and Health, 33*(1): 73–80.

Lacan, J. (1975). *The Seminar of Jacques Lacan Book 1: Freud's papers on technique, 1953–1954*. J. Forrester (Trans.). New York: W. W. Norton & Co.

Lacan, J. (1977). *The Seminar of Jacques Lacan, Book XI: The Four Fundamental Concepts of Psycho-analysis, 1964*. Jacques-Alain Miller (Ed.): A. Sheridan, (Trans.). New York, London: Penguin Books.

Lacan, J. (1980). *D'Ecolage, in École de la Cause Freudienne* (Ed.). Paris: Address book of the École de la Cause Freudienne (11th March 1982).

Lacan, J. (1990a). Note on the child. *Analysis, 2*: 7–8.

Lacan, J. (1990b). The founding act of 1964 *Television*. New York: Norton & Co.

Lacan, J. (1991). *The Seminar of Jacques Lacan, Book II: The Ego in Freud's Theory and in the Technique of Psychoanalysis 1954–55*. S. Tomaselli (Trans.). New York, London: W. W. Norton & Co.

Lacan, J. (1992). *The Seminar of Jacques Lacan, Book VII: The Ethics of Psychoanalysis, 1959–60*. D. Porter (Trans). London: Routledge.

Lacan, J. (1995). Proposition of 9 October 1967 on the Psychoanalyst of the School. *Analysis, 6*: 1–13.

Lacan, J. (2000). British psychiatry and the war. *Psychoanalytical Notebooks 4* (Spring).

Lacan, J. (2002a). *The Seminar of Jacques Lacan Book III: The Psychoses, 1955–1956*. B. Fink (Trans.). New York: W. W. Norton & Co.

Lacan, J. (2002b). *The Family Complexes in the Formation of the Individual*. C. Gallagher (Trans.). Dublin: unpublished.

Lacan, J. (2002c). *The Seminar of Jacques Lacan, Book VIII*: Transference, 1960–1961. C. Gallagher (Trans.). London: Karnac.

Lacan, J. (2004a). *Écrits: A selection*. Bruce Fink in collaboration with H. Fink & R. Grigg (Trans.). New York, London: W. W. Norton & Co.

Lacan, J. (2004b). *The Seminar of Jacques Lacan, Book XX: Encore, 1972–73*. C. Gallagher (Trans.). Dublin: unpublished.

Lacan, J. (2007). *The Seminar of Jacques Lacan, Book XVII: The Other Side of Psychoanalysis, 1969–70*. New York: W. W. Norton & Co.

Lacan, J. (2009). L'étourdit. *The Letter, 41*: 31–80.

Lacan, J. (2015). *The Seminar of Jacques Lacan, Book XXIII: Joyce and the Sinthome*, 1975–76. C. Gallagher (Trans.). London: Karnac.

Landy, D. (1961). An anthropological approach to research in the mental hospital community. *Psychiatric Quarterly, 35*(4): 741–757.

Lanzoni, S. (2003). An epistemology of the clinic: Ludwig Binswanger's phenomenology of the other. *Critical Inquiry, 30*(1).

Laplanche, J., & Pontalis, J. B. (1988). *The Language of Psychoanalysis*. London: Karnac & The Institute of Psychoanalysis.

Laurant, E. (1990). The impact of Lacan's teaching on psychoanalysis with children. *Analysis, 2*: 21–37.

Lawrence, G. (1995). Totalitarian states of mind in institutions. In: D. Armstrong, W. G. Lawrence, & R. M. Young (Eds.), *Group Relations: An Introduction*. London: Process Press, pp. 21–37.

Leader, D. (2011). *What is madness?* London: Hamish Hamilton.

Lees, J., Manning, N., & Rawlings, B. (1999). *Therapeutic community effectiveness: A systematic international review of therapeutic community treatment for people with personality disorders and mentally disordered offenders*. Nottingham: University of York NHS Centre for Reviews & Dissemination and School of Sociology & Social Policy.

Lefort, R., & Lefort, R. (1980). *Birth of the Other*. Chicago: University of Illinois Press.

Lehmann, H. E., & Ban, T. A. (1997). The history of the psychopharmacology of schizophrenia. *Canadian Journal of Psychiatry, 42*: 152–162.

Leonoff, A. (1996). Pioneers of interpersonal psychoanalysis. *Canadian Journal of Psychoanalysis, 4*: 381–384.

Levine, M. (1990). An integrated approach to the treatment of schizophrenia with medications and psychotherapy: The Chestnut Lodge experience.

Paper presented at the USA-Europe joint meeting on therapies and psychotherapy of schizophrenia, September: Perugia, Italy.

Lewin, K. (1952). *Field Theory in Social Science: Selected Theoretical Papers by Kurt Lewin*. London: Tavistock.

Lionells, M. (2002). The William Alanson White institute: Yesterday, today, and tomorrow, Unpublished PhD thesis. Retrieved 2010 from www.wawhite.org/history/brief_history_WAWI.htm

Loewenstein, R. M. (1958). Variations in classical technique: Concluding remarks. *International Journal of Psycho-Analysis, 39*: 240–242.

Long, S. (2006). Organizational defenses against anxiety: What has happened since the 1955 Jaques paper? *International Journal of Applied Psychoanalytic Studies, 3*: 279–295.

Lucas, R. (1985). On the contribution of psychoanalysis to the management of psychotic patients in the N.H.S. *Psychoanalytic Psychotherapy, 1*(1): 3–17.

Luhrmann, T. M. (2000). *Of Two Minds*. New York: Alfred A. Knopf.

Lynn, D. J. (1993). Freud's analysis of A.B., a Psychotic man, 1925–1930. *Journal of American Academy of Psychoanalysis, 21*: 63–78.

Maccoby, M. (2000). Narcissistic Leaders: The Incredible Pros, the Inevitable Cons, *The Harvard Business Review*, January–February.

Mackie, B. (2011). Toiling at the oars. *Analysis 16*: 75–86.

Main, T. (1989). *The Ailment and Other Psychoanalytic Essays*. London: Free Associations Press.

Maltz, M., & Witt, K. (2011). The complexity of leadership: The complexity of the organizational self. *Triadic Consulting Group*, 1–22.

Manning, N. (1991). Maxwell Jones and the therapeutic community movement: A sociological view. *The International Journal for Therapeutic and Supportive Organizations, 12*(2 & 3): 83–97.

Mannoni, M. (1967). *The Child, his Illness, and the Others*. Harmondsworth, England: Penguin Books.

Mannoni, M. (1999). Birth of the Institution: Meeting Artaud and Grotowski. S. Farifield (Trans.). *Separation and Creativity: Refinding the Lost Language of Childhood* 5: New York: Other Press, pp. 105–140.

Masson, J. (1985). *The Complete letters of Sigmund Freud and Wilhelm Fleiss 1887–1904*. Cambridge, Massachusetts: Belknap Press of Harvard University Press, p. 505.

Massumi, B. (1992). *A User's Guide to Capitalism and Schizophrenia: Deviations from Deleuze and Guattari* (4th ed.). Cambridge, MA: The Massachusetts Institute of Technology Press.

May, U. (2008). Nineteen patients in analysis with Freud (1910–1920). *American Imago, Baltimore, 65*(1): 41–106.

McGlashan, T. (1984). The Chestnut Lodge follow-up study; I & II. *Archives of General* Ma *Psychiatry, 41*: 573–601.

McGlashan, T. (1986). The Chestnut Lodge follow-up study, III & IV. *Archives of General Psychiatry, 43*: 20–30 & 167–176.

McGlashan, T., & Nayfack, B. (1988). Psychotherapeutic models and the treatment of schizophrenia: The records of three successive psychotherapists with one patient at Chestnut Lodge for 18 years. *Psychiatry, 51*(4): 340–362.

McGlashan, T., & Carpenter, W. (2007). Identifying unmet therapeutic domains in schizophrenia patients: The early contributions of Wayne Fenton from Chestnut Lodge. *Schizophrenia Bulletin, 33*(5): 1086–1092.

McGorry, P. D. (2004). An overview of the background and scope of psychological interventions in early psychosis. In: J. Gleeson & P. McGorry (Eds.), *Psychological Interventions in Early Psychosis: A Treatment Handbook.* Chichester John Wiley & Sons, pp. 1–22.

McMillan, D. W., & Chavis, D. M. (1986). Sense of community: A definition and theory. *Journal of Community Psychology, 14*(1): 6–23.

Menninger, K. (1962). *A Manual for Psychiatric Case Study.* New York: Grune & Stratton.

Menninger, W. (1982). The Menninger hospitals' guide to the order sheet. *Bulletin of the Menninger Clinic, Vol 46*(No 1).

Menzies-Lyth, I. (1959). The functioning of social systems as a defence against anxiety: A report on a study of the nursing service of a general hospital. *Containing Anxiety in Institutions: Selected Essays* (1988). London: Free Association Books, pp. 43–85.

Menzies Lyth, I. (1990). The dynamics of organisational change: A psychoanalytical perspective on social institutions. In: E. Trist & H. Murray (Eds.), *The Social Engagement of Social Science: A Tavistock Anthology.* University of Pennsylvania Press, pp. 463–476.

Meissner, W. (2006). Finding and refinding the therapeutic alliance: On thinking and thirds. *Journal of the American Academy of Psychoanalysis and Dynamic Psychiatry, 34*(4): 651–678.

Miller, J. (1994). Le Cartel Dans Le Monde. *Lettre Mensuelle: de l'Ecole de la Cause Freudienne, 134.*

Milner, J. (1964). The residential treatment centre. *Annals of the American Academy of Political and Social Science, 355*(Programs and problems in child welfare): 98–104.

Mitchell, A. J., & Selmes, T. (2007). Why don't patients take their medicine? Reasons and solutions in psychiatry. *Advances in Psychiatric Treatment, 13*: 336–346.

Mozère, L. (2002). Reconceptualizing early childhood education research, theory and practice. Paper presented at the Childhood Education Conference, January 5–9 Tempe, Arizona.

Muir, B. (1987). Is in-patient psychotherapy a valid concept? In: R. Kennedy, A. Heymans & L. Tischler (Eds.). *The Family as In-patient: Working with*

Families and Adolescents at the Cassel Hospital. London: Free Association Books, pp. 64–77.
Muller, J. (1999). Consultation from the position of the third. *American Journal of Psychoanalysis, 59*(2): 113–119.
Muller, J. (2007). A view from Riggs: Treatment tesistance and patient authority-IV: Why the pair needs the third. *Journal of the American Academy of Psychoanalysis and Dynamic Psychiatry, 35*(2): 221–242.
The National Institute for Health and Clinical Excellence (2010). Schizophrenia: Core interventions in the treatment and management of schizophrenia in adults in primary and secondary care (updated edition). *National Collaborating Centre for Mental Health, National Clinical Guideline No 82*.
Neri, C. (1993). Field theory and trans-generational phantasies. *Rivista di Psicoanalisi, 39*: 43–62.
Neve, M. (2004). A commentary on the history of social psychiatry and psychotherapy in twentieth-century Germany, Holland and Great Britain. *Medical History, 48*: 407–412.
Norton, K., & Bloom, S. (2004). The art and challenges of long-term and short-term democratic therapeutic communities. *Psychiatric Quarterly, 75*(3): 249–262.
Obholzer, A. (1986). Institutional dynamics and resistance to change. *Psychoanalytic Psychotherapy, 2*(3): 201–206.
Obholzer, A. (1996). Psychoanalytic contributions to authority and leadership issues. *Leadership & Organization Development Journal, 17*(6): 53–60.
Olfson, M., & Glick, I. D. (1993). Inpatient treatment of schizophrenia in general hospitals. *Hospital and Community Psychiatry, 44*(1): 40–44.
Owen, J. H. (2011). Interaction between alliance and technique in predicting patient outcome during psychodynamic psychotherapy. *Journal of Nervous & Mental Disease, 199*(6): 384–389.
Oxford English Dictionary (1989). *Institution*. Retrieved 11th December 2011, from www.oed.com.ezproxy.lib.monash.edu.au/view/Entry/97110
Palmai, G., & Blackwell, B. (1966). The Burgholzli Centenary. *Medical History, 10*(3): 257–265.
Pankow, G. (1974). The body image in hysterical psychosis. *International Journal of Psycho-Analysis, 55*: 407–414.
Pankow, G. (1985). Forms and their structuring power in psychosis. *International Journal of Psychology, 20*: 439–448.
Parish, M., & Elmendorf, D. (2007). A view from Riggs: Treatment resistance and patient authority-V. Silencing the messenger: The social dynamics of treatment resistance. *Journal of the American Academy of Psychoanalysis and Dynamic Psychiatry, 35*(3; Health & Medical Complete): 375.
Parker, I. (2005). Cartels in Lacanian psychoanalysis. Paper presented at the Psychoanalytic Matrix-founding meeting, 1 June Manchester, pp. 1–4.

Peele, R., Luisada, P., Lucas, M. J., Rudisell, D., & Taylor, D. (1977). Asylums revisited. *Am J Psychiatry*, *34*(10): 1077–1082.

Peplau, H. (1952). *Interpersonal relations in nursing: A Conceptual Frame of Reference for Psychodynamic Nursing*. New York: G. P. Putnam's Sons.

Perry, C. J., Fowler, J. C., Bailey, A., Clemence, A. J., Plakun, E. M., Zheutlin, B., et al. (2009). Improvement and recovery from suicidal and self-destructive phenomena in treatment-refractory disorders. *Journal of Nervous & Mental Disease*, *197*(1): 28–34.

Pines, M. (1999a). Forgotten pioneers: The unwritten history of the therapeutic community movement. *The International Journal for Therapeutic and Supportive Organizations*, *20*(1).

Pines, M. (1999b). Great Britain. In: S. Lebovici & S. D. Schill (Eds.). *The Challenge to Psychoanalysis and Psychotherapy: Solutions for the Future*. London: Jessica Kingsley Publishers, pp. 15–28.

Plakun, E. (2001). Making the alliance and taking the transference in work with suicidal patients. *Journal of Psychotherapy Practice and Research*, *10*(4): 269–277.

Plakun, E. (2006). A view from Riggs: Treatment resistance and patient authority-1. A psychodynamic perspective on treatment resistance. *Journal of the American Academy of Psychoanalysis and Dynamic Psychiatry*, *34*(2; Health & Medical Complete): 349–367.

Plakun, E. (Ed.). (2011). *Treatment Resistance and Patient Authority: The Austen Riggs Reader*. New York: W. W. Norton & Company.

Poblome, G. (2002). How a psychotic subject comes to speech. *Courtil Papers*.

Putnam, J. J. (1906). Recent experiments in the study and treatment of hysteria at the Massachusetts General Hospital, with remarks on Freud's method of treatment by psychoanalysis *Journal of Abnormal Psychology*.

Rachman, A. W. (1998). Ferenczi's relaxation principle and the issue of therapeutic responsiveness. *The American Journal of Psychoanalysis*, *58*(1): 63–81.

Rapoport, R. (1960). *Community as Doctor: New Perspectives on a Therapeutic Comunity*. New York: Arno Press.

Redler, L. (2000). R.D. Laing's contribution to the "treatment" of "schizophrenia": Responsible responses to suffering and malaise. *Psychoanalytic Review*, *87–117*(4: Health & Medical Complete): 561–591.

Reggio, D. (2004). *Paper 5: Jean Oury—iatros philosophos*. Unpublished manuscript on Malfatti, Oury, Mathesis, and Philosophy: London.

Reggio, D., & Novello, M. (2007). The hospital is ill: An interview with Jean Oury. *Radical Philosophy: Interviews*, (143): 1–19.

Reich, W. (1972). *Character Analysis*. New York: Farrar, Straus & Giroux.

Richards, A. (1999). A.A. Brill and the politics of exclusion. *JAPA: The Journal of the American Psychoanalytic Association, 47*(1).

Rissmiller, D. J., & Rissmiller, J. H. (2006). Evolution of the antipsychiatry movement into mental health consumerism. *Psychiatric Services, 57*(6): 863–867.

Robertson, M. (2005). Power and knowledge in psychiatry and the troubling case of Dr. Osheroff. *Australianasian Psychiatry, 13*(4): 343–350.

Robinson, C. (2003). Understanding iterative homelessness: The case of people with mental disorders. *Journal of Council to Homeless Persons, After Deinstitutionalisation* (April): 1–6.

Rodríguez, L. (1987). Technical implications of Jacques Lacan's theory of psychosis. *The Australian Journal of Psychotherapy, 6*(2): 128–140.

Rodríguez, L. (1991). The position of the analyst in psychoanalysis with children: The Lacanian contribution compared with other perspectives. *Analysis, 3*: 104–114.

Rodríguez, L. (1999). *Psychoanalysis with children*. London: Free Association Books.

Rodríguez, L. (2005). Destruction and creation of the world in the psychoanalytic treatment of psychosis. *Australasian Journal of Psychotherapy, 24*(1), pp. 1–20.

Rosenfeld, H. (1947). Analysis of a schizophrenic state with depersonalization. *The International Journal of Psycho-analysis, XXVIII* (Part 1): 130–139.

Rosenfeld, H. (1957). Differentiation of the psychotic from non-psychotic personalities. *International Journal of Psycho-Analysis, 38*: 266–275.

Rosenfeld, H. (1988a). Contribution to the psychopathology of psychotic states: The importance of projective-identification in the ego structure and the object relations of the psychotic patient. In: E. B. Spillus (Ed.), *Melanie Klein Today: Developments in Theory and Practice*. London: Routledge, pp. 117–137.

Rosenfeld, H. (1988b). Notes on the psycho-analysis of the superego conflict in an acute catatonic patient. In: E. B. Spillius (Ed.), *Melanie Klein Today: Developments in Theory and Practice: Mainly theory*. London: Routledge, pp. 14–51.

Rosser, R., Birch, S., Bond, H., Denford, J., & Schachter, J. (1987). Five-year follow up of patients treated with inpatient psychotherapy at the Cassel Hospital for Nervous Diseases. *J R Soc Med, 80*(9): 549–555.

Rostek, H. (2003). Norman Elrod (November 22, 1928–July 01, 2002): Unity and conflict of opposites. *International Forum of Psychoanalysis, 12*: 289–295.

Rouillon, J. -P. (2002). The part played. *Courtil Papers*, pp. 1–8.

The Royal Australian and New Zealand College of Psychiatrists (2010). What is psychiatry? Available at: http://student.ranzcp.org/index.php/what-is-psychiatry

The Royal Australian and New Zealand College of Psychiatrists (2010). What is psychiatry?, Availble at: http://student.ranzcp.org/index.php/what-is-psychiatry

Schein, E. H. (2010). *Organizational Culture and Leadership*. San Francisco: John Wiley and Sons.

Schlesinger, H. J. (2007). The treatment program at Menninger. *American Imago, 64*(2): 229–240.

Schreber, D. P. (2000). *Memoirs of My Nervous Illness* I. Macalpine & R. Hunter (Trans.). New York: New York Review of Books.

Schultz, C. G. (1963). A follow-up report on admissions to Chestnut Lodge 1948–1958. *Psychiatric Quarterly, 37*(2): 220–234.

Schulz, C. (1987). Sullivan's influence on Sheppard Pratt. *Journal of American Academy of Psychoanalysis, 15*: 247–259.

Schwing, G. (1954). *A Way to the Soul of the Mentally Ill*. New York: Universal Universities Press.

Scortecci, M. A., Ceroni, G. B., Boccanegra, L., Correale, A., Frangini, G., Licenziati, F., et al. (1993). Severe pathologies and models of comprehension *(Patologie gravi e modelli di comprensione). Rivista di Psicoanalisi, 39*: 191–203.

Scull, A. (1989). *Social order/mental disorder: Anglo-American Psychiatry in Historical Perspective*. Berkeley, CA: University of California Press.

Sealy, P., & Whitehead, P. C. (2004). Forty years of deinstitutionalization of psychiatric services in Canada: An empirical assessment. *The Canadian Journal of Psychiatry, April*: 1–6.

Searles, H. (1963). Transference psychosis in the psychotherapy of chronic schizophrenia. *International Journal of Psycho-Analysis, 44*: 249–281.

Sechehaye, M. (1951a). *Reality Lost and Regained: Autobiography of a Schizophrenic Girl*. G. Rubin-Rabson (Trans.). New York: Grune & Stratton.

Sechehaye, M. (1951b). *Symbolic Realization: A New Method of Psychotherapy Applied to a Case of Schizophrenia*. New York: International University Press.

Sechehaye, M. (1956a). *A New Psychotherapy in Schizophrenia*. G. Rubin-Rabson (Trans.). New York: Grune & Stratton.

Sechehaye, M. (1956b). The transference in symbolic realization. *International Journal of Psycho-Analysis, 37*: 270–277.

Segal, H. (1950). Some aspects of the analysis of a schizophrenic. *International Journal of Psycho-Analysis, 31*: 268–278.

Segal, H. (1957). Notes on symbol formation. *International Journal of Psycho-Analysis, 38*: 391–397.

Seikkula, J., & Olson, M. (2003). The open dialogue approach to acute psychosis: Its poetics and micropolitics. *Family Process, 42*(3): 403–418.

Seikkula, J., et al. (2006). Five-year experience of first-episode nonaffective psychosis in open-dialogue approach: Treatment principles, follow-up outcomes, and two case studies. *Psychotherapy Research, 16*(2): 214–228.

Shapiro, E. (1997). The boundaries are shifting: Renegotiating the therapeutic frame. In: E. Shapiro (Ed.), *The Inner World in the Outer World: Psychoanalytic Perspectives* (USA: Yale University Press), pp. 1–22.

Shapiro, E., & Fromm, G. (2000). Eriksonian clinical theory and psychiatric treatment *Comprehensive Textbook of Psychiatry* (7th Ed.). USA: Lippincott Williams & Wilkins, pp. 2200–2209.

Shapiro, E., & Plakun, E. (2008). An intensive psychodynamic approach for patients with treatment-resistant disorders. *The American Psychiatric Publishing Textbook of Psychiatry* (5th Ed.). New York: American Psychiatric Publishing Inc, pp. 285–298.

Sheth, H. C. (2009). Deinstitutionalization or disowning responsibility. *International Journal of Psychosocial Rehabilitation, 13*(2): 11–20.

Shorter, E. (1990). Private clinics in central Europe 1850–1933. *The Society for the Social History of Medicine*: 159–195.

Silver, A. L. (2000). The 2000 Frieda Fromm-Reichmann lecture: The current relevance of Fromm-Reichmann's works. *Psychiatry, 63*(4): 308–322.

Sliver, A. L. (2001a). Psychoanalysis and psychosis: Players and history in the United States. *Psychoanalysis and history, 4*(1): 45–66.

Silver, A. L. (2001b), Psychotherapy and psychosis: What are promising new developments? *Journal of Contemporary Psychotherapy, 31*(1): 21–30.

Simmel, E. (1921). Symposium on psychoanalysis and the war neurosis *International Psycho-Analytical Library*. Fifth International Psycho-Analytical Congress: Budapest, pp. 30–43.

Simmel, E. (1929). Psycho-analytic treatment in a sanatorium. *International Journal of Psychoanalysis, 10*: 70–89.

Simmel, E. (1937). The psychoanalytic sanitarium and the psychoanalytic movement. *Bulletin of the Menninger Clinic, 1*: 133–143.

Singh, B. S., & Castle, D. J. (2007). Why are community psychiatry services in Australia doing it so hard? *Medical Journal Australia, 187*(7): 410–413.

Skogstad, W. (2003). Internal and external reality in in-patient psychotherapy: Working with severely disturbed patients at the Cassel hospital. *Psychoanalytic Psychotherapy, 17*(2): 97–118.

Soler, C. (1991). A passion in transference: Marion Milner and the Susan case. *Newsletter of the Freudian Field, 5*(1 & 2): 21–49.

Stanton, A., & Schwartz, M. (1954). *The Mental Hospital: A Study of Institutional Participation in Psychiatric Illness and Treatment*. London: Tavistock Publications Ltd.

Stanton, A., & Schwartz, M. (1970). The management of a type of institutional participation in mental illness. In: H. Polsky, D. Claster, & C. Goldberg (Eds.). *Social System Perspectives in Residential Institutions*. 1949 Edn: East Lansing: Michigan State University Press, pp. 323–341.

Stevens, A. (2002a). Courtil: A choice. *Courtil Papers*.

Stevens, A. (2002b). Applied psychoanalysis. *Courtil Papers.*

Stone, M. (1999). The history of the psychoanalytic treatment of schizophrenia. *Journal of the American Academy of Psychoanalysis, 27*(4; Health & Medical Complete): 583–601.

Sullivan, H. S. (1931a). Socio-psychiatric research: Its implications for the schizophrenia problem and for mental hygeine. *American Journal of Psychiatry, 87*: 977–992.

Sullivan, H. S. (1931b). The modified psychoanalytic treatment of schizophrenia. *American Journal of Psychiatry, 11*(3): 519–540.

Sullivan, H. S. (1954). *The Psychiatric Interview.* New York: W. W. Norton.

Sutton, N. (1995). *Bruno Bettelheim: The Other Side of Madness.* London: George Duckworth, p. 532.

Swerdloff, B. (2002). An interview with Michael Balint. *American Journal of Psychoanalysis, 62*(4; Health Module): 383–424.

Talbot, J. A. (1979). Deinstitutionalization: Avoiding the disasters of the past. *Hospital and Community Psychiatry*, 621–624.

Taylor, E. (1988). On the first use of "psychoanalysis" at the Massachusttus General Hospital, 1903 to 1905. *The Journal of the History of Medicine and Allied Sciences, 43*(4): 447–471.

Thompson, C. (1957). The Different Schools of Psychoanalysis. *The American Journal of Nursing, 57*(10): 1304–1307.

Ver Eecke, W. (2002). A Lacanian explanation of Karon's and Villemoes's successful psychodynamic approaches to schizophrenia. *Journal of the American Academy of Psychoanalysis, 30*(4): 633–643.

Vigorelli, M. (1998). Integrated theoretical/clinical and organizational models for institutional treatment of psychosis. In: J. Pestalozzi, S. Frisch, R. D. Hinshelwood & D. Houzel (Eds.). *Psychoanalytic Psychotherapy in Institutional Settings.* London: Karnac for EFPP, pp. 25–44.

Vlassembrouck, M. (2002). One conjuncture of release from the institution. *Courtil Papers.*

Von Bertalanffy, L. (1950). An outline of general system theory *British Journal for the Philosophy of Science, 1*: 134–165.

Wake, N. (2006). The full story by no means all told: Harry Stack Sullivan at Sheppard-Pratt 1922–1930. *History of Psychology, 9*(4): 325–358.

Wallerstein, R. (1989a). The psychotherapy research project of the Menninger Foundation: An overview. *Journal of consulting and clinical psychology, 57*(2): 195–205.

Wallerstein, R. (2000). *42 Lives in Treatment: A study of Psychoanalysis and Psychotherapy; The Report of the Psychotherapy Research Project of the Menninger Foundation 1954–1982.* New York: The Analytic Press.

Warburg, B. (1932). The psychogenesis of organic disturbances and their psychoanalytic treatment: Ernst Simmel (Berlin), communication to the

Psychotherapeutic Congress at Dresden, May 14–17, 1931. *Psychoanalytic Quarterly*, *1*: 166–170.

Warren, F., & Norton, K. (2004). Henderson Hospital democratic therapeutic community: Outcome studies and methodological issues. In: P. Richardson, H. Kächele, & C. Renlund (Eds.). *Research on Psychoanalytic Psychotherapy with Adults*. London: Karnac, pp. 133–153.

Weber, M. (1947). *The Theory of Social and Economic Organization*. A. M. Henderson & T. Parsons (Trans.). London: The Free Press.

Whitaker, R. (2004). The case against antipsychotic drugs: A 50-year record of doing more harm than good. *Medical Hypotheses 62*: 5–13.

Whiteley, S. (2004). The evolution of the therapeutic community. *Psychiatric Quarterly*, *75*(3): 233–248.

Wing, J. K. (1981). From institutional to community care. *Psychiatric Quarterly*, *52*(2): 139–153.

Wing, J. K., & Brown, G. W. (1970). *Institutionalism and Schizophrenia: A Comparative Study of Three Mental Hospitals 1960–1968*. Cambridge: Cambridge University Press.

Winnicott, D. W. (1953). Transitional objects and transitional phenomena: A study of the first not-me possession. *International Journal of Psycho-Analysis*, *34*: 89–97.

Winnicott, D. W. (1960). The theory of the parent-infant relationship. *International Journal of Psycho-Analysis*, *41*: 585–595.

Winnicott, D. W. (1964). *The Child, the Family and the Outside World*. Harmondsorth: Penguin.

Winship (1998). Democracy in psychiatric settings: Collectivism vs. individualism. In: B. Davidson & P. Barker (Eds.). *Psychiatric Nursing: Ethical Strife* Chapter 20). London: Arnold, p. 384.

Winship (2000). The birth of the new asylum. In: P. Barker & C. Stevenson (Eds.), *The Construction of Power and Authority in Psychiatry*. Oxford: Butterworth-Heinemann, pp. 165–177.

Winship (2005). Consciousness-raising and well-being in public sphere organisations: A historical review of psychoanalytical approaches. *Psychoanalytic Psychotherapy*, *19*(3): 233–245.

Winship, G., et al. (2009). Collective biography and the legacy of Hildegard Peplau, Annie Altschul and Eileen Skellern: the origins of mental health nursing and its relevance to the current crisis in psychiatry? *Journal of Research in Nursing*, *14*(6): 505–517.

Woodbury, M. A., & Woodbury, M. M. (1969). Community-centered psychiatric intervention: A pilot project in the 13th arrondissement, Paris. *American Journal of Psychiatry*, *126*(5): 65–71.

World Health Organisation (2005). *ICD-10 (International statistical classification of diseases and related health problems)* (2nd Edn., 10th Rev.). Geneva: United Nations WHO.

World Health Organisation (1998). *Primary Prevention of Mental, Neurological and Psychosocial Disorders*. Geneva: WHO.

World Health Organisation (2011). *Mental Health Atlas*. Available at: www.who.int/mental_health/evidence/atlasmnh/

Zapparoli, G. C., & Gislon, M. C. (1999a). An integrative approach to severe emotional disorders. *Psychoanalytic Psychotherapy, 13*(1): 19–30.

Zelan, K. (1993). Bruno Bettelheim (1903–1990). *Prospects: The Quarterly Review of Comparative Education, XXIII*(1/2): 85–100.

Zenoni, A. (2002). The psychoanalytic clinic in institution: Psychosis. *Courtil Papers*, pp. 1–17.

INDEX

www.ingramcontent.com/pod-product-compliance
Lightning Source LLC
LaVergne TN
LVHW021120300926
849160LV00010B/800
9781782202240